Consuming Television

. . . So, we are left with a dilemma: this medium turns brains to mush, yet its importance is so great that these days the first things revolutionaries think of is to occupy the television stations. 'All revolutions are [now] tele-revolutions', says Timothy Garton Ash, as we saw in Bucharest: 'Romanian television has been telling the world what is going on', an exultant ABC correspondent said . . .

Bruce Cumings (1992), *War and Television*

Consuming Television

Television and its Audience

Bob Mullan

First published 1997

2 4 6 8 10 9 7 5 3 1

Blackwell Publishers Ltd
108 Cowley Road
Oxford OX4 1JF
UK

Blackwell Publishers Inc.
238 Main Street
Cambridge, Massachusetts 02142
USA

British Library Cataloguing in Publication Data

A CIP catalogue record for this book is available from the British Library.

Library of Congress Cataloging-in-Publication Data

Mullan, Bob.
    Consuming television : television and its audience / Bob Mullan.
        p.   cm.
    Includes bibliographical references and index.
    ISBN 0–631–20233–1. — ISBN 0–631–20234–X (pbk.)
    1. Television viewers.   2. Television programs.   3. Television broadcasting.   I. Title
HE8700.65.M85   1997
302.23'45—dc20
                                                          96–23777
                                                          CIP

Typeset in 11 on 13 Palatino by Grahame & Grahame Editorial, Brighton

Printed in Great Britain by T.J Press Ltd, Padstow, Cornwall

This book is printed on acid-free paper

Contents

Tables

Acknowledgements

The author and publishers gratefully acknowledge the following for permission to reproduce copyright material:

Abbot Mead Vickers and Bisto: for scripts for two Bisto commercials;

Broadcasters Audience Research Board (BARB) and Taylor Nelson AGB plc: for tables 2.2, 3.1, 3.3, 3.4 and 8.2 from the AGB Television Year Book;

Broadcasting Standards Council (BSC): for table 7.12 from their 1991 Annual Survey;

Curtis Brown Group Ltd, London: for extracts from the Mass-Observation Archive, Copyright the Trustees of the Mass-Observation Archive at the University of Sussex;

Channel 4 Television Corporation: for table 4.1, compiled from various *Report and Financial Statements*;

FT Telecoms and Media Publishing: for table 9.2;

Independent Television Commission (ITC): for tables 2.1, 3.2, 5.1, 5.2, 5.3, 6.1, 6.2, 6.3, 7.1, 7.3, 8.1 and the table in note 29 for chapter 2.

The publishers apologize for any errors or omissions in the above list and would be grateful to be notified of any corrections that should be incorporated in the next edition on reprint of this book.

Introduction

It is difficult not to concur with Richard Hoggart's recent rather pithy remarks that 'television produces some remarkably good programmes across the whole range of existing tastes, at all levels, and sometimes against heavy odds. It also produces tripe'.[1] What is especially true is that millions of viewers *daily* watch both such 'tripe' and 'good' programmes. And of course if enough people watch such 'tripe' it will continue to be commissioned, produced and broadcast.

Most of us, I imagine, possess our own specific definition of the relative quality of such programming, none the less we will surely agree on some items. Perhaps agreeing to see *Inspector Morse* or *Pride and Prejudice* at one end of the continuum and *Eldorado* at the other. But of course there *will* be disagreement. Some viewers, perhaps only a minority, will cite *The Word* or *The Good Sex Guide* as exemplars of quality, while deriding costume dramas as predictable and *passé.* This indeed is one of the major conundrums of this book. At the very heart, however, are those experiences/attitudes of the television *audience.*

There are very few occasions at which we can now be said to be metaphorically 'glued to the box'. We are so used to the experience; intimately know the conventions and genres of the medium; and watch so much of it, that it is rarely able genuinely to surprise us. This perhaps accounts for Barwise and Ehrenberg's confident assertion that research shows that 'television viewing is often at a fairly low level of involvement' and that the viewers – *we* – 'do not always pay attention and sometimes are even asleep'.[2] None the less, television programmes are produced, repeated, re-commissioned or heartlessly axed on the basis of the *numbers* of viewers allegedly watching them. Indeed the *ratings* mantra is as crucial to the television commissioning process in the late 1990s as it was in earlier moments.

In their view of the 'technologies of audience' James Ettema and Charles Whitney plausibly argue that:

> Those employing measurement technologies usually claim that their methods provide accurate and detailed images of actual receivers so as to reveal . . . the real information and entertainment needs . . . or the real programme preferences of all those who watch television . . .

But, they continue:

> such claims gloss over the fact that measurement technologies and the audiences that they construct always serve particular purposes and reflect particular interests.[3]

Thus, considering our contemporary television system, *audiences* are customarily delivered in quantitative segments to advertising agencies, media buyers and television companies all seeking reassurances as to their 'creative' impulses. However, it was as far back as the early 1960s that it was realized that such a purely quantitative ('number crunching') approach was somewhat limited and far too unidimensional. Even if such gross numbers that were regularly collated were in any sense accurate they would still not speak of the 'appreciation' of content, performance or genre, nor would they tell us anything about the 'how' of viewing. Thus in 1960 the Pilkington Committee called for the Independent Television Authority (as the Independent Television Commission (ITC) was then called) to engage in research to discover what the public thought of the programmes served up to them.[4]

Accordingly the ITC – in its earlier guise as the IBA – has, for almost 25 years, carried out an annual survey into public opinion concerning the performance of independent television and, more recently, Channel 4 and non-terrestrial channels. No one, other than a totally unreconstructed empiricist, has ever claimed wisdom from such surveys but none the less they *do* throw some light on general trends in television viewing – especially given the longitudinal nature of the work, and also if placed in context with other findings and surveys.

This book is based on the ITC's 1994 survey[5] but additionally looks back at comparable surveys over the past two decades, as well as other research and conceptual work, and attempts to glimpse a view of the television future. What will the impact on terrestrial broadcasting be if the audience for satellite television continues to grow steadily? What will the future hold for what we have come to call public service broadcasting in relatively free market conditions? How many channels give viewers programmes they need, as well as those they want? Indeed, it may be asked if such a question is permissible in the ideology of the 'free' market? Although the focus is on audiences I also include a discussion of media ownership and production, and television programmes themselves, in order to describe what has been called the mutually determining interrelationships of the production of programmes, their content and consumption.[6] In other words, a more complete picture of the television experience.

I wish to acknowledge the help given by the following individuals: David Abbott, Chairman of Abbott Mead Vickers; Paul Winstone; Robert Towler, Carmel McLaughlin and Guy Phelps from the ITC; Nigel Floyd; and finally Dorothy Sheridan, archivist of the Mass-Observation Unit. Although the ITC has kindly allowed me access to its data it is, none the less, particularly important to stress that the views expressed here are mine alone.

Methodological Note

The ITC's 1994 survey, as in previous years, asked viewers questions about ITV, Channel 4, satellite and cable channels and the BBC.

The basic methodology of the survey has remained relatively unchanged throughout its history. A quota sample of the adult population (defined as 16 years and over) is interviewed in-home, with quotas set in terms of age, sex and employment status, to reflect the known population profile of the adult population. Typically, sample sizes have been approximately 1,000 adults. The achieved sample is then weighted to ensure that the sex, age, social class and employment status of the analysed sample are fully representative of both national and regional populations. The population targets employed have been those estimated by JICTAR (up to 1980) and, more recently by the BARB Establishment Survey (since 1980).

The major design modification to the study in recent years has been the addition, from 1990, of booster samples for both cable and satellite viewers, to take into account the impact of these channels. The main sample was conducted in a stratified set of 104 constituencies throughout the country. Within each point, quotas were set for age and social grade within sex, with further controls on the numbers of non-working men and women.

The two booster samples were contacted in two extra sets of 15 sampling points. The booster samples were contacted as quota samples within the points selected, with quotas set by sex, age and social class to reflect the known profiles of these populations. As in previous years, all fieldwork was conducted in-home, by interviewers trained in IQCS (Interviewer Quality Control Scheme) standards. The fieldwork was conducted between 8 and 31 October 1994. Interview length was approximately one hour. The survey was conducted on behalf of the ITC by Paul Winstone Research.

1

Audiences

A society is held together by its internal agreement about the sacredness of certain fundamental moral standards. In an inchoate, dimly perceived, and seldom explicit manner, the central authority of an orderly society, whether it be secular or ecclesiastical, is acknowledged to be the avenue of communication with the realm of the sacred values. Within its society, popular constitutional monarchy enjoys almost universal recognition in this capacity, and it is therefore enabled to heighten the moral and civic sensibility of the society and to permeate it with symbols of those values to which the sensitivity responds. Intermittent rituals bring the society or varying sectors of it repeatedly into contact with this vessel of the sacred values. The Coronation provided at one time and for practically the entire society such an intensive contact with the sacred that we believe we are justified in interpreting it as we have done in this essay, as a great act of national communion.

Edward Shils and Michael Young (1953), 'The Meaning of the Coronation'

This chapter describes some of the ways in which the television *audience* has both been defined and how it has in fact been socially *constructed*. In particular the argument that programmes are *polysemic* – capable of bearing multiple meanings for the individual viewer – is described and considered.

Television is unquestionably one of the central features of modern life. Television accompanies us as we wake up, as we breakfast and as we have our tea. It 'comforts us when we are alone. It helps us sleep. It gives us pleasure, it bores us and sometimes it challenges us. It provides us with opportunities to be both sociable and solitary.'[1] We now take television entirely for granted: it is part of the grain of everyday life.

The sheer pervasiveness of television viewing is carefully and painstakingly enumerated by statisticians: virtually everyone in the so-called developed world watches a box in the corner, with the British, for example, totalling over 50 billion hours of television viewing a year. If a typical viewer's total viewing during the year were laid end to end, it would fill two months for 24 hours each day.[2] If our viewing is extensive so is the menu offered to us: currently television offers us 53 hours of illusion for each actual hour of life. Similarly the hours of programmes available weekly in multichannel UK homes totals over 9,000, while real-time hours total a meagre 168.[3]

The reach of television is unparalleled in the history of media: both in terms of numbers and geography – it reaches out in all directions. Television almost magically enters the daily lives of villagers in remote regions of northern India, informs combatants in war-torn Chechnia, instructs schoolchildren in the finer points of geometry, enters the privacy of bedrooms and indeed permeates almost every available space. It is hardly surprising that station-owners and programme-makers alike relish the opportunity to talk to and influence the billions watching. The motivations of such broadcasters vary of course: from pure propaganda, to the desire to inform impartially, to shock or emotionally move, or simply to entertain. There has *never* been such a speedy and pervasive technique of sending messages: performing live in a British theatre, it would have taken Messrs Pavarotti, Domingo and Carreras over 9,000 years to reach their 1994 World Cup Concert television audience.[4]

Fifty years ago television had only recently entered the homes or lives of the British people. In 1945 the diet of information and entertainment usually consumed was of a basic, routine and quite predictable nature. Almost 10 million households possessed a radio set tuned to one of the two BBC stations – one serious, the other consisting of light music and entertainment – or to the somewhat lighter tone of Radio Luxembourg. Short bursts of music could also be heard on wind-up gramophones playing 10 or 12-inch 78 bakelite records. And when not listening to the music of Joe Loss or Enrico Caruso, the British were regular cinema-goers: some 30 million tickets were sold each week in 1945. The short weekly newsreels, a mixture of features and news, gave a foretaste of television news.[5] Then, as now, Hollywood movies dominated, with the 'B movie' added to the main fare and employed to strengthen its hold on the audience.

By the early 1950s television although merely in its infancy, had none the less taken a number of steps forward. For example, a general election had been covered in a simple and rudimentary manner, *What's My Line?* had begun its long and distinguished career, and a prototype of *Top of the Pops* had been launched featuring Cyril Stapleton and his Augmented Orchestra. But it was the Coronation of Elizabeth II which marked the beginning of television's prominence over radio.

On 2 June 1953 much of Britain came to a standstill as millions watched the regal ceremony from Westminster Abbey. In the weeks before the event, over 500,000 sets were sold as 'Coronation fever' swept the land. Despite the fact that there were only two million or so sets in existence, somehow 20 million managed actually to watch the occasion. At the time the Coronation became the 'biggest event in television history' and was broadcast in France, Holland and Germany. It is estimated that ultimately the world audience measured some 277 million.[6]

Socially and culturally the Britain of the 1950s was a far more ordered and predictable place than is our current postmodern landscape of uncertainty, opportunities and nihilism. Diaries kept for the Mass-Observation Unit[7] graphically describe the texture of everyday life at that milestone of television history.

In the immediate post-war period, food was still a scarce and highly valued commodity, and as such came to be seen as a central feature of the television viewing experience. On Coronation day a London schoolteacher took her breakfast at 8.40 a.m., then hurried round to her sister and brother-in-law to invite them to view with her in her own home.

> They came with lots of milk, and their potatoes ready to cook, for I wanted to open a tin of jellied veal, to follow it by an American chocolate pudding with tinned shredded coconut. They came at 10.15 and the TV was ready. I had meant to do some knitting while I watched but my visitors wanted to have the window blind down, so – no knitting. In any case the pictures were too engrossing for us to do anything else. Four of us sat with occasional remarks until 2 p.m. when we switched off the TV to 'give it a rest', and listened to the radio with the blind up till 2.30, when we drew the blind again and watched TV until about 4.40 . . . We did not talk too much during the day as we were too absorbed in watching, and, for most of the time, quite unaware of our surroundings. One remarked that one of the peers had a coronet which looked like a cake; Churchill's antics set up some growling – his showing-off was the limit; the Colonial police and the Ghurka pipeband pleased everybody, and we all fell in love with the Queen of Tonga. My sister remarked how wonderful TV is in spite of its lack of colour.

A 52-year-old male accountant also invited his family members to view the ceremony with him and he too was concerned to give the television set 'a rest'.

> Ida had prepared a lunch of cold meat and salad, followed by hot rice pudding, but although everything had been prepared beforehand, we had not finished when it came to switch on again. So instead of sitting in a nicely arranged semi-circle, we continued round the dining table, the pots still not cleared away. For the repeat of the procession up the Mall, we decided to let the set cool down for a bit.

A retired civil servant expressed his disappointment that there was some talking going on around him while he was trying to concentrate on the 'sanctity' of the occasion: 'Whenever a part of the service was sung or chanted this seemed to be a signal for an outburst of conversation.' This disgruntled viewer added, disapprovingly, that such conversation carried on 'even through the Creed and Gloria', which seemed to him 'most inappropriate'. The uniqueness of Coronation day was captured by a 40-year-old clerk who, in describing his walk to a friend's house where he was to watch the TV, observed that 'there were few people about in Liverpool – it reminded me of Sunday morning – but as the time drew nearer to ten o'clock' he kept passing people in groups 'carrying bags of sandwiches, camp stools, chairs etc., all obviously doing the same as I was.'

Unashamed patriotism characterized the diary entries of a London woman who called on her neighbours to tell them that 'as we do not have as many visitors as expected would you like to come in and watch the Coronation on TV?' Of course they did.

> We got sandwiches and coffee ready and arranged chairs in front of the set. I went into the garden and picked a bunch of large red, white and blue flowers, and another of small flowers. Red poppies, white lilac and blue lupins for the hall, and red geraniums, white and red saxifrage and blue cornflowers for the sitting room mantlepiece. Then I put our flag up – we had fixed a tall pole to the garage . . . We were all ready and sitting in front of the set when the broadcast began, but it was so cold that we had to have the electric fire switched on and later I had to go and change my sandals for shoes as my feet were cold . . . When the Queen appeared on the balcony we stood and drank her health, and then settled down to watch the fireworks. During the day I wore a blue and white dress with a red belt, but the effect was lost as I had to cover the top and belt with a cardigan to keep warm.

When the next major, enthusiastically awaited Royal event graced the screens the impact was even greater. In 1981 700 million television viewers world-wide watched Prince Charles marry Lady Diana Spencer. There were almost 40 million domestic viewers watching the ceremony, and the spectacle was also beamed to 74 other countries. Significantly the wedding also doubled the sales of video recorders: almost three million VCRs taped the royal couple's performance at St. Paul's.[8] Unlike the Coronation year of 1953 this was, of course, no longer television in its infancy, yet the coverage – so meticulously planned – was not without its problems. For example at 11.42 a.m., as the happy couple knelt at the high altar, ITV were without pictures for three minutes. As viewers anxiously switched channels, ITV used fill-in scenes of the crowd: the screen itself was actually blank for all of 12 seconds.

Unlike the immediate post-war period of the Coronation, 1981 was a year which painfully symbolized the social, economic and racial divisions of England's 'green and pleasant land'. Violent riots in Brixton, Toxteth and elsewhere created great anxiety and political concern, and media discussion of the causes and of the 'emerging underclass'. But the spectre of looting and burning streets did not deter those determined to celebrate – either at first-hand or vicariously through television – the 'fairy-tale Royal wedding' as the popular media called it.

Once again Mass-Observation diaries reflect the changes that had taken place in British cultural life since the Coronation year of 1953. One Essex diarist notes how she breakfasted at 8.30 a.m. on their 'usual weekday meal, for me sugar-free muesli and a slice of wholemeal toast', and how they had 'BBC1 on and the hi-fi for the sound, then Vic taped Kiri Te-Kanawa'.[9]

The television set of 1981 was no longer simply a piece of furniture with a dull grey screen, and indeed many diarists described their almost continuous channel-switching and how colourful it all appeared on the screen: 'I avidly watched TV – much impressed by everything, particularly how colourful and friendly the crowds and police were'. The same diarist thanked 'God, that there was no rioting or trouble of any kind', and added that she saw '*High Society* (1956 film) in the afternoon then waited to see the Prince and Princess off on their honeymoon'.

Unlike their 1953 contemporaries, the 1981 viewers did not impassively stare in awe at the proceedings unfolding before them, rather they represented the generation of articulate, critical and occasionally irreverent viewers. For instance a 60-year-old shopkeeper believed that the coverage offered by BBC1 was both inadequate and disappointing.

> I thought the coverage by the producer was too narrow. He may have decided that 700 million viewers only wanted to follow the Royal couple and the queen. I found it disjointed the event . . . Also I felt that the cameras did not convey any sense of the size of the cathedral and barely touched the clergy . . . The Archbishop Runcie, for me, was the fashion star with a beautiful silver cape studied with sapphires . . .
>
> After the Wedding we had a nice salad with a salmon spread; a raspberry dessert in tulip glasses. Difficult to get the spoon in and out!

At her own televised spectacle the Queen had been watched by an adoring and loyal public. But by 1981 such sentiments were not at all universally held. A 41-year-old graphic artist was not afraid of expressing her ambivalence towards the Royal family.

> My mother and I were enthralled by everything, particularly the sight of poor old Spencer turning purple and being helped down the aisle by his loving daughter. I am sorry to say that this made us laugh . . .
>
> [After tea] the children watched the Disney programme with more delight than they had shown hitherto. Then we saw the news on BBC1 which made my husband groan. I suppose on the day war breaks out, Charles and Di will be the headline and the war a poor second. This is one of the reasons ITV news is better than the BBC's . . . We were fascinated by the spectacle but it does not alter the fundamental opinion of my mother and myself that the days of

such an institution are numbered, that it is fatuous, that the commentators are fatuous, that it is interesting to watch as a spectacle, rather as it is interesting to watch a bull-fight in Spain.

Of course by the early 1980s popular television and the tabloid newspapers worked in tandem to create and sustain interest in the Royal family, as they did with show business, sporting heroes and, of course, television too. A 45- year-old fitter found the media's omnipresence somewhat annoying: 'I was determined not to watch it, these pompous state occasions bore me stiff, and besides, I was getting sick of the "media" ramming the wedding down our throats for the last few weeks'. He did, however, succumb to peer pressure and despite himself ultimately found it all interesting.

> I watched until they had said 'I will', and as the speeches and choral works dragged on, the conversation in the room became too much ('I like Princess Anne's hair', 'Is that the Duke of Kent?', etc). At twelve o'clock I made excuses and went to the pub.

There was little evidence of 'channel loyalty' among the diarists, and many reported indecision as to their channel preference: 'we kept switching from one channel to the other, trying to decide which one we preferred, and about 10.00 a.m., settled on ITV'.

Many viewers enjoyed the possibility of identification that the pictures allowed. A 51-year-old telephonist could not help but notice the 'sad look which came over Princess Margaret's face from time to time, so that she stopped singing – was she recalling her own wedding, and regretting its unhappy ending?'

Despite the enthusiasm the colourful pageant received, it was left to a 26-year-old clerk to point out the difference between life as lived through television as compared with life in the flesh.

> I washed my hair quickly during the boring bits, but didn't bother to get dressed . . . The excitement was growing and although I hated myself for it, I was enjoying every moment of it. I shook Dave into life, 'get up man, we're never going to see anything like this again' . . .
>
> I remember thinking how funny it was to see Michael Foot, ex-Labour leader, amongst all this pageantry, but in a way it was comforting – if he could forget some of his principles then so could I . . .
>
> Of course the Prince looked dashing and his bride beautiful . . . I felt a tear threatening, but a man died in troubled Toxteth last night and I remembered just in time . . .

Since 1981 such 'media literacy' has increased even further as has the degree of criticism and irreverence towards television. But television is none the less still enjoyed by the millions who daily tune to their favourite (and other) programmes which will, invariably, be discussed the following day.

Television in the 1990s faces an uncertain future: on the threshold of a truly multi-channel future in a less-regulated marketplace with ITV, BBC and satellite and cable all competing for the attention and purchasing power of the individual viewer. No one is in a position to predict the outcome with any degree of accuracy. What is certain, however, is that the multi-channel household of 2010 will be as different from 1995 as the ordered and seemingly cosy home of 1953 was to that of 1981.

What would the television coverage of, say, Prince William's marriage to some minor Princess in 2010 look like? Who would be watching the ceremony and why? Which channels would actually show it? One scenario could include a picture of a deeply divided Britain, still uncertain of its European identity yet at the same time struggling with four devolved parliaments. The old divisions of north–south, rich–poor, are compounded by the essential division between the 40 per cent who are connected to multi-media and the 60 per cent who are not and who live on the fringes of the information society, refugees from the previous century. The 40 per cent characterize what John Kenneth Galbraith termed the 'culture of contentment',[10] showing little interest in the plight of the 60 per cent have-nots and therefore enabling the governments of the day to stand idly by and watch them perish. The work-force itself is predominantly female and youthful, and the majority of them work from home – they *telework*. Consequently, actual offices and work-places have disappeared from the landscape, as has the term trade unionism from the common language.

Marriage is still a much sought after and valued if precarious institution. The rate of divorce has been on the decline since the turn of the century, especially since pre-nuptial settlements became the norm rather than the exception. As a consequence of this unhappy marriages tend to continue through fear of the fall-out that would ensue from any clean breaks. Very few (self) employed individuals live in families with children. Where children are part of families they tend to be minus brothers or sisters: and legally such children are protected from their parents (or caretakers) through a parent–child contract negotiated by both parties when the child reaches 12 years of age. Issues covered by such agreements include ones of educational opportunity, 'moral behaviour' and financial rewards and sanctions.

From the year 2000 the national governments of the UK recognized that the term 'full-employment' was like that of 'chastity', merely a cry of nostalgia, understandable perhaps but utterly unattainable. After the turn of the century poverty and destitution had been recognized and then institutionalized by successive governments. Indeed, a scenario described by Ian McEwan in his 1988 novel *The Child in Time*, had in fact come true and beggars had indeed become licensed. Allowed to beg in certain places, while being barred from others. In the novel McEwan's central character

'Stephen' recognized some licensed beggars from their bright badges, even though they were a couple of hundred yards away, and in particular he noticed a pre-pubescent child slowly approaching him.

> She had registered him at some distance. She walked slowly, somnambulantly, the regulation black bowl extended . . . He felt the usual ambivalence. To give money ensured the success of the Government programme. Not to give involved some determined facing away from private distress. There was no way out.[11]

Such a situation actually prevailed in 2010.

By the year 2000 the so-called 'interactive' shopping channels on TV had failed to attract audiences and were replaced by 'smart ' supermarkets which enabled people to shop at only one visit while also avoiding the beggars. The supermarkets are no-cash institutions: 'smart' credit or debit cards are swiped by the customers themselves in return for their goods. Very few assistants actually inhabit these stores. The air is scented with coconut oil: 'Best buy that suntan cream now', the shopper thinks, 'before the summer holidays'. Push the video trolley past the fresh-fish counter and a succulent salmon will be grilling on a screen, wheeled by the shopper, only a few centimetres away. Shelves 'talk', or play music to the passing consumer: as the electromagnetic field is broken by a lingering shopper, the shelves chirp into life encouraging lengthier lingering or even a purchase. At the check-out, shoppers total their own bills with handheld scan-guns. If on the visit the shopper has not visited the bakery, a coupon will be automatically issued to them discounting bakery goods. The 40 per cent who have sufficient income to choose what they will eat have returned to the food-faddishness which characterized the 1990s, but which had subsequently fallen out of favour in the early years of the new millennium.

Estimates as to the number of television channels available to the 2010 viewer fell short of the actual figure: some 700. Despite this, or perhaps because of this so-called abundance of choice, Prince William's wedding is too general an event to be considered an item worth fighting over. None the less a number of minor channels compete for the 'rights': for the privilege of being able to supply live coverage of the wedding from Richard Branson's Caribbean island, also post-marriage scenes and most importantly, exclusive interviews with Diana Spencer (*a.k.a.*, Baroness of Kensington) who, remarkably, remains a female icon despite her divorce and partial decampment from England for the more congenial New York.

Diana Spencer excluded, the British royals are largely ignored by the public following the steady erosion of their constitutional powers. In 2010 they are more like members of the royal families of Denmark or the Netherlands: no bodyguards, little pomp and ceremony, they shop in public with little sign of an interested paparazzi. Although the photographers still seek out movie stars and others connected with show business, it is the *children of the rich* who are most sought after: constantly under threat of abduction or kidnapping, such children's photos are thus rare and therefore desirable.

The Japanese networks declined to bid for the wedding rights, a measure of their disapproval of William's divorced mother. The devolved BBC could not find agreement amongst its regional stations and failed to put a package together: the BBC will have to content itself with highlights, although the station's licence payers – as in the previous century – would be very disappointed at the outcome. ITV was uninterested. The potential audience would not deliver enough under 25s to make it a viable proposition. On ITV the wedding would find itself being shown for a minute or so on the only news bulletin of the day at 3.00 p.m.

Prince William's cut-down pageant would be shown as an outside broadcast through a cartel of English cable companies, led by a channel owned by a hardcore porn entrepreneur, convinced his audience will buy into the event, especially as Diana Spencer would be present.

Subsequently no viewer actually watches the televised event for more than a few minutes at a time, if indeed that long. The head of the household – invariably a woman – avoids the televised wedding, preferring instead to watch a niche channel devoted exclusively for the purposes of networking for black business women. She changes channel by barking out channel names and numbers at her voice-activated set: conventional remote-control hardware now being used only by members of the disadvantaged classes, the poor and 'obsolete'. The viewer checks out the women's kick-boxing channel, now the most popular spectator sport in England. Association football lost ground in 2001 after it changed its format for the benefit of broadcasters: nine segments of ten minutes, played only in the summer was deeply unpopular with fans who drifted away. Her son is in his work/bedroom ensconced in an interactive music video.[12] No more 'air guitar' for this 13-year-old, instead he sets foot on a stage replete with musicians and screaming fans. Wearing his lightweight head-mounted display he sees ten thousand adoring teenagers eagerly waiting to hear him play. In his hands he holds a virtual guitar: he's never had to learn to play the instrument, the computer does it all for him. All *he* is required to do is to strum along. The lights dim and he begins his solo: the ultimate music video.

The father worries about his son: will he ultimately graduate to *teledildonics* – virtual sex? However his concern cannot lead to action: his agreement with his son allows the 13-year-old to do more or less as he pleases. This anxious father does not work. Reliant on his wife's earnings and goodwill, he sits for lengthy hours in front of the television, frequently changing channels with his softly spoken vowels. He lingers momentarily on the scenes from the Caribbean as William marries his obscure princess, his still glamorous mother looking on approvingly. As he continues almost mindlessly to change the channels he recalls a distant past when 'men were men, and women were women'.

Of course there are other scenarios that may be drawn, some more optimistic and almost mirroring contemporary life in the 1990s, but others more frightening still. This is, of course, not at all far fetched. After all it was only 50 years ago when Arthur C. Clarke first shared his idea of satellite television, and at the time few believed in such a vision.

As mentioned earlier, increasingly, different channels will compete vigorously for the potential viewers' loyalty and money. As the menu of what to watch lengthens, concerns continue to be expressed about the possible implications for programming itself. Mainstream broadcasters fear that the increased competition from cable and satellite producers and distributors will, inevitably, reduce advertising revenue and hence reduce programme standards. In the 1990s the consequence of those broadcasters dependent solely on advertising revenue is that they will compete more strenuously than ever in order to provide the advertisers with the audiences they require. In the need to maximize audiences the schedule is increasingly ratings-driven and all too predictable. The knock-on effect is clearly evident with the BBC also enthusiastic to maximize its audiences and, in so doing, justify the licence fee and its existence. Perhaps the broadcasting of the *National Lottery* with its crass game show production values epitomizes this so-called competitive edge. This naked exultation of greed seems to be a long way from the Reithian principles of public service broadcasting.

This market-driven politico-economic mentality not only favours the model of the sovereign consumer it also implies that as such consumer choice becomes more and more central to television, the need for strong regulation decreases: for if the viewer disapproves of the menu set before him he will simply choose another programme, a different channel, a new package, or renew or cancel a subscription. Despite the deregulatory rhetoric, new broadcasting legislation has actually increased the protection for particular programming. Some television genres on terrestrial channels – news, current affairs, religion, children's and regional programmes – have to be provided at a certain 'minuteage' and at specific times of the schedule. Similarly some international and domestic news must occur on ITV, for example, during the peak-time schedule.

Under the Broadcasting Act 1990, the ITC (the IBA, as it was previously called) lost its powers to preview and approve ITV television schedules prior to broadcast. Thus no powers of intervention remain. Instead the ITC is only able to react after the transmission of a programme and possibly to provide censure if regulations have been breached. The same act, as we have earlier seen, also requires the ITC to elicit the attitude of the general public on the television programming within its remit. To fulfil this requirement the ITC annually surveys public opinion on a wide range of broadcasting-related topics.

Audience Research

Peak or prime-time television is judged to be successful or otherwise solely in terms of audience ratings. Worthy programmes of minority interest are shunted into the recesses of the schedule, where expectations are somewhat lower, or at the very least different. Audience figures have always, of course, been central to the philosophy of ITV, funded, as it is, by advertisers wishing to see value for their money. Only relatively recently has the BBC been forced to justify *its* existence (and the licence fee) predominantly in terms of audience ratings. In this climate even worthy programmes are expected to fight strenuously for substantial numbers of viewers. Not only does this endless struggle for the largest audiences available tend to lead, for example, to entertainment shows which are celebrity-led, formulaic or aimed at the lowest common denominator, it tends also to ossify the 'audience'. Rather than seen as millions of individual viewers with unique tastes the 'audience' is instead counted solely in terms of its potential disposable income, 'life-style', class (defined crudely), age and gender. Indeed in media research *numbers* have taken on an almost mystical quality, something akin to the politician's use of convenient statistics.

The sheer numbers of people actually watching a programme is a valuable (to advertisers at least) statistic, however unreliable the actual figure may be. They are also interesting statistics. But it is only of limited value if we are interested in the actual viewing experience, which is an immensely varied one: it can range from a family of four barely paying attention to *Blind Date* as they eat their tea, scoffing at the screen from time to time in cynical amusement; a 75-year-old widow tearfully enjoying *This is Your Life*; and two 14-year-old adolescent boys devouring the sea, sand and rippling silicone muscles of the cast of *Baywatch*, becoming sexually aroused as they do so. They are *all* members of television *audiences*. What the counting of audiences can provide are interesting long-term patterns and trends in viewing, approximate though they are. Such patterns and trends provide an overarching framework to work with: a larger canvas for the details later to be filled in.

Over 80 per cent of the UK population aged four and over watch television at some time during a typical *day*, and the figure rises to 95 per cent during a typical *week*.[13] The average amount of time viewers spend watching live television (on all channels) has, from 1986–96, hovered around 3.5 hours per day, or 25 to 30 hours a week, or almost 1,500 hours per person per year. The television sets themselves are on for even longer periods of time, as different members of the same household may watch at different times.[14] We also watch more television during the winter, approximately 10 per cent more than in the summer months. Indeed, in countries like Finland the contrast is even greater, however in the UK these seasonal variations ought not to be exaggerated. Viewing less television in the summer months still amounts to an average of at least 20 hours per week.

Moreover, as Barwise and Ehrenberg point out, the summer schedules are 'full of cheaper or repeated programmes, with new and high-budget material kept back until autumn and winter'. They, therefore, pose the question 'would summer viewing drop off less if the most attractive programming were more evenly spread through the year?'[15] During evening peak hours up to half the UK's population is watching television, some 20 million or so viewers. But even at prime television time the other half of the population is doing something else. Moreover, the most popular programmes attract only about half those watching television at that particular moment, with the other half divided among the 'less popular' offerings available on alternative channels. Indeed the irregularity of our viewing from day to day or week to week leads Barwise and Ehrenberg to argue that 'viewing mostly seems to occur when we have nothing more compelling to do' although, of course, it is self-evident that we *do* make efforts to see certain favourite programmes. Put somewhat differently, it is paradoxical that watching television is such a compelling pastime, yet appears to be carried out at a low level of involvement for most of the time. Given the vast number of 'programmes, newscasts and commercials people actually watch, viewing any one of them can hardly ever be a very significant event'.[16]

It also appears, according to the evidence of broad trends, that we seek to watch a wide variety of programmes, and that there is no special tendency for viewers of a particular programme to choose other programmes of the same type or genre. A contentious conclusion from such trend material concerns the viewing of lengthy or limited-run drama serials, when it is often claimed that only half of those who view even a peak-time programme one week would have seen the previous episode. Such data suggests that very few viewers see the total run, although many see at least some part of such serials. The *Jewel in the Crown* is cited as an illustration: despite each episode's twice weekly showing, only two in 100 saw all 14 episodes.[17]

Viewers tend to choose specific *programmes* rather than *channels*, though so-called channel loyalty to a degree still exists. The 'average' viewer who will watch between 20 or 30 hours of television in the course of a week will typically watch almost 40 programmes, plus a myriad of snatches from zapped material: perhaps in total, thousands of diverse images.

Long-term trend evidence confirms that the '65 and over' age groups watch almost twice as much television as do young adults. In general, children tend to watch less television than adults, partly due to the timing of their sleeping habits. Young teenagers are quite heavy viewers, while older teenagers have traditionally tended to be lighter viewers, preferring to socialize with their peers. However in recent years 16–24-year olds have tended to increase their time watching television.[18]

Audience Ethnography

Counting the numbers of viewers allegedly watching television at certain times of the day or night is essential to the requirements of advertisers as they attempt to target 'audiences' and maximize their promotional messages. And within a ratings-driven context there is the tendency, therefore, for programmes to be made to fit 'audiences' rather than the other way round. In other words, producers learn from the audience figures 'who is watching what, and when', and subsequently make programmes similar enough to pass as 'new' but not different enough to lose such a potential audience.

However, as research quickly demonstrated that audiences could not be construed or turned into an 'objectified category' and indeed that their behaviour was not as predictable as first thought, audience measurement techniques were encouraged to change. As Ien Ang describes in *Desperately Seeking the Audience*, this dissolution of 'television audience' as a social entity

> became historically urgent when 'anarchic' viewer practices such as zapping and zipping became visible, when viewing contexts and preferences began to multiply, in short when the industry, because of the diversification of its economic interests, had to come to terms with the irrevocably changeable and capricious nature of 'watching television' as an activity.[19]

It must be noted, however, that television institutions – including programme managers, producers, advertisers, and market research organizations – are somewhat reluctant to let go of their calculated ignorance of the dynamic complexity of the social world of actual audiences.

What precisely does the more qualitative research show? Firstly, that television viewing is generally a somewhat busy activity, interrupted by many other activities and routinely accompanied by talk, much of it having nothing to do with the programme being watched.[20] Of course this does not, therefore, mean that such peripheral viewing is less enjoyable as compared to being 'glued to the box', viewing styles being a matter of taste and habit. Other research points to the way in which 'television attendance' is cycled into the broader patterns of social life, where there are bursts of concentration one moment, secondary interest the next, followed by 'idling', when the viewer is temporarily and rather unintentionally engaged in viewing.[21] Barwise and Ehrenberg in a similar vein argue that there is 'usually some involvement in what we watch but mostly it does not go very deep: *low* involvement but not *no* involvement'.[22] This relaxed, partially uninvolved mode of viewing is made easier by the sheer familiarity of the programming: genres, similar and predictable plots, same faces, same places, repeats, and so on create one long sequence of programming we are able to dip in and out of.

Secondly, the qualitative research demonstrates that television viewing usually takes place within families. As David Morley has argued, to expect – as the audience measurement industry has tended – that 'we could treat the individual viewer making programme choices as if he or she were the rational consumer in a free and perfect market is surely the height of absurdity when we are talking of people who live in families'.[23] For most people, viewing occurs within the context of what Sean Cubitt terms 'the politics of the living room' where other family members are likely to disrupt, if not shatter, one's communion with the television.[24] In other words, viewing is often non-selective, with members of a family being forced to view programmes selected by someone else.

In his reconceptualization of viewing within the family context Morley centres in on the importance of gender relations:

> the dominant model of gender relations within this society . . . is one in which the home is primarily defined for men as a site of leisure – in distinction to the 'industrial time' of their employment outside the home – while the home is primarily defined for women as a sphere of work (whether or not they also work outside the home).[25]

One of the consequences of this distinction is that women approach television somewhat distractedly or guiltily, given their continuing sense of their domestic responsibilities. In terms of programme choice, masculine power appears to be the determining factor, especially when Remote Control Devices (RCDs) are at hand. The exception to this general rule is when the man of the family is unemployed while his wife is working. In these cases it is *slightly* more common for the man to give ground over programme choice.[26]

One major finding of Morley's is that while men state a clear preference for viewing attentively, in silence, without interruption, 'in order not to miss anything', women describe their viewing as a fundamentally social activity, 'involving ongoing conversation, and usually – given their sense of their domestic obligations – the performance of at least one other domestic activity' at the same time.

If one line of research has highlighted the context in which viewing takes place another tradition concentrates on the *variable meanings* audiences take from the same programme, regardless of what the intention of the programme-maker may have been. The word 'escape' has been far too casually used in the past to characterize the audience's involvement with television: certainly at times attention is minimal, but on other occasions both the heart and mind may well be totally engaged. The example of soaps is a case in point: it seems important to believe, for example, that *Coronation Street* is plausible, if not actually 'real'. Indeed, soaps positively encourage processes of identification, hardly surprising given that the situation invariably is one of an actual family looking at another family on the screen.

Soaps make us laugh and weep, amuse and anger us, and rarely fail to elicit our identification with their characters and story lines. Similarly programmes like *This is Your Life* may well provide emotional comfort to viewers, as it brings together people who were formerly apart: if only such facilities could be made available for one's own relations.[27] Such responses are not always so predictable: *Star Trek* was originally scheduled as a children's programme until adult hippies tuned in and shunted it into a prime-time slot; teenagers guffaw at the more sensitive moments of *Blind Date*; certain programmes inadvertently became 'cult viewing' because of their awfulness; *Charlie's Angels* may be viewed as yet another example of sexist repression, or as an example of moral decay;[28] some viewers mock heroes, praise villains, while Cilla Black has unwittingly, with her camp naffness, become a much-revered gay icon as has Dean Cain, star of *The New Adventures of Superman* – but for different reasons.

It is, then, obvious that one viewer's reading of a programme may not only be different from someone else's, but perhaps different from the one intended by the producer. Viewers often, but not always, engage in meaning-making: they do not always sit there empty-minded awaiting edification. When a viewer watches television they do not leave their histories at the living-room door: neither do they abandon their cultural, class, racial, economic or sexual identities, nor do they forget either their media knowledge of comparable programmes, information in newspapers, and other aspects of the infrastructure of television viewing.

Those theorists concerned with the possible exercise of state power through the media industries ('the dominant ideology thesis') have found a way out of the theoretical cul-de-sac created by the implausible claim that we, the viewers, are continuously duped by messages intended to create compliance in us. Instead theorists like Stuart Hall have, for example, suggested three basic modes of interpretation: 'dominant', where the viewer accepts the prevailing ideological structure; 'oppositional,' rejecting the basic aspects of the structure; or it may be 'negotiated', creating a sort of personal synthesis.[29] Of course further modes of interpretation can be readily imagined, which indeed have led to a somewhat extreme view that it might be possible to argue that every individual interpretation of television content could, in some way, be different. Despite the unlikeliness of this, especially given the dependence of television on shared meanings, a number of critics like John Fiske have claimed that all programmes ('texts') are *polysemic*, capable of bearing multiple meanings by virtue of the varying constructions of audiences. As Celeste Condit puts it, recent 'critical audience studies thus repudiate prior portrayals of television as a sinister social force in favour of a celebration of the ability of audiences' to reconstruct television messages.[30] Television, in this view, becomes a force for popular resistance to 'dominant interests'.

In such a view *all* programmes are polysemic, not only long-running serials like *Coronation Street* or multi-layered series like *Between the Lines*, but news programmes too. Fiske urges viewers to treat 'news texts with the same freedom and irreverence that they do fictional ones',[31] and though there is an important truth to this – that news is a matter of interpretation – another truth is lost. For instance, it doesn't matter whether detectives Simone and Sipowicz (of *NYPD Blue*) actually police the 15th Precinct – or indeed, whether there is a 15th – whether true or not, the meaning is made. But to say George Bush is still President of the United States, though meaning-making, is untrue and does matter.[32] In this full circle 'the audience' has lost its image as a collection of passive individuals to one where the viewer is king. Neither will suffice.

It is correct to observe that audiences do not 'absorb culture like sponges', rather that they are selective, reflective and constructive in their use of television. But, as Michael Schudson points out, this is 'not to say that the popular audience is always critical or creative in its responses any more than elite audiences are'.[33] Supporters of the 'active-audience' view also insist, as we have seen, on its potential for 'resistance', and talk of the 'empowerment' of the viewer. It is surely fair to question 'where this resistance and subversion of the audience lead' or what effects they might have on broadcasting practices or the holders of cultural power.[34] More broadly speaking it is also salutary to remember that individuals and their families are always embedded in larger social and political networks that create collective experience across family walls. To develop a rich textured picture of audiences it is surely necessary to place them within the broader social and economic processes which they are part of: to do otherwise would be to 'romanticize the audience celebrating the supposed autonomy of the viewer to the neglect of issues of power and social structure'.[35] Quite simply, audiences are neither simply resistant or mere dupes. They neither find television always and utterly pleasurable, simply an escape, nor invariably obnoxious and oppressive.[36]

| 2 |

Technology

Sometimes it is watched with great intensity and emotional involvement (quite enough to produce tears of sorrow or tears of joy): at other moments, with an irreverent concern (in which actors and plot readily become more laughing matters). In both cases it is likely to be a subject for conversation and comment among those present either during or after the specific programme. And whatever may have been the case in the past, nowadays, with at least four channels available and a prerecorded film for hire a few hundred yards down the road, choice is likely to be continually exercised . . .

Although 'television conversations' may often be about the comings and goings of fictional characters or 'personalities', they provide ways of talking about a great many other features of the world: sex, sin, retribution and death.

Laurie Taylor and Bob Mullan (1986), *Uninvited Guests*

Given the rapid growth in television technology we can no longer simply talk of the 'box in the corner' humming away and giving us undiluted *television*.[1] The screen now has multiple functions and, similarly, households invariably possess more than one set. In this chapter we examine this growth and the viewer's reactions to it.

In the early 1980s there was considerable talk of the 'third age of broadcasting', a video revolution which would enable the viewer to choose their programmes more freely and rid themselves of the formal constraints of the scheduler. Multi-set homes have indeed allowed sons and daughters to view *Home and Away* in the intimacy of their bedrooms, while their fathers watch the previous Saturday's *Match of the Day* time-shifted on his VCR. Multi-channel cable and direct broadcasting by satellite (DBS) have also added to the potential of freeing the viewer from the 'tyranny of the scheduler' and, indeed, have brought further international programming into the home. The same decade saw the television screen being used for additional purposes other than the conventional ones; videotex, home computers and video games, video disks, home movies produced by video camcorders, and the various so-called 'alphabet technologies', such as 'STV, LPTV, SMATV, and MVDS, which use different parts of the broadcasting spectrum to provide cable-type services in non-cable areas'.[2]

So deeply embedded is the television experience in everyday life, we rarely contemplate its purpose, but simply occasionally complain over programmes we personally disapprove of. But this was not always the case. In 1911, prior to television itself, the psychologist Hugo Munsterberg worried that movies would eventually numb people's senses, but since that time it has been more warmly embraced: 'TV's aim is no more than to keep you viewing. The medium has become an end in itself.'[3]

On 2 November 1936, television entered our lives with the official opening of the BBC's television service. Chinese jugglers, American dancers, newsreel and speeches, and a specially composed song 'Television' sung by Adele Dixon were elements of the initial programming. The following week viewers were entertained by performing Alsatian dogs, tap dancers, the West End play *Marigold* and a lengthy feature on prize chrysanthemums. Four hundred television sets having been sold at the time of the actual opening, a figure which steadily rose through the following years. Pre-war television ended on 1 September 1939, when the screen suddenly went blank during a *Mickey Mouse* cartoon. No explanation was announced. In fact the government believed that the signals from the Alexandra Palace mast would attract enemy aircraft: so that was that. Normal service was returned some seven years later on 7 June 1946 with the same harmless *Mickey Mouse* cartoon. Presenter Jasmine Bligh opened with 'Hello, do you remember me?', while Leslie Mitchell dryly added, 'as I was saying before we were so rudely interrupted . . .'[4]

Tim O'Sullivan, exploring television memories among the generation who were present at its inception, argues, plausibly enough, that in spite of subsequent innovations 'television has never recaptured or replicated the early novelty of its initial appearance and presence'.[5] His interviewees remembered the excitement which accompanied the initial spectacle of TV and many 'recalled the ways in which early television viewing was often an occasion for large numbers of people to gather at friends' or relatives' houses'. Television ownership soon became a status symbol – 'you could tell from the aerials who had and who hadn't got sets'. But sets were also bought for the benefit of children who, it was believed, would benefit educationally from the programmes. Television watching did not, however, easily slip into the texture of everyday life, and for many people the TV had 'colonized' leisure time: 'In the evenings, it (the living room) became the television room . . . it was "what's on tonight?", and everything started to give way to television. It used to annoy me, you couldn't talk to people.'[6]

Some people objected to television taking over meal times or intruding into conversations held with visiting friends and family. Others, however, talked of how television could unite their families and recalled Sunday afternoon films watched in the depths of winter amidst their cosy domestic security. Similarly television acted as a companion when husbands or family were absent from home.

Television has *always* created ambivalence and conflicting opinions as to its worth: many approvingly referred to the way that children's TV had become part of a structured domestic routine. *Children's Hour* gave mothers a break from child care, and time to prepare tea. At the same time the very same mothers expressed concern about the potential exposure their children faced through the somewhat risque television play. A recurrent theme, one with contemporary resonance, centred on the conflict between television and school work or other pursuits or hobbies considered, by parents at least, to be as valuable as an hour in front of the box.

> It wasn't so bad in the winter, but I remember in the summer evenings it used to upset me – I'd come in on a lovely evening and I can remember it now, all the curtains would be drawn and they'd be sat in the gloom, glued to the set. I often got annoyed and turned it straight off – 'get out in the fresh air' I used to say.[7]

Sadly playing outside in the 'fresh air' is no longer such a safe activity in the 1990s of Britain as it was, perhaps, in more recent decades.

Another view which was regularly expressed was the fact that such a novelty was, inevitably, short-lived. For instance, although viewers remembered how mind-boggling it was to see world events taking place 'live' as they happened, and how television opened a window to the world, they also recalled how the excitement soon wore off. Programmes became all too predictable.

Mass-Observation material from 1949 illustrates the now taken-for-granted attitude toward television of the post-1960s generations compared with previous decades. This material emphasizes the ambivalence, as well as the uncertainty, felt towards this novel and luxurious piece of equipment.

In April 1949 Mass-Observation diarists were instructed to concentrate their thoughts and attitudes towards television: in fact for many of the diarists the subject was hypothetical, as their homes lacked the device. For all of them the dilemma was how television would fit in with the rest of their lives, especially their leisure time and family life. *Time* was the central issue. A 32-year-old teacher viewed the possibility of having a set with mixed feelings.

> There are so many things I can do in my leisure time while listening to and enjoying the wireless, for example, reading, carving and modelling. I am so

afraid that television would prove so attractive that my spare time would be spent straining my eyes looking into a distant screen.[8]

These diaries graphically illustrate how dramatically Britain has changed over the past 50 years: the following diarist – a 24-year-old self-termed 'housewife' – worries over the effect on her husband's palate.

> . . . What housewife (middle or any other class) would have the time to sit down and watch television in the morning and afternoon? With the radio women can work and hum with *Housewives' Choice*. With television they would not be able to watch the screen and make the pastry. What mysteries would be brought forth from the oven at dinner time, due to the irresistible distractions of the cathode tube?

Half a century of technological, occupational, social and televisual change would have rendered her concerns redundant. Microwave ovens, part-time work, serial monogamy and cookery programmes would have completely reshaped her concerns.

The many potential effects on family life was of great concern to a number of diarists. Fears were expressed that television would make people unsociable or even anti-social and that it would lure them away from such large public gatherings as in cinemas and theatres for them to retreat to their own firesides. This was seen as part of a tendency for each family to become completely self-contained and for social intercourse to be greatly reduced. A 35-year-old laboratory technician was particularly concerned about the changing interiors of family life.

> I believe that television makes family home life almost impossible. For 2–3 hours every evening the family must sit in darkness gazing at the screen – mother cannot knit, father cannot read, the children sleep through their homework and stay up late. No one can have a conversation, no letters get written, and friends calling are not welcomed since they break the sequence.

It would, however, be wrong to conclude that the majority of diarists expressed such disquiet. Another 'housewife' eloquently spoke of the unique *potential* of television to enhance our lives, especially in our formative years.

> How many children of three have been to the Antarctic and seen the seals and penguins, or viewed the 'antics of a ski-ing school in Switzerland, or laughed with real abandon at Laurel and Hardy's tumbles and horseplay.' Yes, they love it; with sucking thumbs and goggle-eyes they remain glued from start to finish. Television is certainly a very great broadening and enlightening invention.

The culture within which contemporary television is deeply embedded bears little resemblance to that of 50 years earlier: the conundrum is knowing to what extent television itself has wrought the cultural changes that have taken place, and how much it has itself been altered by other cultural forces. We will return to this puzzle.

British Television in the 1990s

It may be a slight exaggeration to argue that the 'British television market has been transformed more in the early 1990s than in any other period in history',[9] but it certainly is almost unrecognizable from that of two decades earlier, let alone 50 years. Despite the intention of the 1990 Broadcasting Act to introduce more domestic competition, previously forbidden mergers between large ITV companies have been allowed to take place, producing large TV channels capable of potentially competing in the global marketplace. At the same time Channel 4 has been successfully selling its own advertising, and Channel 5 is now newly established. In its search for more efficiency the BBC has, through altered working practices, made thousands redundant. Most significantly, perhaps, is the 'third dimension' of cable and satellite television, especially BSkyB. Satellite channels are competing strenuously for programme rights (as in sporting events) and the 'British public are slowly coming to terms with the concept of pay-TV'.[10] And although television advertising continues to grow in volume, ITV's share of such revenue is likely to be reduced by the continued competition from satellite channels, especially if their programming improves and household penetration increases.[11]

It is important to understand, and not forget, that these changes in television are part of broader changes in the communications industry as a whole. These broader changes include the integration of press, broadcasting, telecommunications and computers within new corporate structures; a reduction in the number of individual media owners; alterations to the range and distribution of film and television products internationally; and a dilution in regulatory practices. But it would be wrong to contend that such broader changes are the direct and inevitable consequences of new technologies such as satellite communications, and that societal changes have been caused by new technologies. As Patrick Hughes correctly argues, such technological determinism 'ignores the people, social institutions and political forces which are all part of innovation'. Particular changes in communications technology are not inevitable, rather they are aspects of the more general changes in the ownership and control of major sections of the national and international economy. These general changes themselves are the result of particular *choices* made by national governments and international corporations. New television technologies such as video and satellites are similar to any other technological innovation: 'they have the potential to reinforce the current structure and operation of their industry *and* also to challenge it'.[12]

Indeed, many new communication technologies simply enable old jobs to be more profitably carried out while at the same time reinforcing patterns of ownership and distribution: satellites enable television and film companies to continue to distribute their products globally, but in new ways which undermine national control over the 'availability of ideas'. Hughes concludes in arguing that the

> real innovation associated with these technologies is the integration of the machinery and companies involved in television with those involved in apparently diverse areas such as computers, telephones and homeworking. Video, satellite, and cable help such companies such as Philips, Thorn-EMI, and Warners to recognize the ways in which knowledge, ideas and culture are produced and distributed.[13]

It is within this conceptual framework that the findings of the ITC's 1994 survey have to be understood.

Previous research has highlighted the continued expansion of the *multi-set* households, especially in families with children under 15 years old. (The percentage of households with more than one set has risen from 5 per cent in 1974 to 39 per cent in 1984 to a figure approaching 53 per cent in the 1990s.) Not surprisingly such households have also enthusiastically embraced such items as home computers, video cameras and games. Two-thirds of those questioned in 1994 claimed to own at least two television sets, while a quarter of the viewers claimed ownership of at least three sets. Families with teenage children were more likely than other groups to claim possession of at least three sets. Just ten years earlier a mere one in four households claimed to have two or more sets.[14] Predictably the sets themselves were spread throughout the home; the main set in the 'living' room, followed by sets in the parental bedroom, children's bedroom and kitchen. Barwise and Ehrenberg note that some media analysts, aware that there is often family tension over what to watch, thought that this would lead to substantial changes in the patterns of viewing in multi-set households. This, in fact, has not happened. They suggest that 'second sets are hardly ever used to extend the choice of programmes' and for most of the time only one television set is on, 'possibly a different one at different times'. When two sets *are* on, half the time they are tuned to the same channel: allowing people to watch the same programme while moving around the house. During the rest of the time when both sets are on, different programmes *are* watched, but this accounts for less than 10 per cent of the household's viewing.[15]

Obviously this state of affairs may well change with the gradual decline of 'family programming and family viewing' and with the increase in niche programming. Let's face it, which 9-year-old wishes to view Sumo wrestlers stealthily embraced in combat? Indeed, the survey found that those viewers who were able to receive either cable or satellite channels tended to have more sets than those only equipped for terrestrial channels.

Since the late 1980s the purchase of home entertainment equipment has continued to grow steadily, with almost every viewer claiming possession of at least one extra home entertainment item in addition to their TV set. While a comparable survey in 1984 found almost half of the respondents expressing no desire for a video recorder (VCR), the 1994 survey found four out of five viewers claiming possession of one. Similarly the rate of growth of ownership of teletext sets rose from 14 per cent in 1984 to almost 50 per cent a decade later.

Not surprisingly the younger age groups (16–20 and 25–44) were far more likely to claim ownership of VCRs and items like compact disc players and home computers. None the less over half the over-65s also claimed ownership of VCRs.

Table 2.1 Home entertainment equipment

In percentages	1987	1988	1989	1990	1991	1992	1993	1994
Video recorder	55	58	70	75	72	77	80	83
Teletext	23	25	30	41	40	46	49	55
Compact disc	n/a	n/a	n/a	n/a	22	29	27	35
Home computer	23	18	26	22	22	30	29	29
Video games	10	10	11	11	12	17	20	23
Satellite TV dish	*	*	2	4	8	10	12	14
Video camera	1	2	3	4	5	9	10	11
Nicam digital stereo television set	n/a	n/a	n/a	n/a	5	6	7	10
Cable TV	1	1	2	1	3	3	3	7
Widescreen television	n/a	n/a	n/a	n/a	n/a	n/a	n/a	7
Cable phone	n/a	n/a	n/a	n/a	n/a	n/a	1	5
Video disc player	1	1	2	2	2	3	2	4
Have one or more of these	65	67	77	81	80	83	86	89
Have none of these	35	33	23	19	20	17	14	11

Notes: (1) * Less than 0.5 per cent. (2) n/a = Not asked.

The survey confirmed the increased growth of satellite television, with, in 1994, a reach of almost one in seven viewers. Not surprisingly it was, again, the younger viewers (16–20, 25–44) as well as those working classes termed 'C2s' who were likely to be connected. Cable TV grew too, quite dramatically from 1983 after years of somewhat gradual growth. Overall it is the middle-class (ABC1) households who are more likely to be more fully equipped with television-related items than working-class (C2DE) households – although it is apparent that the majority of the population is more than well-equipped to extend their choice of viewing, should they wish to do so.

A separate analysis of equipment ownership concentrated on those in households with children: again, unsurprisingly, these households were even more likely to claim to have additional items to the TV set (98 per cent).

Video games and home computers were particularly prominent. Those cabled or dished households reported a higher possession of VCRs, teletext sets, home computers, CD players, video games, video cameras and NICAM digital stereo sets than those not connected to such services.

VCRs

Four out of five viewers claimed to possess a VCR, while one in five claimed to have more than one VCR. Viewers in the age range 16–20 were the most likely to make such claims, while having teenagers in the household also positively influenced the likelihood of having more than one VCR.

The VCR is one technological device which has radically altered our relationship with television, allowing us a previously undreamed of degree of choice of what we actually see on the set. Barwise and Ehrenberg itemize the four distinct uses of the VCR. Firstly, VCRs overcome the 'transient nature of television' by allowing us to record 'off-air'. In other words we time-shift programmes in order to view them at a more convenient moment, or merely to collect them for our television 'library'. Secondly, the VCR offers us access to an 'almost infinite variety of programmes', especially hired-in movies. Thirdly, in tandem with a camera, the VCR creates the possibility of home videos. It is perhaps ironic that this consumer control over the outpourings from television, has, according to my aesthetic taste, rebounded: a number of popular programmes on all channels celebrate home videos – the majority of which are highly embarrassing, both aesthetically and personally. Finally, when playing a tape we may control how we watch. Zip fast-forward, utilize slo-mo, freeze-frame, and so on. Most used is the fast-forward button pushed to escape commercials, however strong the narrative might be or however high the production values. The VCR, although limited in many respects, is the stepping-stone to interactive video disks where the viewer may jump between different items.[16]

Some estimates put VCR viewing at approximately five hours per week per household, with over half of the allotted time used to view time-shifted material, and about half for watching movies (and other pre-recorded hired or bought tapes). There is considerable debate as to the degree that viewers actually look at the time-shifted material: the feeling being that good intentions are swamped by competing material as well as little available time. Ann Gray's research on VCR use in working-class households did, in fact, find numerous cases of women time-shifting serials which were indeed subsequently viewed. One of her informants however, explained that she felt less guilty watching 'real time' television than she did when watching a videotape. Her reasoning was that television transmitted programmes whether she personally decided to watch or not, whereas the use of a videotape implied a decision to view, an act totally in her control.

Gray also believes that the distribution of tapes within the households she researched confirmed her view that, compared to their children and partners, very few women owned tapes of their own or archived tapes for themselves. She concludes that the 'organisation and maintenance of an archive would seem to be a predominantly male and middle-class activity', and that the whole concept of 'an archive is based on the assumption that there will be more than one viewing of the product, something that would appear to be a predominant male activity'.[17] This is a plausible enough argument given the degree of guilt women expressed at watching for what they considered to be excessive amounts of time: in working-class households, the male tended to be allowed more clearly demarcated leisure time, hence television and video viewing was more readily allowable.

The theme of gendered relationships to forms of communication has been noted by numerous researchers both in the UK and elsewhere. For example, German research suggests that many women 'reluctantly conform to masculine styles of media use', and also that the media activities of parents often serve as an example for the children. From the woman's point of view it is the new media in particular, especially VCRs and computers, which are part of the 'masculine domain'.[18] Despite the 'IT skills' that women increasingly possess, it may well be that gendered roles will continue to operate in the realm of domestic media activities. Research in the USA suggests that 'women's attendance to the VCR' is minimal and often takes place at times when men are unlikely to be present. The same researchers observed that children as young as three years old understood, albeit in an elementary manner, both the conceptual and practical aspects of the VCR: 'where the child is given specific guidance in the functional aspects of the machine, he or she can become very adept at fast forwarding past undesired material as well as locating and replaying favourite parts'.[19]

Those who believed that the emergence of the VCR might herald a total cultural change were soon disappointed, as people have never used them as an *alternative* to television, but invariably as a way of watching more of it. The viewer certainly has been given more choice, but it has never dented the 'mould of television culture'. Rather it has given people access to more of the same.[20] In other words, video has not, in any true sense, created an alternative source of programmes to that of the broadcasting and film companies. The majority of hired or bought movies on video, for instance, have already enjoyed a cinema release and possibly an outing on broadcast television. This is due, in part, to the collaboration by the video-machine manufacturers with major film companies to carry only their material on pre-recorded tapes.

Rentals of feature films is big business. In 1986, for example, 350 million feature films were hired in the UK, obviously a significant trade for the US film industry. In the same year it was estimated that nearly 15 times more people in Britain watched a rented film on video than went to the cinema.[21] Moreover, a glance at the top twenty most popular time-shifted programmes during 1994 illustrates the power of the film narrative. For

Table 2.2 Top 20 time-shifted programmes for all individuals, in millions, all channels, Jan.–Dec. 1994

Programmes	Channel	Day	Date	Live ('000s)	Timeshift ('000s)
1 *EastEnders*	BBC1	Mon	18.04.94	8,153	2,673
2 *Mind The Baby Mr Bean*	ITV	Mon	25.04.94	10,026	2,570
3 *Do It Yourself*	ITV	Mon	10.01.94	13,077	2,527
4 *One Foot In the Xmas Grave*	BBC1	Sun	25.12.94	13,077	2,052
5 *Basic Instinct*	ITV	Tue	16.11.94	5,539	1,814
6 *Terminator 2*	BBC1	Sat	03.09.94	9,201	1,777
7 *Back To School Mr Bean*	ITV	Tue	26.10.94	12,703	1,749
8 *It'll Be Alright On The Night*	ITV	Sat	10.12.94	12,040	1,696
9 *Wrong Trousers*	BBC2	Mon	04.04.94	6,675	1,635
10 *EastEnders*	BBC1	Tue	12.04.94	14,281	1,485
11 *Silence Of The Lambs*	ITV	Sat	22.10.94	9,027	1,452
12 *Blind Date*	ITV	Sat	19.11.94	7,754	1,437
13 *Christmas Hear*	ITV	Sun	25.12.94	12,361	1,428
14 *Robocop*	ITV	Sat	19.03.94	7,689	1,414
15 *Coronation Street*	ITV	Mon	03.01.94	14,899	1,399
16 *Coronation Street*	ITV	Wed	29.06.94	15,149	1,380
17 *Look Who's Talking*	ITV	Sun	20.02.94	7,805	1,347
18 *EastEnders*	BBC1	Thu	27.10.94	17,978	1,336
19 *Gremlins 2*	ITV	Mon	26.09.94	6,504	1,329
20 *Sleeping Beauty*	ITV	Sun	25.12.94	6,742	1,327

Source: Taylor Nelson AGB/BARB/AGB Television, 1995.

example, *Terminator 2*, broadcast by BBC1 was watched by over nine million viewers 'live', and almost another two million who recorded it and watched it within the following week. And, no doubt, these films were subsequently watched on a few further occasions. In order to maintain and maximize profit margins, given that time-shifting reduces rental volume, film companies are in a position to demand premium payments from broadcasters for the showing of successful or popular movies. The watching of movies on video appears, according to some research, to be a gendered activity. There is evidence of an unwillingness on the part of women to impose their choice of movies on the other members of the household, the reason being that when they have chosen what to watch the movies were not considered a success – perhaps an indication of the trend that sees both boys and girls (in addition to their father) expressing a preference for, say, *Terminator* than *Sleepless in Seattle*. The consequence of this process is that women find themselves watching movies they don't especially like in order to avoid domestic friction and the disapproval of their husband and children.[22]

In the 1994 survey of those viewers who possessed a VCR, three out of four said its main use was for time-shifting programmes while one-quarter talked of hiring pre-recorded tapes. Not surprisingly, watching hired movies was more likely to occur in those households with children under

15 years. There were few differences in such VCR use between satellite and cable households and terrestrial-only viewers: the most obvious one being that those with cable or satellite were less likely to hire movies, as such material was already available in abundance down the cable or from the dish. When asked about their VCR use the overwhelming majority talked of the attraction of being able to watch what they liked, *when* they liked. A close second was the view that it extended choice, although it is worth mentioning that over 60 per cent agreed that they often had difficulty finding enough time to watch all the programmes they had so, previously, enthusiastically taped. A further illustration of the ever-increasing privatization of family life was that three-quarters of viewers trumpeted the VCR for the reason that it saved them 'the trouble and expense' of going to the cinema.

It has already been remarked that one of the VCR's fond uses is that of skipping through commercials on time-shifted material. This desire was itself one of the major reasons why another device entered the lexicon of television – the remote control device, or RCD. Through 'grazing' viewers are now able to redefine dramatically the structure of television programming by combining seemingly disparate elements of content to their own individual taste. Viewers *zap* in order to avoid commercials or what they see as boring or unnecessary television, so no longer does viewing consist of a few programmes: rather, it resembles a vast collection of programme segments selected by the viewer.[23] Advertisers have nowhere to run: viewers *zip* through recorded programmes too, avoiding commercials however attractive in production values or novelty they may well be. It could well be argued that one of the growth areas in television creativity is the production of unusual – even esoteric – commercials, with expensively funded high-production values in a desperate attempt to keep viewers watching. Perhaps they occasionally succeed, especially with younger viewers, but they do so often at the expense of the product promoted: the music is hummed, the 'storylines' recalled, the beautiful faces adored, but the product remains unrecognized, rarely recalled.

This cruel little device, the RCD, has its most recent origins in the USA of the 1950s. Since the beginning of both radio and television, devices were sought to control unwanted programming and, in particular, commercials. One early attempt consisted of a hand-held device which simply involved a 20-foot cord being attached to a television loudspeaker. One click of the switch turned the sound off but left the picture on so the viewer would know when the unwanted sound material had ended. Click – the sound returned.[24] By the 1980s such primitive devices as the amusingly named 'Blab Off' were long forgotten. Manufacturers now spoke of 'remote-controlled homes', with RCDs linked to computer-based home controllers: it could change television channels, list chores on the screen, doors could be locked, lights switched on, as could the oven. By the end of the decade devices were available that allowed individuals from the comfort of their living rooms to start their cars on a cold winter morning.[25]

And the future? Palm-sized remotes are now a reality, while voice recognition remotes are on their way. A Californian manufacturer has developed a RCD utilizing voice recognition which operates all VCR functions in addition to the actual TV set. It can, allegedly, learn to recognize up to four different voices from up to 40 feet away. If voice-recognition technology proceeds at its current rate RCDs will all but disappear: users will simply command the component with two-step commands. The VCR, say, will be spoken to, then ordered to behave: 'VCR, rewind'.[26] Also promised are devices which can automatically change channels during commercials while real-time viewing, or delete them when recording.

The RCD deserves a more prominent place in the lexicon of television. It has fundamentally altered television watching, a fact which of course has not been favourably received by the advertising industry, television producers or those in the business of audience measurement. In the USA, for example, statistics suggest that almost 40 per cent of viewers with remotes switch channels at least half the time when commercials grace the screen.[27] And with over 70 million USA households equipped with remotes, such behaviour is deeply significant.

The 1994 ITC survey asked questions concerning the use of and attitudes towards 'teletext'. Launched in Britain in 1973, teletext allows viewers with a suitably equipped set[28] to look up the latest news items, sporting information, weather forecasts and television schedules. A speedy and flexible service, it is more up to date but more limited than newspapers, but also free once the relevant TV set has been purchased. Three-quarters of satellite-dish owners in the sample claimed teletext ownership, a figure a little higher than those of cable viewers and much higher than terrestrial-only viewers of which only half claimed ownership. It appears that teletext is either used almost every other day or hardly at all! Men tend to use the service more than women, and the young and early middle-aged adults (25–44) were more likely to report wide usage.[29]

The most popular items mentioned by teletext users surveyed in 1994 were TV programme guides – mentioned by half of the viewers – and national news, which a third noted. Also popular was sport, holiday information and travel items. Such teletext services as problems pages, education, dating services, consumer advice and computer games were hardly mentioned at all. Opinions were then sought as to the quantity of such services and although sport and the TV programme guide remained popular, a number of other less often used information items emerged as highly appreciated: thus subtitles, financial pages and music news were also spoken well of. However it was racing information that topped the appreciation poll, perhaps unfairly fuelling the stereotype of the unemployed satellite-dish-owning *Sun*-reading male hoping against hope for a windfall.

The majority of those surveyed knew of the teletext subtitling service, but tended *never* to use the facility. Since older viewers are more likely to have hearing problems such a service could well be valuable to them, however they under-use the service compared to younger viewers. Some research has suggested that older viewers in particular find teletext sets too complicated,[30] although technophobia is, of course, not limited to the older person.

Satellite and Cable

My first encounter with cable television was in New York a number of years ago when, in a hotel room, I inadvertently tuned into a 'new age' channel. A group of men were laconically discussing some of the more esoteric aspects of the *Tibetan Book of the Dead* – *bardo* states, moment of death and the cycle of reincarnation. From time to time a contributor would pop into frame from nowhere and seat himself in front of the camera's gaze. Occasionally one of the discussants would mention his telephone number for the benefit of any interested viewer wishing to take matters further. This was live and basic television: no rehearsals, no cutting, no graphics and no editing. Shambolic, but somehow appealing through its lack of professionalism or gloss veneer.

It is cable, together with satellite, that constitute the major media talking points of the 1990s. The potential of new technologies, new distribution channels and cross-border activity has encouraged massive investment, acquisition activities and avid speculation. The application of digital compression will mean – in the next few years – a vast increase in broadcasting capacity, potentially allowing UK viewers access to up to 500 or more channels. Indeed, the number of channels available in Europe currently stands at 80 key national channels, 900 local and regional channels and 140 satellite channels.[31] Before looking in more detail at cable and satellite it is perhaps wise to add a salutary note of caution: European television audiences predominantly watch their domestic channels. One such estimate is of 94 per cent of total consumption, with pan-European and global channels such as MTV and CNN accounting for a very small proportion of viewing.[32]

The contemporary multi-channel household is merely the tip of the iceberg, yet it could have hardly been envisaged a decade or so ago. Cable operators transmit local channels and satellite channels while the satellites themselves beam in material directly. In the UK a galaxy of well-known branded channels and more esoteric or niche offerings compete for attention. MTV Europe, Sky One, Sky Movies, Bravo, are examples of better-known brands, but the list is impressive in its apparent scope: Christian channels such as Vision, the Greek language programming of Hellenic Television, PTV (The Persian Channel) offers Iranian singing and dancing, Japansat and Asianet, while Identity Television broadcasts Afro-Caribbean programming. More esoteric is Muslim Television Ahmadiyyah which consists, in the main, of Koranic readings, discourses and discussion. Such offerings rub shoulders with home shopping on QVC and bullfighting at tea-time,[33] not to mention the slashed-down hardcore porn ('no genital *detail*') of The Adult Channel, and Babylon Blue.

It was some 50 years ago that Arthur C. Clarke demonstrated the theoretical possibility of 'parking' satellites above the earth in a geostationary orbit thereby enabling the continuous provision of communication services.[34] By the 1980s technological advances following the early success of the Early Bird enabled powerful satellites to reach directly to homes (DTH). Massive reception dishes were no longer necessary nor was the associated redistribution via cable. The history of satellite TV in the UK can be told quickly: since its official launch in 1982 and following the acquisition of the only competitive satellite broadcaster, BSB, Sky Television has proceeded to increase its operation to its present base of almost three million subscribers. BSkyB also dominates programming as the majority of channels available on cable TV are produced by BSkyB. Many of those are not owned by BSkyB but they benefit from being sold and marketed as part of one of these packages. The vast majority of subscribers take the Sky Multi-Channels package which includes encrypted (scrambled) channels such as Sky One and Discovery and the unencrypted Sky News, QVC and MTV. Such subscribers would also receive the unencrypted 'free' channels such as Eurosport, but to have access to the film and sport channels, TV Asia or the Adult Channel, extra payment is required. Further services are potentially available with the appropriate dishes, decoders and cards.

Of the 97 per cent of all UK households equipped to receive television, almost 16 per cent are now either cabled (4 per cent) or in possession of a dish (12 per cent) to receive non-terrestrial channels. Compared to 22 million conventional television households, a total of three million dishes may not sound too impressive. However, if compared with the figure of half a million in early 1990 the total is immediately more significant.[35] The penetration of both DTH and cable varies widely between the different nations of western Europe.

Table 2.3 Western Europe, penetration of DTH and cable, 1993

	All TV households ('000s)	DTH households ('000s)	percentage penetration	Cable households ('000s)	percentage penetration
Germany	31,390	4,430	14.1	16,660*	53
France	20,900	180	0.9*	1,200	6
UK	22,168	2,571	11.6	611	3
Italy	20,166	0	0	0	0
Spain	11,249	880	7.8	202	2
Belgium	3,765	0	0	3,637	97
Netherlands	6,076	182	3	5,468	90

* Estimate
Source: Carat, Datamonitor.

Viewers in the 3.5 million households with access to cable and satellite channels watch a little more television than those without such services. The attraction of the BSkyB package is apparent as Sky One and the pay-TV service Sky Movies attract somewhat higher audiences than both BBC2 and Channel 4. Perhaps the following speculative equation suggests one possible shape of the future: the two BBC channels have a combined share of about 30 per cent, while ITV with Channel 4 settle at something under 40 per cent. The remaining 30 per cent is dominated by the BSkyB channels (20 per cent), with the other channels in the multi-channel package fast emerging. Clearly there will be fluctuations in such viewing figures: but the long-term trends are persuasive. Further audience fragmentation will invariably occur, the degree of which being determined by the rate of growth of cable and satellite services, which in itself can only remain somewhat uncertain.

As a result of government funding policy, cable television has developed at different rates in Europe. When governments have taken the initiative in funding the cable infrastructure, subsequent penetration is much higher. Thus Germany, Belgium and the Netherlands have significant cable networks while in the UK 'broadland cable is in its infancy'.[36] Although satellite television (DTH) has developed where cable was initially absent the two now compete where cable networks are laid. While DTH offers the potential of multi-channel TV, cable has the added potential to supply interactive services and telephony.

The origins of cable television are to be found in the USA in the late 1940s, predominantly as an attempt to improve television reception in remote rural areas where the broadcast signal was poor in quality, or where it was limited to only a few stations. The 'stampede in growth' of cable was the decade of the 1970s and particularly significant was HBO which tapped into viewers' interest in uncut feature films.[37]

The UK cable television has developed slowly, mainly due to governmental insistence that development ought to be financed by private capital. Almost 700,000 households in the UK are currently cabled, a significant increase on the 1987 figure of 249,000 and that of 423,000 in 1990. Although the Cable Authority was actually established in 1984 substantial growth in cable did not occur until the early 1990s. Importantly, the 1990 Broadcasting Act allowed, for the first time, foreign companies to become directly involved in the UK cable industry. Accordingly, recent statistics on the ownership of the 127 cable franchises show that only 14 per cent are wholly UK owned. More significant than overseas investment was the 1991 *Duopoly Review of the Telecommunications Industry* which subsequently enabled cable companies operating their own switches to enter the telephony market in competition with BT and Mercury.[38] Indeed, it has been the attraction of these less expensive telephone services rather than cable television itself which has been the driving force behind the spread of UK cable.[39] In the year January 1994 to January 1995 the number of telephone lines installed by cable franchises providing telephony rose from just over 300,000 to a little over 700,000.[40]

To a considerable degree, cable is still essentially a retailer of satellite programmes, especially as so few operators have invested in 'local programming' despite their franchise application promises that they would do so.[41] The Sky package remains the basis of all cable systems, with the cable operators charged for taking the channels. Premium channels meanwhile are available on further payment. There has, however, been the gradual introduction of cable-only channels like Wire TV, Live TV, the Parliamentary Channel and Channel One (Associated Newspapers' news channel for London),[42] and in addition there are a few local-only channels and elementary interactive services like The Box, a channel which plays videos on numerical demand and which has overtaken MTV in cabled homes. It is perhaps the features of uniqueness or distinctiveness – in The Box's case, the element of interactivity – which are required for a channel to begin to prosper.[43]

Despite the current reliance on Sky for programming, as cable television 'matures' this relationship might well change. There is, as indicated, the as yet untapped *potential* of local programming. It could be argued that such programming both meets and expresses minority interests: Cable London has actively encouraged Hellenic programming for the local Greek and Cypriot communities, while Yorkshire Cable is enthusiastically planning to cater for Asian needs. Another possible thrust of local programming lies in interactivity: for example, in dating services, property advertising, banking and home shopping. The existing major shopping channel QVC, imported from the USA in 1993, is not yet fully interactive, as viewers are obliged to telephone the channel to place their orders.

In its place of origin, the USA, home shopping has not been 'widely profitable' and is largely limited to trinkets and non-essential goods. Media analysts argue that for such channels to succeed in the cable mainstream 'improved programming, interactivity and changes in consumer attitudes will be required'.[44] Perhaps, more significantly, specialist interactive channels will invariably cost the viewer extra in subscription: and as such demand is difficult to predict, the scope of such services is somewhat unknown.

Cable and Satellite Viewers

What do we actually know of those viewers who are able to view non-terrestrial programming? To begin with it is clear that they are enthusiasts of Hollywood movies and also early British ones, and all manner of sports programmes, but especially football and cricket, and lovers of classical popular television from the archives: *Star Trek*, *M*A*S*H*, *Some Mothers Do 'Ave 'Em*, *Kate and Allie*, *thirtysomething*, *Colditz*, and other memorable television moments. Perhaps even more significant is the interest in the various music channels and children's programming: *The Muppet Show*, *The Simpsons*, *Teenage Mutant Hero Turtles*, *The Super Mario Brothers* and other television heroes.

The ITC's 1994 survey added more detailed information to this emerging viewer profile: children continue to be heavier viewers of cable and satellite channels than adults, to the point where almost half their viewing time is spent watching those channels; not surprisingly, the viewing of cable and satellite channels decreases with increased age; that viewers in the upper socio-economic groups continue to be relatively light viewers of cable and satellite programmes, although significantly, socio-economic differences in viewing patterns are less marked than in previous years. It is obviously far too early to discern any fundamental patterns of viewing especially as the growth of such channels steadily continues, the audience fragments and segments even further, and as the terrestrial channels compete more strenuously in this uncertain media market-place.

The 1994 survey asked all non-cable and satellite viewers whether they were interested in receiving extra channels through such systems. Almost three-quarters expressed disinterest, while one in six were interested in satellite and one in nine in cable. Of these minorities the younger in age the more enthusiastic the interest expressed. Indeed, it was those who were *single* who showed the greatest degree of interest in receiving satellite (34 per cent) or cable television (20 per cent): further proof perhaps of the companionability of the box in the corner.

The majority of viewers were also disinclined to imagine they would ever pay for such services, either on a general subscription basis or in terms of a pay-per-view basis. Similar sentiments were expressed for the video-on-demand (VOD) option, although the younger (16–24) age group were, not surprisingly, more enthusiastic. Video-on-demand whereby viewers have the opportunity to select a programme from a catalogue to watch whenever they please, could well be an interesting test as to the future of the competitive media market-place. Several companies are pursuing the technology involved, including British Telecom. For BT video-on-demand represents a 'strategic move, an attempt to redress the competitive imbalance imposed by the regulators whereby it is prevented from offering broadcast services while cable companies have been given free rein to develop cable telephony'.[45]

Such viewer disinterest in such subscription and pay-TV services is hardly surprising given the extensive range and quality of terrestrial television: besides which, when viewers become disappointed with such television they are able to console themselves with the thought that they still have only to pay the BBC licence fee (the *hidden* costs of ITV remaining *hidden* in their mind). Interestingly enough, the attitude that there were 'enough channels' or that there was 'sufficient entertainment on the four main channels' was expressed by at least a quarter of those asked. Another quarter considered that more channels were 'too costly' while another quarter was simply 'not interested'.

The most popularly received channels in satellite households were claimed to be Sky News, Sky One, Eurosport, UK Gold, MTV, and UK Living, with a similar profile for cable viewers. Given the claim of the *postmodernists* that a multi-channel future will lead to even greater information graffiti, it is interesting to observe that viewers can indeed be confused or at least uncertain about which channels they can receive or may be *actually watching*. Some satellite households claimed to receive channels which were *not* satellite distributed like The Box which is only available on cable. On the other hand the response from cable viewers tended to *underplay* the availability to them of certain channels – The Learning Channel, Landscape Channel, Euronews, etc. – as compared with the ITC's quarterly statistics showing the number of homes to which they are actually supplied.

Some households, it appears, cannot get enough of these new channels: indeed, some consumers are prepared to go to extra expense to obtain more than one decoder for the household. Other viewers subscribe to cable and in addition also possess a dish. On the other hand, some viewers take up a 'subscription' package only subsequently to 'disconnect' their dishes or cable connections, an activity comically termed by the industry as 'churn'.

The 1994 survey uncovered evidence for both activities – of multi-decoder purchase and, on the other hand, churn. Although the great majority of those questioned possessed one decoder, a modest proportion (7 per cent) claimed they had two or more. This was more likely to be the case in cable households. Such second and third decoders appear to be acquired to enable viewers to watch non-terrestrial channels in more than one room, as unlike terrestrial channels which can be viewed anywhere within a home, the same is not automatically true for satellite and cable channels. Those with extra decoders tended, not surprisingly, to view in bedrooms – parental or child's – in addition to the main 'living room'.

To investigate the possibility of future 'churn', satellite and cable viewers surveyed were questioned as to the likelihood of them still subscribing in a year's time. Almost 80 per cent claimed that they would be, while those who strongly imagined they would not (9 per cent) tended to be found among the middle classes (ABs). Relatedly, the survey uncovered viewers who had indeed once subscribed to such channels but had subsequently disconnected: the main reasons offered for such a decision were either the cost, the number of repeats or the quality of the programmes (especially those questioned in cable households).

It is overwhelmingly obvious that the future contours of television are yet to be accurately drawn: that audiences will fragment is an undeniable fact, but to what precise degree and in which direction cannot be accurately predicted. Much will depend on whether or not the British television viewer agrees to the principle of pay-TV and, more importantly, whether programming on cable and satellite channels is seen to be worth the money paid to receive it.

As we have reported, home entertainment media of all sorts continue to develop, with, for example, TV sets and computer screens increasingly sharing the same space. However, there are isolated cases of more simple systems too, remnants of a more predictable past as well as alternative evidence of an extensive multi-channel future. Thus, a few viewers can still be found peering at small black and white sets, perfectly attuned to those mid-afternoon 1950s movies or repeats of *The Cisco Kid*, while other households appear to be literally swamped with television images, invariably American in origin: different rooms offering *Denver the Last Dinosaur* and *NBA Basketball*, or the more conventional *Roseanne*, but enjoyed in the luxury of stereo surround-sound.

3

Programmes

There is a limit to what can be said about television; and much of what can be said will be tautologous. Formulas are arrived at, programmes are programmed; however many channels we are eventually blessed with, there will be nothing remotely comparable to the book published in a short print run for a small audience. To bring to bear the critical scrutiny appropriate to the novels of Dickens or the poems of Donne would be the depth of absurdity. Television needs attention, but attention of another and, alas, more uncertain and hazardous nature.

D. J. Enright (1990), *Fields of Vision*

In this chapter we consider the on-screen 'successes and failures', genres that thrill, and others which depress the viewing appetite: and, in particular, we consider the changes taking place which will invariably affect the future TV diet we are urged to consume.

From its humble beginnings some 50 years ago television has eased itself into our everyday lives, to the point that we are almost addicted to it. None the less, and despite this, there has *always* been a degree of ambivalence towards it. Some critics blame television for all manner of human folly or societal disease or crisis: delinquency, divorce, family discord, sexual crimes, financial greed, the decline in literacy – the list is extensive. Other people, meanwhile, exercise equanimity towards television, recognizing its virtues as well as the potential for harm. Others simply point to the existence of the 'off' button.

It is unquestionably true that television calls forth imitative behaviour, although the range and extent of such imitation is an unanswered question and one to which we will return in chapter 8. More significant, perhaps, is the extensive degree of *distraction* that television offers us. Why learn a second language, engage in lengthy and discursive conversations, play with our children, or visit the cinema or theatre when from the comfort of our homes a diet of sitcoms, game shows, news and drama can effortlessly fill the empty time?

The impression that television is all-pervasive, that television surrounds our very existence, is reinforced by the ever-increasing tendency for it to act in a self-referential manner. All art forms actually exhibit self-referring tendencies, perhaps a tribute to artistic continuity and community, but narcissism in television is 'something else – blatant and habitual'. Television refers to television in the 'calm assurance that nothing of significance exists outside television'. As D. J. Enright remarks, 'situation comedies make knowing allusions to other situation comedies, while newscasters take part in quiz shows', and 'adverts feed off programmes, programmes feed off adverts, and participants in game shows can win a TV set, a video-recorder, a freezer containing three months' supply of TV suppers . . . '.[1] All of this, he adds, is carried out in a spontaneous and un-calculated manner, as 'natural' as breathing.

It is, indeed, this ambiguous but lingering sense of unreality created by television that has so concerned a number of cultural critics. Television, they argue, intersects with two related themes: on the one hand, the un-relenting rise of the celebrity, and relatedly the desire to live vicariously through others more well-known than oneself. The argument is as follows. Television creates an illusion of intimacy when celebrities enter into our living rooms, appearing as they do so in a physically manageable size. Absent is the alienating distance of the big screen, theatrical stage or lecture platform. It is, therefore, not impossible to confuse what we see on the television screen with our daily reality.[2] This smallness of screen size together with the domestic context pull television towards all that is familiar, homely and, perhaps, even boring. But it is, however, rescued by the 'magic of stardom', the feature which gives television such a central role in the political economy of mass communications.[3] Indeed, Neil Postman acutely comments that television's strongest point is that it 'brings personalities into our hearts, not abstractions into our heads'. He adds, somewhat caustically, that that was the reason why CBS's programmes about the universe were called *Walter Cronkite's Universe*: 'one would think that the grandeur of the universe needs no assistance from Walter Cronkite'.[4]

Fred Inglis recalls the work of Leo Lowenthal who perceives a deep change in the imagery of popular culture when, 'checking through the mammoth weeklies of American domestic life, the *Saturday Evening Post*, *Harper's* and the like, he finds a shift completed by the 1920s from heroes who are captains of industry to heroes who are "celebrities", a quite new category including sportsmen, star actors in film and theatre, all alike in that their fame is to be looked at, not to do'.[5] Thus, the argument continues, the history of fame is the history of the shifting definition of achievement in a social world, and the moment at which capitalism moves from its pro-ductive to its consumerist phase.

In one respect television is merely the latest form in the progression from oil painting to copper-engraving, to photography and movies as an influence on self-presentation and cultural focus. But the reproducibility of the image and, therefore, the fame both widened its appeal and undermined its uniqueness. As fame was dependent on a mass audience, so it was more closely tied to the audience's gaze towards the famous.[6]

In *The Image* Daniel Boorstin develops this argument further. He suggests that the household names which populate our consciousness are not actually heroes, rather they are *celebrities*: persons known for their well-known-ness, and manufactured by us in response to our exaggerated expectations. Celebrity-worship and hero-worship should not, he adds, be confused, yet daily we do so, and by doing so deprive ourselves of all role models. As Boorstin puts it, celebrities are the receptacles into which we pour our own purposelessness. They are nothing but ourselves seen in a magnifying glass. As a result of this the lives of these entertainer-celebrities cannot possibly extend our horizons. Indeed, the names which were once made by the news now make the news themselves, and whereas the hero was distinguished by his achievement the celebrity is recognized by his image. The hero created himself, the celebrity is made by the media.[7] The connection between this process and the tendency to live life vicariously is made by Christopher Lasch:

> The mass media, with their cult of celebrity and their attempt to surround it with glamour and excitement, have made Americans a nation of fans . . . The media give substance to and thus intensify narcissistic dreams of fame and glory, encourage the common man to identify himself with the stars and to hate the 'herd' and make it more and more difficult for him to accept the banality of everyday existence.[8]

Thus, there is this tendency, in a sense, to exempt ourselves from our own lives and live them through the 'reality' of television. Søren Kierkegaard, the nineteenth-century Danish philosopher, tells the story of the absent-minded man so abstracted from his own life that he hardly knows *he* exists until, one fine morning, he wakes up to find himself dead.[9]

This, then, is one line of cultural criticism. Others, conversely, warmly embrace the shared culture which television has both partially created and greatly contributed to. Such critics point to the wide range of programming which acts like a 'net or membrane stretched round society', holding it together, trying always to include newcomers, and creating a texture of narratives which gives them a voice too.[10] Daily conversations are merely refractions of the previous evening's television, while children share visions of heaven and hell through communal exposure to television's heroes and villains – and *everyone* knows either David Frost, Jeremy Paxman, Cilla Black or Chris Evans. But this shared culture is itself partial: some members rarely watch television and then only selectively, while others have literally fallen in love with it. None the less, it *is* deeply embedded in the wider culture it both creates and is part of. And television watching is, as we have earlier argued, obviously a subjective experience: personal circumstances and biography enter the viewing process. My taste might not be yours. A blissful schedule for me would include substantial episodes of the earlier episodes of *NYPD Blue*. I personally identify with the Catholicism and touchy-feelyness of original character John Kelly, enjoy the handheld jerky camera, the sex and sensuality in the shadows, and the subtle characterizations, not least Kelly's preference for rhetorical questions – 'am I right?' Other viewers, not least the American Family Association, find the show appalling, or badly crafted, perhaps difficult to understand, or just plain boring.

The fact that we do not always agree on what constitutes 'good television' renders media analysis a problematic activity. How, for instance, do we compare (say) different decades of television programming? By the highlights, or the average programmes? Can we actually agree on what the highlights were?

An intrinsic problem is that as many television formats and templates were devised in the early experimental years of the 1960s and 1970s, it is subsequently difficult to produce novelty from a predetermined framework. Additionally, there is the other in-built tendency that we have seen most things already – programmes, genres, faces, sounds – thus, a process of desensitization sets in. Consider some of the important television of the past decades: *This is Your Life* (1955), *Coronation Street* (1960), *Z Cars* (1962), *That Was The Week That Was* (1962), *The Prisoner* (1967), *Star Trek* (1969), *M*A*S*H* (1973), *Fawlty Towers* (1975), *I, Claudius* (1976), *Grange Hill* (1978), *Minder* (1979) and *Black Adder* (1983). Many still show on either terrestrial or satellite channels. More significant is the fact that the important programming of the 1990s – *NYPD Blue*, *The X-Files*, *Cracker* and *Inspector Morse*, from drama, for example – has to be developed within a context far different from earlier ones. Over and above the obvious fact that the creative process cannot be turned on at will, there are those constraints imposed by budgetary considerations and also the critical context of a ratings-driven mentality. This is why there are so few *Morse*-type programmes on the screen.

The 1990s have seen established genres continue to be explored, some less successfully than others: note, for example, the paucity of current sit-coms, compared to the continuation of both new and well-established soaps. At the same time the decade has introduced into the lexicon a number of hybrid formats. The conventional chat show has now been all but replaced by the so-called 'nuts and sluts' show, in which both guests and audience indulge in self-humiliation as they divulge personal fantasies and secrets – be it stories of transvestism, binge-eating, dilemmas of slimming, or agonies of rape, incest or murder. A recent *Ricki Lake* show set a standard with an infidelity special entitled 'I can't believe you left me for *that*'.

Factual entertainment continues to be broadcast either on daytime television, with cyclical themes, guests and even audiences; early morning discussion programmes cover the same material as the 'nuts and sluts' shows but with more decorum and restraint; while core daytime programmes use presenter-celebrity-couples to present a mishmash of cookery, fitness, astrology, 'welfare', make-overs, celebrity interviews and phone-ins, all carried out crisply and cheerily. Reconstructions, either of crimes or disasters or emergencies appear to be popular in the mind of the producers, as do self-humiliating home-video programmes which are both inexpensive to make and allow us to laugh at each other's misfortunes.

Drama in particular has been severely affected by budgetary constraints. Consequently drama serials have been formulaic in the extreme, with the 'stories' simply being vehicles for 'stars'. There are moments in contemporary drama when the screen appears awash with doctors, patients, nurses, policemen, criminals, lawyers, victims and vets all working to a musical or *muzak* accompaniment. Of course *in theory*, the most marketable series would centrally feature a police doctor who shared his bachelorhood with a lovable mongrel named 'Patch'. Indeed, perhaps the template for the future is the BBC's serial *Dangerfield*: here is a doctor who also happens to be the local police surgeon, is a single parent with a confused son and flaky daughter, is accompanied by a lovable pet dog, has a doctor girlfriend, while the whole series is shot in rural England at a time when it never rains. Even the high-quality offerings are none the less formulaic: '*ER* is a smartly-woven, technically sophisticated medi-soap, pressing the laugh/cry/tough/tender buttons to rollercoaster you through a predictable but irresistible Kleenex-Catharsis . . . [it breaks] . . . its plotlines into two-minute attention-bites, using the relationships between the doctors and their nearest and dearest as scaffolding.'[11] Besides which, truly to understand the action of *ER* the viewer requires a postgraduate qualification in medico-linguistics.

Programmes

The 1994 ITC survey asked viewers questions about issues concerning audience share. Viewers reported that ITV was watched most of all (35 per cent), followed by BBC1 (28 per cent), then Channel 4 with 14 per cent and BBC2 with the same percentage. Finally satellite and cable channels attracted 9 per cent of viewing. Such figures are roughly in line with actual industry figures. What *is* clear from the evidence of the mid-1990s is that, of the terrestrial channels, it is ITV in particular that has suffered from the emergence of satellite and cable, with somewhat smaller inroads being made into BBC1's audiences.[12] Channel 4, meanwhile, continues steadily to increase its share.

The impact of cable and satellite channels is more vividly illustrated

Table 3.1 Channel share based on average daily hours of live television viewing

In percentages	BBC1	BBC2	ITV	Channel 4	Cable/Satellite	Total
1984	34.4	12.5	46.9	6.3	–	100.0
1985	31.6	15.8	47.4	5.3	–	100.0
1986	33.3	10.3	48.7	7.7	–	100.0
1987	38.2	11.8	41.2	8.8	–	100.0
1988	36.1	13.9	41.7	8.3	–	100.0
1989	37.1	11.4	42.9	8.6	–	100.0
1990	35.5	11.8	44.1	8.8	–	100.0
1991	36.4	11.8	44.1	8.8	–	100.0
1992	33.3	12.8	38.5	10.3	5.1	100.0
1993	33.3	11.1	38.9	11.1	5.6	100.0
1994	31.4	11.4	40.0	11.4	5.7	100.0

Source: Trends in Television, AGB/BARB, 1994.
Note: (a) Live viewing is defined as viewing of the broadcast material at the time of transmission; (b) The figures are averages for the month of April in each year.

when viewers in households receiving such services were questioned as to their viewing habits. Both ITV and BBC1 combined did not equal the non-terrestrial share. Industry figures for 1994 show a total terrestrial share of 65 per cent compared with 35 per cent for satellite and cable viewing. The slight difference cannot disguise the obvious longer term trends towards what is termed 'audience fragmentation'.

Table 3.2   Claimed share of viewing

In percentages	Total '94	Terrestrial only homes				Satellite dish homes				Cable homes			
		'91	'92	'93	'94	'91	'92	'93	'94	'91	'92	'93	'94
ITV	35	39	39	39	38	24	26	24	24	25	25	23	22
Channel 4	14	13	13	15	15	7	9	8	8	7	7	8	9
BBC1	28	34	34	32	31	19	19	20	18	19	19	20	18
BBC2	14	14	13	15	15	7	7	8	8	6	6	7	9
Satellite or cable	9	–	–	1	–	44	39	40	43	44	38	42	43

Source: ITC, 1994.

What people actually like to watch is inevitably a somewhat subjective issue and one which changes over time, although it is useful to remember that viewers are born into existing schedules, programme types and programme combinations, and quickly become habituated to the existing pattern: so their 'preferences' are somewhat constrained. None the less there are trends in such patterns which provide a useful starting point.

Viewers tend to choose a mixed diet of programmes: light entertainment, news, films, sport, drama and features. Of this menu, something over 60 per cent of viewing time is spent consuming entertainment programming including 'non-demanding' drama, while 30 per cent of the time is taken up with more demanding, informative programming including 'substantial drama' and news. The residual time covers a myriad of programming opportunities.[13] Significantly, the pattern is remarkably similar between the higher socio-economic groups and the lower ones: a demythologization of the idea that only working-class women watch soaps, and that only the more affluent immerse themselves in more 'highbrow' programming.

The viewers were asked of their interest in a broad range of 35 different programme types. Most popular were: national news, recent movies, natural history programmes, local, regional and international news, adventure or police series, sports, soaps, movies in general, game shows, drama, drama-documentaries and sit-coms. Least popular were programmes for older children, chat shows, programmes about politics, church services, business and financial items, arts programmes, programmes for schools and the under-5s, and at the bottom of the list, religion. Such a list clearly tells a story of the nation's priorities as to what it expects from television and, indeed, perhaps of its wider interests and concerns. From the box we seek entertainment, not education. It is also a highly predictable list. There is, of course, substantial 'minority interest' in such programming as politics and arts but it has to be understood that in the contemporary television environment even so-called minority programmes have to aim for higher-than-average ratings. A consequence is the rise of the formulaic and safe, at the expense of risk and innovation.

The Question of Gender

In keeping with established trends there were considerable differences between men and women in their preferred viewing: men were more likely to be interested in sports, current affairs, 'alternative' comedy, adult films, science, European items, politics and business, while women showed a preference for soap, game shows, drama, 'women's programmes', health and medical programmes, chat and programmes for the under-5s. All very predictable: men and movies, men and sport, men and politics, as women immerse themselves in soap while they entertain and occupy the children.

The following tables amply illustrate, in crude terms, this division of interest. Six sports programmes featured in the top twenty entries for men of that year. Their popular viewing patterns differed to some extent from those of women, despite the fact that a considerable amount of viewing was in the evenings when both sexes were 'available to view'. Presumably on several occasions different members of the same household watch different television sets. The most popular genre for women is, as if it need be said, soap, while conversely they watch less sport but more 'variety', game shows and drama. The only sporting events likely to unite the genders are such competitions as champion ice skating when there is British interest, the Grand National or the Olympics.

It has been argued that the claims men tend to make about only watching

Table 3.3   Top 20 programmes for men by TVR, Jan.–Dec. 1994*

Programme	Channel	Day	Date	TVR	000's	Channel Share
1 Torvill and Dean	BBC1	Mon	21.02.94	42.5	8,686	72
2 National Lottery Live	BBC1	Sat	19.11.94	37.4	7,667	68
3 Olympic Ice Dance Championship	BBC1	Mon	21.02.94	35.9	7,351	62
4 Licence To Kill	ITV	Mon	03.01.94	33.1	6,772	58
5 Coronation Street	ITV	Mon	14.02.94	33.1	6,762	68
6 World Cup/Final Grandstand	BBC1	Sun	17.07.94	33.0	6,760	63
7 World Cup Grandstand	BBC1	Tue	28.06.94	32.5	6,651	75
8 Coronation Street	ITV	Fri	14.01.94	32.4	6,625	70
9 Coronation Street	ITV	Tue	26.01.94	32.1	6,566	65
10 Touch of Frost	ITV	Sun	30.01.94	32.0	6,537	64
11 F.A. Cup Final 1994	BBC1	Sat	14.05.94	31.9	6,534	85
12 One Foot In The Xmas Grave	BBC1	Sun	25.12.94	31.3	6,433	53
13 It'll Be Alright On the Night 7	ITV	Sun	02.01.94	31.3	6,386	60
14 London's Burning	ITV	Sun	20.11.94	30.7	6,308	56
15 Utterly Worst/Night	ITV	Sun	10.04.94	30.8	6,306	60
16 Heartbeat	ITV	Sun	13.11.94	30.7	6,305	58
17 You've Been Framed	ITV	Sun	04.09.94	30.3	6,223	62
18 EastEnders	BBC1	Thu	27.10.94	30.2	6,195	67
19 Big Fight Live	ITV	Sat	05.02.94	30.2	6,169	62
20 EastEnders	BBC1	Tue	25.10.94	29.7	6,102	67

Table 3.4   Top 20 programmes for women by TVR, Jan.–Dec. 1994*

Programme	Channel	Day	Date	TVR	000's	Channel Share
1 Torvill and Dean	BBC1	Mon	21.02.94	55.6	12,786	78
2 Olympic Ice Dance Championship	BBC1	Mon	21.02.94	48.3	11,104	70
3 Coronation Street	ITV	Mon	14.02.94	46.3	10,653	77
4 Coronation Street	ITV	Fri	07.01.94	45.7	10,522	80
5 Coronation Street	ITV	Tue	26.01.94	45.4	10,444	77
6 EastEnders	BBC1	Thu	27.10.94	43.0	9,929	75
7 EastEnders	BBC1	Tue	25.10.94	41.1	9,500	73
8 Heartbeat	ITV	Sun	20.11.94	40.5	9,347	68
9 National Lottery Live	BBC1	Sat	19.11.94	38.9	8,987	63
10 Peak Practice	ITV	Tue	10.05.94	38.4	8,841	68
11 Soldier Soldier	ITV	Tue	13.12.94	38.2	8.823	66
12 Emmerdale	ITV	Thu	06.01.94	37.7	8,665	71
13 London's Burning	ITV	Sun	20.11.94	36.8	8,492	59
14 Casualty	BBC1	Sat	05.02.94	36.7	8,453	66
15 Emmerdale	ITV	Tue	05.01.94	36.7	8,442	65
17 The Bill	ITV	Fri	18.03.94	35.9	8,268	73
18 Charles: Priv. Man, Public Role	ITV	Tue	29.06.94	35.8	8,261	70
19 Touch of Frost	ITV	Sun	30.01.94	35.9	8,248	65
20 Cracker	ITV	Mon	05.12.94	35.7	8,245	59

Note: * Excluding multiple occurrences.
Source for tables 3.3 and 3.4: Taylor Nelson AGB/BARB/AGB Television, 1995.

'factual' television may misrepresent their actual behaviour, with their anxiety over admitting to watching fictional programmes fuelling their deceit.[14] Lull, however, believes that perhaps the apparent factual interests of men and the fictional interests of women are not, actually, so distinct. He argues that while sports programmes are obviously factual, games and matches are not, however, merely informational events. They are 'stories, too. They provoke emotional reactions'. A 'good game' is a drama, full of suspense and surprises: you don't know the ending until the last scene. 'News stories' too, he sees as dramatic forms. So, Lull concludes, perhaps men and women may be expressing preference for 'a type of story' rather than for programming that at first appears to be completely different.[15]

Programme Types

Two decades ago when the IBA carried out a similar survey to that in 1994[16] a majority of viewers, including men, *claimed* that they wished to see less televised sport. Given, however, its considerable presence on both contemporary terrestrial and satellite channels the contours of the past two decades' programming is indicative both of televisual and more wider cultural changes.

The top ten programmes for 1974 consisted of three sit-coms, *This is Your Life*, three comedy-entertainment shows, *News at Ten*, the *British Screen Awards* and *Miss World*. This last offering in itself was not without its own dramatic elements, but the controversy did not surround sexism or bimboism. Rather, in keeping with the mores of the time, the winner – Miss UK, Helen Morgan – was only allowed to keep her crown for five days, after it was revealed that she was an unmarried mother. The runner-up, from apartheid-ridden South Africa, was subsequently crowned.

The 'three-day week' meant that the television year of 1974 began with a 10.30 p.m. curfew. More importantly it was the year that heralded the introduction of domestic VCRs. The screen was regularly filled with popular sitcoms: *Love Thy Neighbour*, *Bless This House*, *Porridge*, and the contentious *It Ain't Half Hot Mum*, about a British platoon organizing a wartime concert-party in India. For this show Michael Bates 'blacked up' as Rangi Ram, while the cast shivered with glycerine 'sweat' on their foreheads in the Norfolk 'Jungle' where it was made.[17] The viewer was assumed to find the racist jokes about Indian servants funny, though the programme-makers claimed it was 'only entertainment', not to be taken too seriously. But, as Stuart Hood rightly remarks, 'a racist joke is no less racist for being funny or even witty'.[18]

Two decades later sit-coms fail to appear so significantly in popular successful programme lists, although they litter the schedules. Perhaps it is more difficult to craft them, or maybe the audience has simply tired of them? Certainly compared to the best of the US offerings – *Roseanne, Grace*

Under Fire, Ellen, Frazier – the domestic UK programmes generally pale into insignificance. D.J. Enright characterizes the popularity of sit-coms as offering 'concealed therapy by representing humorously some small failing or eccentricity, or mild misfortune or problem: lack of competence or confidence, the trials of retirement, shared accommodation, a change of job, grown-up children who decline to leave home.[19] Therein possibly lies the explanation. Perhaps we generally have less to laugh at these days, or perhaps feel less inclined to do so. Our misfortunes are multiplied. Therefore, only the best will succeed: *One Foot In The Grave*, a rare example of the craft.

The documentary series *The Family* made the headlines in 1974, when the BBC decided to make a Reading working-class family the subject of a twelve part fly-on-the-wall account of their lives: 'we are not a problem family, we are a family with problems'. The series was a somewhat depressing tale of poverty, quarrels, pregnancies, swearing and an illustration of poor nutrition. The producer admitted to the mistake of screening early episodes while recording later ones: the pressures of 'ordinary family life', which the series had set out to reflect, had become pressures of coping with 'extraordinary publicity'.[20] *The Family* was none the less innovative and trend-setting. It was easily recognizable as a documentary, but nevertheless different enough from other forms of the genre.

At this time documentaries were well-established and identifiable elements of the schedule: for example, the previous year had seen the transmission of the award-winning *The World at War*. The genre itself has a lengthy and distinguished past beginning formally with Robert Flaherty's 1922 film *Nanook of the North*, but with earlier origins in the Lumière films of 1895.

In the 1960s documentaries were still being made by film-makers and the influence of *cinéma vérité* was evident in such films as Marcel Ophüls's *The Sorrow and the Pity* (1970). And Denis Mitchell was making impressionistic documentaries for Granada as was Michael Apted who, in 1963, launched *Seven Up*, a longitudinal study of children. In 1982 the BBC's *Forty Minutes* was launched, beginning a lengthy series of well-crafted films on subjects as varied as lavatories and pigeons, religious cults, child prostitutes, the London Underground and prize leeks. Varied in format and creative execution, all were attempts at getting *close* to 'truth': while keeping interpretation and editing to a minimum.

In the 1990s the documentary has, to a great extent, changed its spots. Indeed, factual television itself is now more a hybrid creature than it ever was. In 1975 Raymond Williams saluted some of the 'best television of the time', and in doing so cited those wide-ranging 'features' which the BBC led the field with: 'the personal television essay or journal, such as *One Pair of Eyes*, the personalized social report, such as *The Philpott File*; the television argument, such as Clark's *Civilisation* or Berger's *Ways of Seeing*; the television exposition, such as *The Restless Earth*; the television history, such as

The Great War; the television magazine, *Horizon* for science, *Chronicle* for archaeology, *Aquarius* and *Omnibus* for the arts; *The Countryman* and *Look, Stranger*; the many reports of exploration and natural history'.[21] Such features are still present in the schedules of the 1990s, but in fewer numbers and less centrally placed. More noticeable still is that the range of so-called factual programming has both embraced newer forms and, at the same time, narrowed its focus.

Documentaries have to an extent been edged out, in general terms, by the current affairs programme: the 'triumph' of journalism over the free-ranging mind. There is also the increase of the foot-in-the-door factual programme, epitomized by Roger Cook in which it is *de rigueur* for the presenter to be abused while campaigning, and there are also more seasonal and subjective offerings symbolized more graphically by the ever-increasing camcorder diary programmes. Cheap and popular.

There also exists a whole raft of programming somewhat difficult to label: informational, yet not educational, programmes fronted by celebrities – *How Do They Do That?*; the worthy yet somehow self-congratulatory programmes in which 'the missing' are searched for – their privacy invaded in the process – in an attempt to reunite them with those they (sometimes deliberately) left behind; while continuously and relentlessly programme managers are urging that the barriers are pushed back even further, not *always* in the name of 'truth', but rather in search of the ratings-grabbing headline. A case in point is the film *Death on Request*, which follows the last few months in the life of Cees van Wendel de Joode up to the point where his doctor administers him a lethal injection, then consoles his widow. On its first showing in the Netherlands it prompted television companies world-wide to buy the rights to it. Most, however, were 'only interested in the last few minutes, featuring the death scene'.[22] Drama-documentaries continue to be a popular item in the scheduler's armoury, despite the continuing misgivings expressed over the genre: the overlap of drama and fact is often confusing, to say the least.[23]

This is not to say that factual television has changed beyond its initial remit but, with endless formulaic current-affairs series taking up most of the available screentime, it is difficult to believe that public argument, discussion or indeed imagination has been genuinely broadened in the 1990s. Too much 'investigative' programming leads not to truth, simply to viewer desensitization and exhaustion. And where are the irreverent, eccentric, oddball and unique documentaries? Too few.

The year in which the AIDS virus was discovered, 1984, was another pointer to the changes taking place in television. It saw the launch of *Spitting Image*, a puppet-driven satire which mocked all and sundry, especially the Royals, politicians and anyone the programme-makers decided was pretentious enough to deserve it. It was yet another indication that little was safe from the gaze of television. *'Allo 'Allo* mocked all who were involved in the Second World War, especially the French, Germans and the British, while other sit-coms simply plodded on. Factual entertainment began to be given 'shape' with *Surprise, Surprise!*, another programme reuniting families, critically slated but popular with the viewers. Thames Television meanwhile attempted to revive the BBC's *What's My Line?*, but with its new team of panellists the once popular formula failed to succeed. Significantly the BBC succeeded in the ratings war when it transmitted a glossy lowbrow serial *The Thorn Birds*, which centred around a priest who absconded the Vatican for sex on the beach, while at the same time ITV broadcast the critically acclaimed 14-part *The Jewel in The Crown*. Interestingly enough research discovered that when subsequently questioned many viewers believed *The Thorn Birds* had been shown on independent television.[24] So perhaps the BBC's lapse from the lofty heights of art to second-rate schmaltz, had gone unnoticed. But certainly the divisions between drama on both channels have been somewhat reduced, and in the 1990s they tend to merge more in response to the call to maximize audiences.

The most popular programmes of the decade were also indicative of the changes that were to continue into the 1990s. For example, the top programme of 1984 – now watched by 20 million viewers, doubling the figures of the leading programme ten years earlier – was *Coronation Street*, a trend of soap-domination which continues unabated into the 1990s. Other top ten entries included, again, *Miss World* and *The Royal Variety Show*, *Porridge*, *Minder*, *Bullseye* and, significantly, four Hollywood movies, including *Raiders of the Lost Ark* and *Airplane*.

In the 1950s the 'mass audiences' began to desert the cinema for the convenience of the domestic television screen. This trend has continued with the preponderance of movies on television: together with soaps they represent most symbolically popular television. The range of movies seen on television is in principle broad: Hollywood, Bollywood, Bengali cinema, European 'art house', British black and white, all continue to grace the screens, although it is those from Hollywood – with their tidy narratives and closed endings – that achieve peak-time slots and sizeable audiences. In the current multi-channel environment those responsible for bringing movies to the screen, tend to simply buy indiscriminately – except on those special occasions, like the Christmas season. Competition is fierce, and time has to be filled. For television viewing many movies are censored, with swearing excised and graphic sex scenes reduced and, at times, many are shown in the wrong ratio: widescreen movies are not always 'letter boxed', leading to a subsequent 50 per cent loss of picture. But television audiences none the less love movies.

In addition to movies made for the cinema the 'made for TV' (or 'B' movie) has become an important part of television programming. The 'TV movie' tends to be a glossy but relatively cheap production, produced at top speed and aimed at the 'middle-of-the-road audience for whom so many cinema films are now thought to be unsuitable'.[25] In critical terms made-for-TV movies have been unfavourably compared to 'real' movies, and labelled 'quickies'. By virtue of the relative smallness of the television image, the medium shot and close-up dominate, while huge crowd scenes and on-location spectacles cost more than their smaller budgets allow. As television audiences tend to be less attentive than cinema-goers, TV movies tend to emphasize *sound* to attract the viewer's glance: hence the tendency in these movies to rely more on dialogue than cinema films. Thematically made-for-TV movies often are factually based, occasionally centring on sensational stories, injustices or social problems, although many of those issues are somewhat de-politicized when seen through a domestic narrative. However as Lawrie Schulze compellingly argues, 'the TV movie's politics cannot be taken for granted', as in its search for ratings through the controversial, 'the TV movies frequently brings the socially marginalized – women, people of colour, gays and lesbians, the working class, the homeless and unemployed, the victims – onto popular terrain'.[26]

Games and Quizzes

In 1984 *Bullseye* was the most popular competition-based show on the screens, although it was ITV's *The Price is Right*, with its hysterical-hooligan audiences and passionate contestants in search of the prize, that raised some central questions about the genre. *Competition* has always been an aspect of television's programming – *Come Dancing*, cricket, *Mastermind*, boxing and *Blankety Blank* to name but a few – but despite such varied expressions it has been most evident in game and quiz shows. Such shows have always been attacked, in some quarters, for being merely 'a form of celebration of consumption, glorifying consumer goods',[27] although there is evidence that there is no direct relation between the popularity of game shows and the size of prizes they offer. One explanation, for example, of the huge success *The Price is Right* enjoyed was that viewers revelled in seeing large numbers of people raucously enjoying themselves.[28] None the less, as Garry Whannel points out, it simply 'cannot be denied that in the last analysis the experience [of *The Price is Right*] is structured around the competition to win commodities'.[29]

In the 1990s quiz and game shows resolutely remain in the weekly schedules: around 40 different such shows feature each week on terrestrial channels as well as the hybrid *National Lottery*. Increasingly, ITV's relationship with tabloid newspapers enables them to boost their potential audience, by conniving to allow viewers to 'join in the game from their armchairs'. Formats change as do set designs, as do the size of prizes, presentational style and type of contestant: but winning and losing remains the central leitmotif of the event.

Quiz and game shows have their origins in Victorian parlour games, fairground side-shows and such popular activities as bingo. Indeed, the huge popularity of bingo is 'proof enough that broadcasting must be regarded as appropriating, rather than inventing, a national penchant for games that combine skill and chance'.[30] But it was radio that immediately preceded television in developing such shows: in the late 1940s Wilfred Pickles' *Have a Go* regularly enjoyed an audience of up to half the population. Of special significance was the arrival of ITV which, Peter Black argues, 'ushered in a major shift in the public manifestation of popular taste'. Up until its arrival the British public had 'never seen anyone earn a pound note for correctly distinguishing his left foot from his right'. Black argues that such shows as *Double Your Money* and *Take Your Pick* which were the first television quiz games to offer cash prizes were central to the building of a big ITV audience.[31] By 1957 there were eight quiz shows a week.

It is fair to say that few television forms have enjoyed as low a cultural status as the popular quiz or game show, with only the exceptions of *Mastermind* and *University Challenge* escaping such censure. From the 1980s onwards the importance of answering questions on the basis of 'facts ' was no longer the sole criterion of contestant participation. Shows like *The Price is Right* celebrated the 'personalities' of its contestants, while other formats – *Family Fortunes* or *Play Your Cards Right*, for instance – relied more on guess work. Many of these shows trade on the contestant's fascination of the world of glamour and celebrity, the desire to live vicariously: game and quiz shows suggest that some people 'with luck can be transported briefly into this world'.[32]

In Pursuit of Crime

Minder topped the 1984 ratings for fictional programmes concerning 'law and order', though it was hardly a conventional cops and robbers show: more a story of a spiv and his minor fiddles. But the same year saw the beginnings of *The Bill*, a police soap, still running in the 1990s and much more a conventional police series. And despite being shot on the less expensive videotape (as opposed to film), the series uses the medium to great effect in creating a sense of urgency, immediacy and 'reality'.

The fascination with fictional crime and its investigation will continue, despite less confidence in the police, their activities and their abilities to solve crime. Quite simply, by perceiving crime and violence from a distance, it enables the viewer to believe it is happening elsewhere, not to them, and, additionally, there appears to be a deep interest in the misfortunes of others: similar to the behaviour of crowds who flock to gaze at disasters.

The genre is particularly associated with such diverse offerings as *Dixon of Dock Green*, *Z Cars* and, more recently *The Sweeney*. Based on a character from the 1950 film *The Blue Lamp*, Dixon first appeared in 1955. He was an 'ordinary copper' policing a predictable world, free of racial intolerance, cynicism and the excesses of human brutality. In 1986 when some viewers were asked when *Dixon of Dock Green* had been on air, the general consensus was that it was 'ages ago, twenty years or so': in fact the last live transmission was in 1976. What seemed to be happening was that Dixon's traditional approach to policing was not remembered as a particular fictional style, but as 'a mirror of the reality at the time when he made the programmes. Historical time had to be adjusted to television time'.[33] Certainly such series as *Dixon* and *Z Cars* portrayed a sense of social conscience towards crime: underlying causes of crime might well be explored, as would be the criminal's individual problems, wrapped in an embracing moral message of the threat to the community that crime brings. But the 'spirit of co-operation and optimism which the shared values of *Dixon of Dock Green* suggest' was replaced in the 1970s especially by *The Sweeney*, characterized instead by its 'world-weary cynicism'. In this series there is little time for contemplation or indeed moralizing. The job in hand is simply to stop the country being 'swamped by the crime wave'.[34] *The Sweeney* was a world of hard liquor, squealing tyres, infidelity, dispassion and with uncertain boundaries between the criminals and the police, the methods of whom were somewhat suspect.

The end of *The Sweeney* saw the return to more conventional series, like *Juliet Bravo* and *The Bill* in which bloody violence is less evident. In *The Bill*, for example, all manner of crimes are represented, but less graphically so, while at the same time much screen time is devoted to both police and legal procedures and the indigenous conflicts between the 'uniformed officers who follow the book and the CID officers who need the convictions'.[35] Not only does this fictional genre continue to flourish but, more controversially, so does the raft of 'crime reconstruction' programmes which, undoubtedly, increase some viewers' fear of crime, who may be led, inadvertently, to the view that they are prey to marauding criminals.[36] Perhaps part of the problem is that the viewing of such reconstructions necessarily takes place *within* our fictional knowledge of crime and violence. *Crimewatch*, for example, does not provide a heroic detective with whom the viewer may identify. Neither does it provide the other consolations of the crime genre, 'a clear motive for the central crime or a nice dénouement in which mysteries are solved and wrongs righted'. Instead, the picture sometimes conveyed is 'of a relatively arbitrary act committed by unidentified villains who are still on the run'.[37]

Sports and Soaps

As we have earlier seen the genders divide quite significantly in their television preferences, particularly over soaps which women prefer and sports to which men are equally attracted.[38] At particular moments in the schedule the screen is either resplendent with Australian suburban families breezing through life's travails; Australian doctors finding romance as difficult to understand as medical techniques; high-powered family shenanigans in California's *Knots Landing*; the mythical Manchester of *Coronation Street*;

hyper-reality in Brookside Close and the East End of London; or J.R. Ewing still grinning menacingly amidst the skyscrapers of *Dallas* and from the even loftier heights of satellite television.

Between them, the major soaps can attract well over 60 million viewers in a week, a figure which demonstrates a degree of multiple loyalty to the programmes. Traditionally, the genre commands strong audience loyalty: though it is not essential to watch all episodes, the incentive does exist to watch regularly enough to stay in touch with the story. Their very success on ITV drew the BBC into the genre once more in the 1980s with the launch of *EastEnders*, some 20 years following *Compact* in the 1960s. Despite audience research which had suggested that soaps were not the kind of programme viewers associated with the BBC, it felt that it simply had to develop such programming to compete with commercial television. *EastEnders* soon reduced the evening audience gap between BBC1 and ITV.[39]

Soaps have their origins in the US radio serials of the 1930s which were sponsored, in large part, by Procter and Gamble the soap corporation. Subsequently the term 'soap opera' came to be associated with a melodramatic style of drama serial. Soaps attract good audiences, even when poorly scheduled or badly crafted. Why is this so? D.J. Enright suggests that when television is content to be 'lowbrow', as in British soaps, it can become 'middlebrow'. He opines that the 'obvious secret' of soaps is that, 'in however undistinguished a manner, they deal with basic and relatively homely situations'.[40] Soaps are watched world-wide, due mainly to the export successes of such series as *Dallas* and *Dynasty*, although similar indigenous forms are found in various parts of the globe. For example, the Venezuelan networks broadcast five hours of home-produced *telenovelas* daily. Not strictly soaps – they run to approximately 100 episodes – the aim, none the less, is similar in that 'the audience suffer, enjoy, and laugh with the things that are happening on the screen as if they were happening to themselves'.[41]

In 1995 the most popular soap in the US is the lunch-time *The Young and the Restless* which plays five times a week. Currently playing to 12 million viewers daily, the programme was first broadcast in 1973 and helped launch the career of *Baywatch's* David Hasselhoff. Predictably enough the stories surround three wealthy business families in Genoa City, a fictional Mid-West town. As well as the US *The Young and the Restless* is seen in over 20 other countries, including Australia, Puerto Rico and Liechtenstein.

In contemporary France, however, the soap diet contains more existentially angled ingredients. In *Les Coeurs Brûlées* (*The Burned Hearts*), which on its once-weekly showing on TFI plays to some ten million viewers, every one of its characters appear to be going through their own personal-yet-recognizable hell.

It is indeed the process of identification that is central to the success of soaps: psychologists have referred to our relationship to television characters as a *para-social* one.

When they are 'real' to us they may take all sorts of shapes, serve quite different functions. They may be surrogate parents or spouses or lovers who help to show us how to behave and how to feel in many normal situations . . . They may be companions or friends or acquaintances who make us feel less lonely and less dissatisfied with our own existence.[42]

These soap characters are complex multi-faceted beings composed of fiction, fact and pseudo-fact. Their 'existence' is partly brought to life by the millions of conversations which take place about them, such talk fuelled by the additional information about the 'stars' who play the characters to be found in the showbiz pages of the tabloids. Such background knowledge substantially reinforces the overall pleasure of soap watching.

UK soaps tend to locate the relationships that texture their programmes in and about the home or pub, and significantly less so in the workplace. Issues of fidelity and adultery, generational conflict, mere gossip, family tension, love, hatred, indifference, violence, sexual attraction, normal neurosis, and other sentiments are the stuff of soaps and as such are seen to be the woman's domain. This is, of course, only partly true but true none the less.

Soaps are characterized by a number of distinct features: the speed of production and the continuous use of sets, large casts and convoluted story-lines which are spun out for weeks on end, and, most importantly, as Dennis Potter remarks, the central purpose of the soap is 'never to end'.[43] Soaps without peak-time status, those lost in the vast afternoon television wasteland – the likes of *The Young Doctors*, *Shortland Street* and *A Country Practice* – tend to be produced on low budgets: as is evident with the clumsy and plodding direction, the implausible storylines, and the all too predictable sets. All soaps, however, share a sense of timelessness which clearly is part of their attraction. As D. J. Enright shrewdly observes, soaps contrive to provide the 'exciting feeling that things are about to ensue, along with the assurance that nothing untowardly radical is likely to occur'. Following them, he argues, even irregularly, can import a 'sense of immortality or at least of timelessness'.[44] Soap watching, then, is an absorbing but relaxing and always comforting experience.

If abundance is the condition most vividly and extravagantly portrayed in American *prime-time* soapland, it is the notion of *community* which underpins British ones – both in the sense of the mythical communities visible on the screen and the feeling of community created between the familiar characters on view and their loyal audience. In this view, soaps function to bind us together: in the 'Middle Ages religion was the glue of society', but today 'television is the binding agent that helps us cohere' – soaps instill a sense of continuity, a sense that life is still going on.[45]

Although British soaps differ in their precise conceptions of 'community', all tend towards the optimistic, perhaps even the utopian in the notion of individual needs being able to be met communally. Endless tapestries are created of shared problems, moments of camaraderie and individuals 'pulling together'. *Coronation Street* is the classic example, conceived as it was as a nostalgic celebration of 1950s working-class culture where its image of community has stubbornly remained. As Verina Glaessner has pointed out, the programme has appeared 'increasingly nostalgic for an (imaginary) past, and has had trouble incorporating and representing the process of change of work within inner-city' Manchester of the 1970s and onwards. This 'magical recovery' of an organic and almost entirely white-skinned working-class community is, 'it must be assumed, a significant element in its appeal'.[46]

Unlike *Coronation Street*, other soaps – *Brookside* and *EastEnders* in particular – have attempted to reflect contemporary problems and have enthusiastically taken up a number of social issues, like AIDS, race and gay rights. In doing so they have faced the intrinsic tension and conflict between on the one hand the desire to be positive about a particular issue and, at the same time, a commitment to maintaining the credibility of the characters. Additionally, it is clear that such 'realism' does not necessarily lead to increased audience figures, as a comparison of *Coronation Street* and *Brookside* demonstrates. The *Street* has consistently relied on characterization and a particular type of humour to build its huge loyal audience: there have been no widespread cases of sexual assaults, murders, suicides, drug addicts, prostitutes, battered wives, only a sprinkling of thieves and a few terminal illnesses. *Brookside*, already at a disadvantage on being shown on a minority channel, has conversely always deliberately attempted to portray the Close as a microcosm of actual Liverpool life: by 1996, rapes have occurred twice, five murders have been committed as have the same number of suicides, drug addicts too have numbered four, while comas, heart attacks and cancers have rapidly spread as has the number of thieves, battered wives and runaway children. Such 'social realism' has, undoubtedly, given the programme a particular loyal audience, albeit somewhat small.

Politically speaking the socially aware soaps simply cannot win. Theirs is a *catch*-22 situation. If, say, their gay or black characters are integrated into the programme and become 'normal' familiar members of the 'community' the soaps will be accused of ignoring sexual and racial problems, but if the same characters are treated in a 'special way' the programme will be accused of marginalizing them.[47]

Soaps will continue to attract the largest television audiences, each with their own distinctive agenda and style: the minor morality tales of *Neighbours*, the nostalgia and brilliant double-acts of *Coronation Street*, the raw-edged and gritty *EastEnders*, and the class warfare of *Brookside*. Despite the débâcle of *Eldorado* the future will inevitably see the steady introduction of more home-produced soaps, whether funded jointly by ITV companies as in the case of the appallingly scripted *Revelations* or perhaps by European co-producers. Soaps will continue to vary in the degree to which they reflect and refract social realities. Realism has, in any case, built-in limits: a truly 'realist' soap would see the characters of *Coronation Street* watching themselves on television.

Despite being a stated preference by women, soaps are none the less watched by a substantial proportion of men; similarly televised sports have a considerable female audience in addition to male viewers. This in itself is hardly surprising, especially given the 'politics of the living room'. Although the audience for most sports television is indeed predominantly male, there is evidence that females have increasingly been entering the sports audience. This trend is partly due to the diversity of sport made available by the proliferation of channels, and possibly also due to changing gender roles within families. What *is* clear, is that unlike men women prefer *non-team sports*, such as tennis and figure skating.

Unlike soaps, sports programmes *will* continue to change over the coming decades and in so doing will change sport as it does so. This, of course, is a process which is already occurring.

As George Comstock recalls sports programming has been prominent in the USA television schedule since the 'very first days of broadcasting: on May 17, 1939, the first broadcast baseball contest, Columbia versus Princeton, was televised by NBC using a one-camera mobile unit positioned behind third base'.[48] In the UK over 2,000 hours of sports a year is broadcast on terrestrial television and numerous satellite channels are solely devoted to the genre. The ways in which television has already altered the face of sport are numerous and significant: quite simply, sports events are reconstructed to fit the needs of television. For example, over the past three decades television has altered the morning scheduling of West Coast basketball to suit East Coast television, forced baseball players to play World Series games on freezing October evenings, altered surfing events for the convenience of the schedule and without regard to weather conditions and forced tennis players to compete on both all-weather surfaces and indeed indoors.

More specifically in 1995, in boxing, Lennox Lewis fought Oliver McCall for the World heavyweight title at Wembley at 2.00 a.m. for the benefit of American prime-time television; in golf the final day of the 1995 British Masters started particularly early so that it would finish before Sky's live Premiership football match; while in the money-rich world of grand prix motor racing, aspiring race promoters are told that 'tight circuits' are preferable because they make trackside advertising more visible on television. In the context of boxing Hodgson neatly summarizes the synthetic relationship between TV and sport: 'Colin McMillan is typical of the type of boxer that television executives are scared of: he can move, he has fast hands, he barely gets hit but he rarely knocks people out. In short, MacMillan is a TV nightmare'.[49]

Television has thus rearranged the sporting calendar and separated sports from their familiar relationships with the natural seasons. Spectators of live sports events anticipate the action replay and the close-up, and so, increasingly, giant TV screens are installed to fulfil this very need. And, in association with sponsorship, television in the UK (and elsewhere) has brought snooker and one-day cricket to prominence, has enabled some sports to thrive and others to decline, introduced shirt advertising in football and, in a very real sense, has encouraged sport to become 'a branch of the advertising and public relations industries'.[50]

Although televised sports consist of news as well as entertainment, it is the latter element which has flourished most in recent decades. Indeed, the term 'quasi-sport' has been used to describe the merging of sport and show business: the merging of celebrity and competition. The popular ITV *Gladiators* programme is a case in point, a hybrid of games and sport played by 'celebrities' in front of a live 'hysterical' audience. Such prominent examples of quasi-sport programmes, such as *It's a Knock Out* and *SuperStars* have, however, long since disappeared from the screen. It may well be that as 'real sport' is forced to conform to entertainment values the need for quasi-sports is accordingly reduced.[51]

It is unquestionably the case that television coverage of sport – with intrusive and revealing close-ups, variety of camera angles, and ground-level audio – has created a novel sense of excitement and immediacy for the viewer. But what fundamentally appeals to the viewer is, not only such visual delights or occasions of team identification – or even winning or losing – rather it is the uncertainty that sport itself brings: sport entertains, but also frustrates, annoys and deflates. It is this very uncertainty that gives its 'unpredictable joys their characteristic intensity'.[52] It might also be added that the viewing of sport allows those so inclined to vent their anger against the foreigners that are paraded before them: they may *stereotypically* view the natural grace of Caribbean cricketers, the robotic yet successful German athletes, and the creative, but lazy black footballer.

If satellite sporting channels succeed as profit-making enterprises, it is likely that in the long-term some – if not all – of sport's major spectacles will only be found on such channels. Events which have always been 'free' to the viewer – as belonging to the 'nation' – will only be available on subscription or on pay-as-you-view. At the same time there will be the continued determination of programme-makers to find more ways of creating drama and suspense, even through the introduction of contrived sporting events. And such success will inevitably lead the channels into more uncharted territories in the search to fill the schedules: for example, the Basque national sport *Jai lia*, a centuries-old squash-like game, will soon grace the mid-afternoon screen.

The irony inherent in all this is that television did not, of course, create the major sports it now systematically disassembles. Rather television (and radio) satisfied and extended an 'already developed cultural habit'. Yet, as Michael Novak laments, the invasion of sport by the entertainment ethic breaks down the boundaries between the 'ritual world of play' and the sordid reality from which it is designed to provide escape.[53]

Drama

As we have argued it is drama, be it in the shape of soaps, movies or in any number of series of varying lengths, that has continued to capture the attention of audiences, regularly attracting substantial audiences. This centrality of drama is deeply ingrained in our everyday life and is highly significant. As Raymond Williams has observed, it is clear that 'watching dramatic simulation of a wide range of experiences is now an essential part of our modern cultural pattern'. The scale and intensity of dramatic performance which television brings is without precedent: more drama is watched in a television week by an average viewer, than would have been watched in a year or in some cases a *lifetime* in any previous historical period.[54]

The 1980s and 1990s have seen the rise not only of soaps but also drama series of varying lengths: *Brideshead Revisited*, *Edge of Darkness*, *Paradise Postponed*, *The Beiderbecke Trilogy*, *London's Burning*, *Heartbeat* and *Inspector Morse*, to name but a handful. Not only do such series create substantial loyal audiences they also sell to overseas markets. The rise of the drama series has its counterpoint in the decline of the televised single play, most evident and much favoured in the 1960s. Indeed, though theatrical work commanded cultural prestige, many believed that much of the best new work of the dramatists of that decade went directly into television. The BBC's *Wednesday Play* is in this regard, regularly cited. The single play, less subject to management interference, has conventionally been seen as the best vehicle for asking awkward social questions. Its demise may well have been accelerated by the Thatcherite cultural offensive but, more likely, it was rather due to the importance of ratings: it being easier to build up audience loyalty over time for a series than for a one-off drama. In addition there are the economics of scale involved in longer-running productions – the saving in sets, rehearsals and costumes.

In his overview of television drama, George Brandt argues for the importance of Channel 4 in generating drama in the 1980s and 1990s, particularly through its commitment to film. Despite the impressive number of completed films the Channel has been involved in, doubts have lingered as to their value: that, perhaps, the initiative has unfortunately taught British cinema simply to think *small*. Brandt himself desists from such a view in arguing that rather than muscling in on a flourishing film industry, the Channel has helped keep an ailing industry afloat. Another feature of these two decades has been the increasing number of co-productions. Enthusiasts welcomed the sharing of budgets and the more international vision such dramas might bring. Those less optimistic have instead worried about the loss of a national or regional voice, which invariably accompanies such co-productions.

We have earlier commented on the rise of the formulaic drama series of the 1990s: policemen, detectives, doctors and nurses. Interestingly enough, although these models were already popular fictional types before television, it is doubtful, before the epoch of television serials and series, that anything like the current proportion of dramatic attention to crime and illness had ever existed.[55] Presumably the trend is directly related to the increasing preoccupation that people have over such matters in their everyday life. The precise impact of these fictional representations on such preoccupations is, clearly, a matter of debate.

Jurrasic Park author Michael Crichton has himself recently entered the world of television with his medi-soap *ER* and his views on television drama are perhaps a pointer for the future development of the genre.[56] American audiences, he maintains, are incapable of watching television for any length of time unless it is a 'news reality' programme like *Cops* or a courtroom drama like the O.J. Simpson trial. The only way forward, he believes, is to make drama more dramatic than the news and reality programmes. Result: action, super-realism, quick-fire story-lines within well-marked segments. A lengthy sustained attention span is not required.

The Significance of Age and Class

Programme preferences obviously radically change with age as well as with gender: the over-55s prefer *Last of the Summer Wine* to *Top Gun*, while the 16–34-year-olds clearly are more at ease with Hollywood and adult-movies than with *This is Your Life*. Such findings are predictable, and indeed the 1994 survey confirmed such trends.

All kinds of news were preferred more widely with increasing age: a window on the world is particularly welcome to those who are more home-bound and who, perhaps, feel life is gradually passing them by. The need still to feel involved, if only vicariously. Viewers aged 55 and over reported a greater than average interest in natural history programmes, game and quiz shows, older movies, variety, drama and church services. Those under 65 were keen to view holiday programmes and adult education items, while those over 65 were more likely to be more interested in consumer programmes. Again hardly surprising, with less disposable income available spending choices must be thoroughly considered.

Conversely, younger viewers stated a preference for contemporary movies, soaps, rock music programmes, 'alternative comedy', adult-only movies and 'women's programmes'. Both findings are in line with recognized national trends. As for those viewers who fall in the 35–54 years age band, their preferences are predictable too: light entertainment, drama and serials. Unlike their younger counterparts they tend to watch more sport and fewer movies.

The amount of time spent watching television varies considerably with age: on average, the '65 and over' age group spends almost twice as much time watching television each week as the 4–15 age group. The unskilled and working classes (social group DE) tend to watch 50 per cent more television than the highest socio-economic group, the upper and middle classes (the ABs). Interestingly, in recent years the only age group unique in going against the general trend of a slight reduction in the total amount of time spent watching television, is the 16–24-year-olds. Over the past decade their proportion of television viewing compared to the population as a whole, has risen from 63 per cent to 80 per cent. The explanation for such an increase in homely pursuits does not lie in a reduction in the exercise of testosteronic activity, rather it is the increased programming of films and the targeting of the audience by programme-makers that has effected the change.

Religion and Talk

Religious programmes and church services came lowest on viewers' programme preferences. Not far behind were the once widespread chat shows, those moments of conversations with celebrities orchestrated by other celebrities, like Wogan, Parkinson and Harty. Both formats are victims of changing social mores.

Chat shows suffered through audience expectations of two distinct kinds. *Viewers* wished for questions to be more relevant, risqué and controversial, a desire which could not be achieved within the prevailing format. If they did so the continuous flow of guests would simply abruptly end. Secondly, *studio audiences* felt they could do better themselves: a manifestation of the fact that 'ordinary people' are more media literate. People are all too ready to talk, to confess or to quarrel – all for one's edification. The result of these two tendencies is the emergence of the so-called 'nuts and sluts' shows, like *Donahue* and *Oprah Winfrey* and copied, with varying degrees of taste, by *Kilroy*, *Ricki Lake* and *Vanessa*. Such shows claim to raise and discuss 'controversial matters' like AIDS, date rape, transvestism, obesity, plastic surgery and other such emotional, personal or bodily items but, we might ask, what precisely is *controversial* about such issues? Actually, only the propriety of discussing them on television, in such a humiliating and debased manner.[57] Because of their low cost, the sense of false camaraderie created, and because of the tendency to wallow in other people's misfortunes, the genre will continue to exist in its present form for some time to come.

When asked in surveys, almost three-quarters of the population will claim some religious affiliation, a proportion which has remained the same since the late 1960s. When doing so, the majority of such people ally themselves to one of the major Christian churches. However, *in reality*, enrolled adult membership of such churches currently represents a mere 15 per cent of the total UK adult population. And, indeed, such membership has fallen almost 20 per cent since 1975. Meanwhile, over the same period the membership of other churches has greatly increased, and the numbers of Muslims and Sikhs more than doubled. The broader canvas of Europe shows that the UK has the lowest level of active church membership amongst adults, with a figure approaching some 15 per cent. The Irish Republic is highest at 80 per cent, followed by the Netherlands, Austria, Norway, Finland, Spain, Switzerland, Denmark and France. *All* with higher rates than the UK.[58] Despite the evidence of such a steady growth in secularization many people none the less turn to various cults or New Age ideas in their search for transcendental knowledge or deeper meaning to their earthly lives. Or they simply live private spiritual lives. It is against this backcloth that religious programming must be considered.

Both commercial television and the BBC are enjoined to provide religious programming, however, the subsequent output is neither as favourably scheduled as it once was, nor so warmly received. In recent decades the most popular items have been music-based like *Highway* and *Songs of Praise*, programmes valued by their audiences as uplifting and as a legitimate substitute for real church-going.[59] Not surprisingly, it is the older rather than the younger viewers who are more likely to partake of televised religion.

Research has suggested that the most common reason potential viewers give for *not* watching religious television is that they do not wish to have religion 'rammed down' their throats. Additionally such people believe that the programmes are aimed at the religious, not them.[60] None the less there is evidence that the majority of potential viewers *are* interested in ethical and moral issues, so perhaps the challenge for religious broadcasters is to make religious programmes through explorations of such moral and ethical issues. In a sense, religion through the back-door.

Certainly it seems likely that the future will not see any discernible increase in religious programming, unless such programming emerges 'locally' on cable television, and especially those channels aimed at minority communities – the Muslim, Asian or African–Caribbean, for example. Programmes like *Witness*, *Everyman* and *The Heart of the Matter*, and others which eschew formal religious themes and focus more on matters of spirituality and morality, will continue to develop. These will be invariably journalistically crafted and character or story-led in style.

In the longer term the issue will centre around the increase of the deregulation of religious programming and, also, will concern the degree to which religious programming on cable penetrates the market-place. For example, the US-owned *New World Channel* provides hours of such programming per day, subsequently distributed in numerous languages to such countries as Belgium, France, the Netherlands, Sweden and Switzerland.[61] Similarly the *Christian Channel Europe* spreads its message on satellite for three hours a day, between the unearthly hours of 4–7.00 a.m. Another potential broadcaster, *Ark 2*, has reputedly hired Saatchi and Saatchi to recruit corporate sponsors keen to associate themselves with the allegedly wholesome family values of a Christian channel.[62] It is a matter of speculation as to the degree of UK penetration such channels will achieve, or indeed the effect their sectarian Christian message will have.

It is difficult not to see the future of programming as one dominated by the formulaic, especially given the necessity to compete with the most popular of programmes and the anxiety not to run risks. Niche programming too looks likely to grow, especially through the mechanism of subscription viewing, as in the case of sport, films and children's programming.

4

'Quality Television'

Most episodes [of *Northern Exposure*] employ the voice of Chris Stevens, the Disc Jockey of K-BEHR, to both organize and comment upon each episode's day-in-the-life-of-Cicely structure, in a fashion reminiscent of *Hill Street Blues'* morning 'Roll Call'. Chris's eloquent musings draw upon a range of cultural sources, from Native American writers to Jung, Thoreau, Proust, Albert Einstein, Maurice Sendak, and Chicken Little, among others. Chris is this community's philosophical troubadour: he narrates the town and its stories, and by extension, ours . . .

> Betsy Williams (1994), '"North to the Future": *Northern Exposure* and Quality Television'

In the late 1980s the debates surrounding the Broadcasting Bill thrust to the fore the problematic issue of what constitutes 'quality television'. In this chapter we consider whether such a conundrum is in any sense answerable.

Raymond Williams has interestingly described the television experience as one of 'flow'. For although the screen consists of a sequence of varied and numerous items, station 'idents', programmes, trailers and commercials, some short others lengthy, some colour others merely black-and-white, some loud others barely audible, the television experience in itself, in a sense, unites them all. This sense of 'flow', indeed, conceals the fact that a description of an evening's viewing would in fact be akin to describing 'having read two plays, three or four newspapers, three or four magazines, on the same day that one has been to a variety show and a lecture and a football match'.[1] We might add that to such a list could be included such items as a number of trips to various supermarkets, stores and shops – again visual feats. Breaking such a flow into discrete parts is, however, necessary for the broadcaster, the advertiser *and* the viewer. When the television schedule was less competitive and crowded, this was of course a much easier task. Also remote control devices have merely functioned to cloud the issue: in zapping channels it is not always clear what has been discovered – an actual programme, a trailer or perhaps a story with a commercial message?

In television's earlier pioneering years the structure of the television experience was clear-cut and served additional functions: notably to structure the viewer's everyday life, by marking *time*. Indeed, in the early days of mass television, it was much more customary for the set to be switched on for general viewing at certain times rather than left constantly flickering alone in the corner. Viewers would know that Saturday evenings meant a particular sequence of programmes at a predictable time: *Dixon of Dock Green* would follow *Dr Who*. Such ritualized viewing structured the evening.

A more formal example was the so-called 'toddlers' truce' when, between 6 p.m. and 7 p.m. every evening, transmission ceased in the belief that parents would put young children to bed. This truce was initiated in 1955 – when the broadcasting hours for both channels were set at 50 hours a week per channel – and lasted until February 1957, when the BBC subsequently launched the current affairs programme *Tonight* into the vacant slot. Similarly breakfast *time* has obviously been restructured since the introduction of specific early-morning programming in the year of 1983: and as television is now a 24-hour medium, bed*time* too has perhaps changed its precise meaning.

Amidst this kaleidoscope of pictures and cacophony of sound, how does the viewer set about choosing what to watch? When asked this question the majority of viewers, almost three-quarters in total, claimed that they watched the same programmes again and again, so knew their precise timings from repeated experience. They were *loyal* to their programmes. The next most common strategy was to read the specialist high-circulation TV magazines or the television or entertainment pages in the newspapers. In the latter example this is almost impossible to avoid given that the tabloids in particular devote scores of columns to television programmes, personalities, previews and criticism. David Morley's research discovered that it was men, on the whole, who talked of checking through such listings on teletext to *plan* an evening's viewing. Very few women appeared to plan, except in terms of already knowing which evenings and times their favourite series were on, and thus not needing in fact to check the schedule. This, Morley argues, is an indication of a different attitude to viewing as a whole: 'many of the women have a much more take-it-or-leave-it attitude, not caring much if they miss things' except for their favourite soaps and series.[2]

Obviously a number of viewers found programmes by grazing aimlessly through channels or simply watched programmes other family members had chosen, while a smaller minority claimed they were often persuaded by programme trailers. Very few viewers planned days in advance, or followed the recommendations of friends and very few indeed stuck to one channel only by steadfastly ignoring the fare available on other channels.

The notion that there might be 'races' of BBC1 or ITV people is, generally speaking, no longer tenable. Of course, some may declare themselves to be BBC2 types or Channel 4 *aficionados*, however their actual viewing habits provide no support for such claims of allegiance.[3] None the less viewers do retain ideas about channel images which, in turn, may affect viewing habits. As we have already noted, the BBC's *The Thorn Birds* was incorrectly seen by many viewers to be an ITV programme, one example among numerous others that could be cited. And in spite of the tendency to graze through channels, and regardless of the fact that channel loyalty has largely been replaced by programme loyalty, all channels nevertheless have distinctive viewer profiles which distinguish them from each other.[4]

BBC1's profile suggests it is broadly a channel for *all* people, but with a slight tendency to have an appeal for older viewers. In terms of social class the channel's profile closely matches the actual distribution of classes in society as a whole, thus including both the upper classes and the state pensioners, casual workers and the underclass. The corresponding viewer profile of BBC2 somewhat belies the channel's image of catering to special interest and minority groups, as it has a markedly larger proportion of older viewers than BBC1, although its mid-age profile is broadly the same as for BBC1 as is the overall class profile of its viewers. Both channels, however, suffer from a sharply declining proportion of its viewers (in the 1990s) from the skilled working-class group, matched by an equally sharp increase from the lower middle classes.

The age profile of ITV is virtually the same as that of BBC1, which is hardly surprising given that both channels aim for mass appeal. But unlike BBC1, ITV has a much higher audience of semi- and unskilled working classes and correspondingly less of the upper and middle classes. Channel 4, perhaps predictably so, has a markedly younger age profile than the other terrestrial channels and again, like ITV, claims more lower working-class viewers than the upper and middle classes, although less significantly so.

The satellite channels, taken collectively, present an age profile quite different from the terrestrial channels with 20 per cent of viewers in the 4–15 age group and over 50 per cent under the age of 34. By comparison only about 35 per cent of BBC1's viewers are under 34. The bias of the satellite channels towards younger viewers is made even clearer if compared to the age distribution within the underlying population. These channels actually have a larger share of ages 4–15, and a smaller share of the 55 and over age group, than the population as a whole – unlike any of the terrestrial channels. Similarly, the class profile of the satellite channels is quite different, with a high concentration of lower middle class and skilled working-class viewers relative to other channels and also to the population as a whole.[5]

So perhaps there are no great surprises here: 'traditional, slightly establishment' BBC1, none the less appealing to the mass of the population; ITV, a little less 'up-market'; while BBC2 appears to be viewed in the same light as BBC1, despite the different range of programming, while Channel 4 lives up to its somewhat rebellious image with its younger-than-average viewers and increasingly lower working-class audience. The profile of the satellite channels is the one they have systematically cultivated by the precise targeting of audiences – programmes for the young and their parents who have money to spend, and with few programmes for the over 55s who, it is believed, do not have the money to spend or if they have are unlikely to use it on home entertainment.

Despite the emergence since the 1980s in particular, of *programme* loyalty rather than *channel* allegiance, it remains a fact that despite the availability of popular programmes with wide appeal, heavily promoted and trailed, Channel 4 and BBC2 fail to achieve 'large' audiences. There is no mystery here: viewers can of course find these programmes through listings, television literature, on-screen promotion, through grazing and by friends' recommendations, yet they decline to do so. Moreover, Channel 4, for example, is no longer merely a bastion of left-wing agitprop, with multicultural, Marxist or gay programming, neither is BBC2 simply a channel presenting worthy items of a non-didactic but nevertheless educational type. Rather, such channels increasingly compete with the two major channels for the same audiences and in doing so produce and broadcast popular television: *Don't Forget Your Toothbrush, Cheers, Roseanne, Countdown, Oprah Winfrey, Brookside, Heartbreak High, Food and Drink*, movies, Italian football, *Bottom, Sesame Street, Star Trek, Ricki Lake, The X-Files, Adult Oprah* ('Gay Men who only Date Married Men') and *The Big Breakfast*. It may well be true then that, by and large, channel loyalty is an archaic expression of television behaviour, but it is unquestionably true that a simple shift sidewards from Channel 4 to ITV would see *Brookside*'s audience double.

Scheduling

The television scheduler's task is to 'out-think' the opposition, co-operate with the competition when the need arises and to develop and sustain both channel and programme loyalty. Amidst the kaleidoscopic cacophony of sounds and pictures, and in an increasingly competitive environment, this is no easy task; indeed, since the introduction of the VCR, second and third TV sets and the remote control device, some might say almost impossible. Essentially the scheduler's task centres upon the exercise of judgement. A successful example would perhaps be the placing of *Neighbours* at tea-time; while a less victorious one finds the BBC's *Nine O'Clock News* directly competing with an ITV drama already 30 minutes into the plot.

Despite contemporary concerns over 'quality demographics' and niche marketing, some basic scheduling strategies remain intact. The key to the ordering of programmes across a day, week after week, remains, as it always has, one of *repetition* and *continuity*. *Coronation Street* has been on air since 1960, *World in Action* since 1963, *The South Bank Show* since 1978 and *News at Ten*, since 1967. And many television viewers remain creatures of habit. No one, in the prevailing model of television programming, particularly benefits from the element of surprise.

The scheduler's lexicon contains many terms which are simple in their meaning but none the less crucial to the craft: 'inheritance factor' – a programme which follows a successful one – can expect to inherit a proportion of that audience; 'pre-echo' – if viewers tune in early to watch a programme, they may see a little of the preceding one and, perhaps, subsequently decide to watch all of it the following week; 'hammocking' – a less popular programme can be hammocked by placing it between two popular ones, so that it benefits from inheritance at the start and pre-echo towards the end – for instance the scheduling of *World in Action* after a sitcom and prior to a drama; 'common junction points' – when an opportunity arises for promotional cross-tailing when two programmes start at the same time on either BBC1 and 2, or ITV and Channel 4.[6]

In addition to such strategies there are two prevailing concerns for the scheduler, one being much easier to deal with than the other more difficult task. Matching programmes with their target audiences is the first task, much of it an exercise in common sense – 'children's programmes' scheduled at tea-time and early weekend mornings, and 'adult-only movies' in the late evening. But of course on occasions schedulers learn lessons directly from the audience: as we earlier mentioned, in 1969 *Star Trek* was initially scheduled as a children's programme but was (successfully) moved to 'prime time' when it was discovered the actual audience for it was youthful and adult. More problematic, especially for the two major channels, is the scheduling of special interest or 'minority' programming. Usually such programmes are hammocked, successfully or otherwise, or discarded into the graveyard slots of the schedule.

More and more trailers grace the screen annually in an attempt to keep audiences tuned to a specific channel: their precise placement being a question of the scheduler's intuition, rather than the application of any obvious logic. Drama trailers do indeed sometimes follow an actual drama, but often at a different time on a different day. On this point there is a lack of equity between the two main channels: for the BBC the space between programmes – trailers, presentation announcements, and the station ident – is an important factor in carrying 'the image of the BBC's diverse programming and in ensuring a continuity of audience from one programme to the next'. On ITV, in contrast, 'such material has to jostle for space and attention alongside advertising'.[7] As the 1990s unfold, the number of such trailers increase, as does the amount of off-screen promotion in the form of listings magazines and newspapers.

Richard Paterson observes that in parallel with the working practice which defines 'repetition as a fundamental structuring principle of most of its programming', on the basis that viewers watch what they are familiar with, the schedule is also 'determined by notions of family life'.[8] The tacit assumption is that, for example, in the early evening domestic life is centred around meals and children are in control of the TV set until about 7.30 p.m., when the 'mother' then organizes family viewing up until about 9.00 p.m. After this 'watershed', programme content changes substantially catering more to adult tastes; at this time parents determine what their children should be allowed to watch. This assumption also includes the idea that as the evening unfolds the 'father' of the house takes a more determining role in programme choice. It hardly needs pointing out that such a model is anti-quated, somewhat Blytonesque. For instance, since the late 1960s there has been a dramatic rise in lone-parent families, fewer couples with children (through the strategies of either delaying having children or choosing to remain childless), and the growth of reconstituted families with their various permutations of step-children and step-parents. Moreover, some children simply go to bed as *they* please, or watch 'unsuitable' programmes on their own bedroom sets, or watch videos in private, sometimes material graphically more awful than their parents might possibly imagine.

With the ever-increasing numbers of multi-set households, the television audience can thus be fragmented at any time of the day or night. Such a scenario is perfectly suited to those thematic or minority channels available on cable and satellite; and if *they* succeed, terrestrial broadcasters will indeed be pushed further into matching them with similar programming. Perhaps, then, the notion of 'scheduling for the family' may well become merely a historical curiosity.[9]

The Significance of Television

When asked about the amount of time they spent watching television, almost 60 per cent of the 1994 survey believed they watched about the right proportion. However one-fifth believed they watched too much, while a similar number felt that they simply didn't have the opportunity to see enough. Such frustrated viewers were predominantly those younger viewers aged 16–34. Viewers were then asked a number of questions centring on the reasons why they actually watched television; not surpris-ingly, the overwhelming majority of respondents simply said they watched the box in order to see a programme they enjoyed. Such a response may safely be taken as evidence that not all viewers always watch the television aimlessly.

None the less other reasons for watching television included the notion of watching for the sheer pleasure of it, regardless of the actual program-ming available. Also viewers reported that on occasions they would watch television as there was 'nothing better to do at the time', or would turn the set on 'just for company'; or would tune into one programme and then find themselves 'watching for the rest of the evening'; or would watch it 'just for background, when doing something else' or would turn to it as an 'escape

from everyday concerns'. A smaller minority claimed that they used television as a means of putting off something else they ought to be doing, or
as a strategy to ignore the people around them.

The younger viewers (especially those aged 16–24) were much more
likely to endorse passive reasons for their viewing, like saying that 'there
was nothing better to do' or to put off 'something else they should do'. They
also used television, to a greater extent than other viewers, to tune out those
around them. Older viewers on the other hand, were much more likely to
talk of the attraction of specific programmes, and of television's informative
potential or indeed that viewing was a pleasurable way to spend an
evening. These older viewers were also not surprisingly more ready than
other age groups to admit to using the television as 'company'. Interestingly
enough, women were more likely than men to say they often watched television for company, perhaps this is because they spend more time alone, or
are more bored and lonely than men. Or perhaps for women an unpalatable
truth is that the television is more companionable than the men in their
lives?

Nearly *all* viewers claimed that they could find other things to do if there
was nothing of particular interest on TV, yet only 40 per cent of them
believed they would find it easy to live without it. Such a response exemplifies the power of television and its place in our lives, but also our
ambivalence towards it: TV viewing, especially among older groups,
remains an activity tinged with *guilt*.

The overall impression gained from the viewers' responses confirms the
view that television is *so* popular because it 'provides large amounts of
distraction and relaxation at a trivial cost and with minimum effort to the
viewer'. And that its *main* role in people's lives is to 'entertain, more often
by soothing than by stimulating'. Most television simply 'washes over us'.
As Barwise and Ehrenberg put it, most of us spend the majority of our daily
leisure time unwinding or simply passing the time rather than, say, reading
Tolstoy or going to see an Ibsen play, or, we might add, reading a novel by
Tom Clancy or seeing a Willy Russell play. It follows, they argue, that we
must not expect too much from our television viewing; nevertheless, it is
an undeniable fact as is often cited, that 'more people have seen
Shakespearean drama in 40 years of television than in 400 years of the
theatre'.[10]

The viewers surveyed were asked a number of questions concerning television censorship and programme choice. The overwhelming majority of
viewers – over three-quarters of the total – believed they themselves should
be able to choose what to watch, rather than the choice being made for them
either by broadcasters or regulators. A majority of viewers also felt that if
people wished to pay extra for 'violent' or 'pornographic' material then
they should be allowed to do so, though this view was expressed more
keenly by satellite viewers and cable viewers than terrestrial viewers.
However, at the same time a majority *also* agreed that pay channels should

have exactly the same restriction on what they are allowed to show as other channels. While 80 per cent of terrestrial-only viewers tended to agree that they had ample choice of what to watch on BBC1, 2, and ITV and Channel 4, the figure dropped to only a third of cable and satellite viewers; which is why, of course, they subscribe to these extra services.

There were less clear-cut views about whether or not items that were likely to upset people should *ever* be shown on television. Disagreement (61 per cent) somewhat outweighed agreement (38 per cent) with the belief that potentially upsetting items should *never* be seen. On the other hand, a substantial majority – especially among cable and satellite viewers – disliked the slashing of films, even those broadcast in the late adult-only slots. Not surprisingly the desire for censorship *generally* grew with increasing age. Older viewers, of course, have with their own eyes witnessed the changes on television that have resulted in full nudity appearing in the middle to late evening, and the seemingly inexhaustible supply of violent images. Younger viewers, however, only know television as *it is* now; future generations, it may reasonably be argued, will be even less shocked and, accordingly, will desire even less censorship.

On questions concerning 'pay-TV' almost all the satellite and cable viewers believed that such channels were well worth the financial outlay involved – they certainly did not regret signing up for those extra services as they believed that the channels could offer a far wider choice of programmes and made viewing a more satisfying experience. However, terrestrial-only viewers, on the other hand, expressed mixed views as to the question. It can safely be assumed, however, that their views manifest a considerable degree of ignorance about these actual new channels. Interestingly enough, of the same satellite and cable viewers, at least three-quarters of them believed that they were in fact offered more channels than they could possibly manage to watch and that they seldom watched more than just a handful of the channels available. Half of these cable and satellite viewers felt that the four main terrestrial channels were 'staid and boring' compared to the channels they subscribed to. Significantly, only a third of them claimed that they had been attracted to cable by the possibility of cheap telephony; rather for these viewers, the predominant attraction to cable was the additional television channels rather than the prospect of cheaper telephone services. It is difficult not to conclude that increasingly there appears to be some satellite and cable households where viewers – invariably a younger audience – have radically different expectations and television experiences than terrestrial-only viewers.

Quality Television: 'Brideshead in the Crown'

Both the BBC and terrestrial commercial television are required, to a greater or lesser degree, to produce a diverse schedule of programming consisting of both entertainment and information. Additionally, these programmes

are expected to be of high *quality* regardless of genre or precise time of transmission. Meaning what? We may well ask: for while diversity may be
measured by the provision, or otherwise, of different types of programmes,
the notion of 'quality' is almost impossible to define.

At first glance the issue appears to be simply a matter of taste: of personal,
individual, subjective judgement. And of course the emergence of so-called
cultural populism has energetically brought into dispute absolutist criteria
of 'quality': undiluted cultural elitism, it is argued, no longer washes. As
Jim McGuigan puts it, cultural populism has dealt cultural elitism a fatal
blow: 'opening up the range of "texts" worthy of study (from grand opera
to soap opera, from lyric poetry to disco dancing), evincing humanity
towards popular tastes and installing the active audience at the centre of
the picture'.[11] In other words, our evening spent in front of *Brookside* or
Baywatch may well be as worthwhile as Bernard Levin's at Glyndebourne.
Just as *cultural*. But more of this later.

In her review of the issue of 'quality' Charlotte Brunsdon argues that television does not easily 'fit' into established aesthetic discourses, and that
there is no genuinely agreed way of speaking *about* television. It is certainly
true that there is no language which would enable us to identify 'quality'
with any ease or certainty.[12] The relentless experience of diversity which
centrally characterizes television makes the issue additionally problematic:
what precisely can 'quality' mean when 'television' means, say, an expensive costume drama like *Martin Chuzzlewitt* or *Pride and Prejudice*, the
controlled excitement of *Football Italia*, the cheaply made and consumerist
celebration of *Supermarket Sweep*, or the revealing stories of *Cutting Edge* in
which, for example, mothers make lengthy and emotional journeys to meet
their children abducted by their Libyan fathers.[13] *All* of this is television.

In recognizing this problem Brunsdon believes that such diversity must,
therefore, always be taken into account in any discussion of quality, but 'not
in ways which makes quality "genre specific", creating certain "sink" or
"trash" genres of which demands are not made'.[14] In other words, it is her
belief that soap operas are *not* to be compared with, say, high-budget
costume dramas, rather they are to be discussed within the rules of their
own genre.

Arguments forwarded by the Broadcasting Research Unit (BRU) illustrate this point. Thus, factual programmes ought to be evaluated above all
other considerations in terms of impartiality. So when facts are relevant to
the item under investigation they are to be treated with care, accessibly
offered to the viewer, placed in context, obtained with sensitivity and sensibility, while the manner of presentation must be honest, truthful and
plain. Similarly, opinions should be put forward fairly, with alternative
viewpoints also expressed. At all costs, it is argued, broadcasters must not
be 'seduced, for any reason, in order to satisfy viewers' supposed cravings
for "human interest" stories, into the coarse devices of sensationalism and
spurious confrontation'.[15] Drama, on the other hand, ought *not* always to

aim for impartiality but instead attempt to offer challenge, controversy, scope for experiment, and an opportunity for the voices of dissent to be heard: 'drama of quality, to hold the attention and provoke a response from the viewers, may require passion and directness, combined with respect and simplicity'. And, the BRU continued, 'originality cannot be evolved to order. Its life and sustenance require freedom in which to grow (and make mistakes)'.[16]

This of course merely represents *one* account of the fundamentals of genre-specific programme standards. The notion of 'quality', however, still remains elusive. Mary Warnock, in her important review of the 'quality and standards in broadcasting', analyses the conventional definitions of 'quality' in an attempt to provide a more satisfactory one. Firstly, she opines that 'good broadcasting' is much more than simply broadcasting which does not offend, and more than merely technically efficient broadcasting. She adds, somewhat diffidently, that it is instead broadcasting which is, in some sense, *worth receiving*. Helpfully she proceeds to unpack this personal value judgement. Warnock believes that 'good quality' in television is something that cannot be 'precisely specified in advance' because good broadcasting is *creative* and, therefore, always 'liable to surprise us'. It is her belief that fixed criteria lead to formulae, and as such are 'death to broadcasting. Nothing can be done by rule of thumb; nor can high-quality broadcasting be ensured by negative rules prohibiting such evils as bias, undue violence or bad language'.[17] The argument that it is 'variety' that gives central meaning to quality in broadcasting, also holds little attraction for Warnock. Even if variety was ensured, either by the number of available channels or by the idea of regionality ('often confused with the local'), there would, she believes, be no guarantee that it would be a 'source of excellence'. Instead, she prefers the importance of a property seen in individual programmes, which Warnock refers to as 'non-triviality'.

> It is a general mark of the human imagination, in whatever sphere it is exercised, that it excites in us the feeling that an experience, a sight, a sound, a piece of information, a joke, is somehow significant; it is worth pondering; it opens a door to something besides itself. Enjoyment of it seems to promise more enjoyment. And so it is with non-trivialising broadcasting.[18]

Across the many different genres she sees the potential for intrinsically educative non-trivializing broadcasting – programmes which are rarely, if ever, boring, but instead always capable of releasing the viewer's imaginative capacities.

Such an idea as Warnock's might appear merely to be a refraction of the more general culturally elitist notion of quality; but it is not, however, easily dismissed. More problematic, though, is that Warnock takes the individual programme as her unit of analysis whereas it is surely more appropriate that quality should be ascribed to the overall provision of television: an evening or a week's output, or indeed a channel's.[19] Also she assumes that viewers do not differ in what they find stimulating and that all agree on which programmes fire the imagination. Besides, as we have earlier seen, for a good deal of the time viewing television is a somewhat passive and relaxing activity, even if the audience is potentially 'active' in its interpretation of programmes, for much of the time TV is more a barbiturate than an amphetamine.

It was the British Government's 1988 White Paper, *Broadcasting in the '90s: Competition, Choice and Quality*[20] which initiated much of the debate of recent years about the issue of quality in television. Specifically, under the proposed legislation television companies seeking lucrative ITV franchises were to be required to pass 'quality thresholds' in order to do so. It is within this context that it is essential to remember that there are *always* issues of power at stake in notions such as quality in broadcasting. As Charlotte Brunsdon expresses it: 'Quality for whom? Judgement by whom? On whose behalf?'[21] In other words, some voices are more likely to be heard than others, or it may be that their message will be taken more seriously than other competing ones.

Brunsdon in her comprehensive and insightful analysis enumerates what she terms the various 'discourses of quality' competing against each other for supremacy: *traditional aesthetic discourse*, which conventionally concentrates mainly on dance, drama and music; *professional codes and practices*, in which channels are differentiated as are genres (current affairs are more prestigious than soaps), while ratings may signify 'quality' or indeed its opposite; *realist paradigms*, in which the emphasis is on objectivity in factual programmes and issues of representation in drama (for example, black characters in crime programmes); and *moral paradigms*, which include the principles of public-service broadcasting, notions of impartiality and the 'justification of censorship and controls on broadcasting'. Brunsdon summarizes the contemporary institutional and managerial–broadcaster's position as being located within the traditional *realist* and *moral* codes, in which complexity and contentious issues are avoided.

One of the strategies employed to side-step critical arguments about quality television, Brunsdon argues, while still being able to 'attest to its existence and virtue is to refer to specific programmes, which can then function as shorthand for taken for granted understandings of "quality"'.[22] Over the decades particular programmes have functioned in this way, including *The Forsyte Saga*, *Civilisation*, *Jesus of Nazareth*, *Roots* and, more recently, *Brideshead Revisited* and *The Jewel in the Crown*. She argues that these two Granada productions have come to be seen as 'uncontroversial' indicators of 'quality' and unlike *The Singing Detective* or *Boys from the Blackstuff*, these are programmes which everyone can perceive to be quality productions. They incorporate 'already established taste codes of literature, theatre, interior decoration, interpersonal relationships and nature'. For Brunsdon these two programmes produce a 'certain image of England and

Englishness which is untroubled by contemporary division and guaranteed aesthetic legitimacy'.[23] It is undemanding, and under-utilizes the medium's uniqueness. For her argument she turns to Raymond Williams whose own definition of 'serious television' is insistently 'cross-generic', including such diverse programmes as *Z Cars*, *Monty Python*, *Match of the Day* and *Panorama*. The aesthetic Williams develops is formed within the 'two major cultural traditions of the West'. It is realist in that he believes in television's *capacity* to inform us about the way we and other cultures live. But it is also modernist, in that he believes that television should develop *its own specificity*: as Brunsdon concludes he 'consistently searches for, and applauds, programmes that utilize the resources of television to their full extent'.[24] He was less impressed with those productions which merely reproduced existing cultural habits and values.

Programme Standards

In the survey viewers were asked a number of questions about programme standards. Just over half of the sample said they believed that the standards on television had generally remained the same since the previous year. Almost a third disagreed however, arguing that standards had worsened, while 10 per cent perceived an improvement. Younger viewers (16–24) were more likely to talk of such improvements than older (45 plus) viewers: this of course is hardly surprising, given that such younger viewers had not such a back-catalogue of programmes to compare the current ones with. Those viewers from multi-channel households were more positive about the additional channels they subscribed to, again a predictable response given that they had chosen to pay for them.

In terms of the terrestrial channels the prime source of criticism was that there were far too many repeats, an opinion forcibly expressed in the earlier comparable 1974 and 1984 surveys. Interestingly, in 1974 the majority of viewers both complained about the excessive number of repeats but nevertheless also the merits of such repeats for those viewers who had not previously seen the programmes.[25] Such generosity towards the issue was, however, absent in the 1994 survey. But this is hardly surprising given the relentless increase in repeat programming, a process which invariably will increase.

The only exception to such condemnation of the process is when those programmes held in almost universal esteem like *Fawlty Towers* are repeated. Otherwise, viewers experience a sense of being cheated, or of their intelligence being insulted.

Programmes are thus repeated; movies grace the television screen following a sometimes lengthy theatrical (cinema) or video release; television programme formats are relentlessly copied, sequels are enthusiastically produced and, at the same time, the same faces appear on the screen with incessant regularity. And of course, there are niche channels like UK Gold which broadcasts re-runs only, raiding the vaults of terrestrial channels and providing instant memories for the viewer. As audience fragmentation continues and niche programming further develops, repeat television on terrestrial channels will come to be seen as unacceptable, as the specialist channels will be seen as the appropriate channel for such programming.

The sheer volume of repeated programmes leads David Thorburn to observe that the 'system of re-runs has now reached a point of transforming television into a continuous living museum which displays for daily or weekly consumption texts from every stage of the medium's past'.[26] Indeed, the present system and volume of re-runs would allow a truly dedicated viewer to watch no fewer than 10,000 repeats a year, as well as the same number of older films. In multi-channel households viewers are able to return to the early episodes of *Neighbours* or *EastEnders* and then may tune into a terrestrial channel to watch the very latest episode.

For all the major terrestrial channels the figure for repeat transmissions stands at a reasonably stable one of one-third of total programming.[27] It is of course the more expensive productions (drama serials, sit-coms, or costume dramas) or the expensively acquired feature films that are most likely to be repeated. Repeats, quite simply, keep the costs of broadcasting down. In a highly competitive media environment this process will invariably increase.

In purely economic terms reproduction costs are relatively minor compared with the huge costs incurred by original programming: as Inglis puts it, each original programme in fact 'resembles the development of a prototype'.[28] When the television industry conjures a success naturally it attempts to replicate it as speedily and easily as possible. Given the fact that sequels rarely work, repeats, therefore, are the most viable option open to them. Of course the success of any unique or novel creation is a matter of luck or accident, thus commercially an extremely risky venture. Repeat programming is a much more manageable strategy.

Creative risk-taking remains, none the less, central to *anyone's* definition of quality television; indeed, perhaps no one in their right mind desires a *constant* re-run of the past. Yet, as television continues speedily along the path towards a relatively free and deregulated market-place, such creative risk-taking is an activity which market forces, left unfettered, are unlikely to encourage. Although clearly the issue is not without complexity. For example, in the case of US television, Betsy Williams claims that there is widespread agreement that whatever 'quality television' actually means, one show which satisfies the term is the comic-drama *Northern Exposure* set in the 'Alaskan Riviera' and which can be seen as a 'kinder, gentler *Twin Peaks*'. At the centre of a 'remarkable ensemble cast' is New Yorker Dr Joel Fleischman, reluctantly working off his medical school loans in the remote and somewhat surreal Cicely. The programme explores a range of cultural oppositions central to Joel's life: east versus west, frontier versus civilization, science versus mysticism, male versus female.[29] Reflecting on the success of *Northern Exposure*, Williams argues that as the television audience continues to fragment, the networks are clearly aware that even a very popular show will only bring in so many households. And while the quality series of the 1970s and 1980s didn't have to reach a mass audience, the quality series of the 1990s simply *cannot* reach a mass audience. Accordingly, she argues, the networks have begun to show a greater propensity to target specific audience groups. Thus, Williams concludes, a 'quirky, introspective show like *Northern Exposure* has greater chances for survival', and perhaps the 'narrowly targeted but polyvocal series is the way of the future for quality network television'.[30]

The Range of Programmes

The viewers in the survey who claimed that programme standards on terrestrial channels had in fact improved, were asked to give their reasons for this belief. In general terms such improved standards were linked to the perceived availability of a wider range of programmes, and a greater quantity of 'quality' dramas.

This perhaps is an appropriate moment to introduce an element of caution: the viewer's responses to all number of questions conceal as much as they reveal. Take, for example, the widespread claim of those who believed that the 'range' of programmes had increased. A cursory glance at the statistics demonstrates that, on the terrestrial channels, the range of programmes has, in actuality, been systematically narrowing over the decade, and not widening. This is an issue we will return to, but perhaps it is instructive here to cite the illuminating case of Channel 4.

The remit of Channel 4[31] is that it is to be a public service which will provide information, education and entertainment: its programmes must be 'distinctive', appeal to tastes and interests not generally catered for by ITV, encourage innovation and experiment, include a number of educational items, include programmes which are European in origin and supplied by independent producers, provide 'high-quality' news and current affairs, and overall 'maintain a high general standard and a wide range'. In some quarters, however, concern has been expressed that Channel 4 will increasingly be unable to fulfil its remit in the face of strong pressures from advertisers for them to deliver large audiences. The statistics suggest there may well be some justification in such concerns. For example since the beginning of the 1990s news output has halved, documentaries and current affairs programmes have been substantially reduced, arts and music programmes have been reduced by some 75 per cent, while over the very same period entertainment programmes have almost doubled. There is no doubt that this new programme menu has proved popular with the viewers, and the Channel's audience figures have indeed continued to grow steadily. The central question remains, however,

Table 4.1 Channel 4 television: analysis of output by programme category

	1990 Hours	%	1991 Hours	%	1992 Hours	%	1993 Hours	%
Drama (a)	400	7.6	719	10.2	706	9.7	613	8.4
Entertainment	952	18.2	1,190	16.8	1,859	25.5	2,246	31.0
News	403	7.7	638	9.0	558	7.7	277	3.8
Documentaries	354	6.7	494	7.0	374	5.1	282	3.9
Current Affairs	438	8.4	613	8.7	385	5.3	429	5.9
Education (b)	549	10.5	779	11.0	890	12.2	937	12.9
Arts and Music	434	8.3	364	5.2	294	4.0	167	2.3
Feature Films	945	18.0	1,378	19.5	1,245	17.1	1,187	16.4
Sport	445	8.5	569	8.1	602	8.3	671	9.2
Quiz	117	3.4	148	2.1	205	2.8	255	3.5
Multicultural	76	1.4	98	1.4	121	1.7	139	1.9
Religion	72	1.4	76	1.1	50	0.7	52	0.7
Total	5,245	100	7,066	100	7,289	100	7,255	100

Source: Channel 4 *Television Corporation; compiled from various Report and Financial Statements*.
Notes: (a) Including *Film on Four* and *Film on Four International*;
(b) including schools.

to what degree ought viewers' tastes and preferences take precedence over broadcasting aims.

Consumer choice is the oft-repeated mantra of the market-place: and if it is indeed the case that for most of the time viewers seek entertainment programming, Channel 4 is clearly giving them what they want. Many critics though believe that to lose sight of the educative function of public service broadcasting would inevitably lead to a decline in 'standards and quality' in broadcasting: it is all well and good giving people 'what they want', but do they actually know what possible alternatives are available so the argument goes, or are their 'choices' merely superficial, based on their addictions and habits, and further reinforced by other influences?[32] Such a critique is immediately perceived as one of cultural elitism but surely the issue is more complex? This is an issue we will return to in the post-script, although as a preliminary observation it is useful to recall Michael Schudson's stricture in his discussion of 'sense and sentimentality' in broadcasting: 'The fact that popular audiences respond actively to the materials of mass culture is important to recognize and understand, but it is not a fact that should encourage us to accept mass culture as it stands or popular audiences as they now exist'.[33] He believes it to be vitally impor-tant to accept that not all cultural forms are equal or that all interpretations are valid, or indeed beyond criticism.

5

News

Serving up the world in ninety-second slices is, on television journalists' own admission, a poor second best to the explanatory power of a good newspaper. In moments of self-doubt and self-examination, good television journalists will admit that if the general population were entirely dependent on their nightly bulletin for their understanding of the world, they would be exceedingly poorly informed . . . [and] . . . if the nightly news were replaced by magazine programmes and documentary features with open-ended formats, the institutional preconditions for a Journalism that respects itself and the terrible events it covers would begin to exist . . .
    Michael Ignatieff (1985), 'Is Nothing Sacred? The Ethics of Television'

The social construction of 'news' is one of the most researched areas of media studies. In this chapter we describe such processes whereby 'events become news', and also consider the audience view of the news.

In the early months of 1995, Kabul, the capital city of Afghanistan, remained under blockade and relief workers predicted a mass exodus of hungry, frightened people. Some estimated that as many as 200,000 refugees would flee the capital and make their way towards the already overcrowded refugee camps of Jalalabad, situated near the Pakistan border. The city had been under siege since 1992 and a number of estimates put the total of deaths at some 6,000, with over 21,000 seriously wounded.[1]

Whether or not such 'news' reaches our television screens depends on a number of factors somewhat unconnected, with Kabul itself, *viz*, the ability of 'suitable' pictures and indeed of reporters in the region, and the quantity and quality of other competing 'stories', the issue of whether death in Kabul is 'new or old news', and finally, and crucially, the extent of British 'interest' in the carnage taking place.

This is not to be overly critical. Rather, it is simply to point out that 'news' is a process of *selection* and *construction*. As Neil Postman observes, the 'news of the day is a figment of our technological imagination', it is, in fact, 'a media event'.² Particular *events* are what count as news: if other things occur which do not easily fit the 'news-processor's categories', they are either transcribed until they *do* fit, or they are ignored. Thus news-collecting agencies cannot report *process* or the uneven development of history, rather they must be able to frame news as a succession of 'news-as-events' and have the pictures and voices to match.³

News comes in a variety of shapes and sizes: simply compare, for example, the rolling reporter-led CNN news, the more 'entertaining' *News at Ten*, the discursive Channel 4 programme of the early evening, and the conventional and painstakingly presented BBC bulletins.

It is unquestionably true that the pictures news programmes deliver are memorable: the dismantling of the Berlin Wall, the massacre at Tiananmen Square, Mikhail Gorbachov's ticker-tape welcome in New York and Nelson Mandela's release from his South African prison, after serving 28 years of a life sentence. Indeed, in numerous surveys, viewers consistently state that they would like to see *more* news, and express the view that such programmes are an essential part of their television lives. For broadcasters too, the news is – as ITV has discovered in recent years – a central and presently unmovable item of the schedule. However, research by Taylor and Mullan which required viewers to compile *their* ideal evening's schedule, discovered that many omitted any mention whatsoever of news in their schedule. For them watching news was a duty, not a desire, something they felt they 'ought' to do.⁴

News programmes invariably employ a presentational style designed to create a sense of importance and authority. Despite variations depending on the channel watched or the time of the transmission, news programmes establish a certain formality by their reliance on stiff postures, fairly formal clothes, grammatically complete sentences, a general lack of emotion and the use of the conventional medium close-up shot.

World News

From the 1950s onwards numerous surveys of public opinion have demonstrated that the public learns about world news primarily from television. Mass audiences have consistently identified television as their main source of national and international news information, well ahead of newspapers. This finding was repeated in the 1994 survey when almost three quarters of viewers mentioned television as their main source of world news, followed by newspapers and then radio. This figure is 10 per cent higher than in the comparable survey a decade earlier. However, as with previous surveys, women (76 per cent) were slightly more likely than males (68 per cent) to nominate television as their first source of world news, whereas the men were more likely than average to nominate newspapers (19 per cent).

The over-65s of both genders were also more likely than average to cite television as their first source, than the younger groups. And upper and middle classes were less likely than the working classes to cite television as a first source, but more likely to name the radio (14 per cent versus 8 per cent).

A somewhat predictable enough picture thus emerges: the majority of viewers turn to television for world news, although the middle classes also refer to broadsheet newspapers and, additionally, radio programmes for information. But what precisely is the *point* of world news, and what do audiences take from such bulletins? Put another way, why should the television news be elevated on to a 'protective pedestal, rather than original drama or children's programmes or experimental comedy?'[5] Is it because news is pre-eminently *informative*, and as citizens it is believed that we need such information to contribute rationally to the democratic decision-making process of a democracy? Is that what audiences actually take from news? Essentially, very little is known of the impact or effect of news bulletins on audiences, such impact depends on how much background knowledge the viewer already has, how much the item directly affects them or can be seen in personal terms, and also upon exactly where the item occurs in the bulletin's running order.

The problem with *world* news is that the majority of it is not directly relevant to the personal lives of the viewers watching. For instance on 26 April 1986 the nuclear reactor of the Soviet power plant at Chernobyl in the Ukraine went completely 'out of control'. Following this catastrophic event there was widespread, extensive and detailed news coverage of the radiation that followed the explosion. Subsequent research on this issue showed that such bulletins had very little effect or impact on the viewers.[6] Even when there *is* British interest in world affairs, as in the Gulf conflict of 1991, the audience is hardly glued to the main news bulletins for information. There *was* interest in some of the in-depth programming – *Newsnight* and *Channel 4 News* for example – however, at the time the two mainstream news bulletins did not greatly exceed their average audiences. Steven Barnett's analysis of the ratings at the time leads him to conclude that most viewers of the news are 'simply bored very quickly'.[7]

There is no denying television's spectacular reach. No other medium could have had the world-wide impact in terms of the vast numbers reached and the effect on individual viewers that the 1984 BBC broadcast on the Ethiopian famine achieved (or of the Live Aid concert that followed). Yet even in cases such as these television created 'awareness' and subsequent gift-giving, but not deep involvement in the issues of famine.[8]

Michael Ignatieff, in his penetrating analysis of the news coverage of the Ethiopian famine, recasts the issue and asks the question 'Is nothing sacred in such television broadcasting?' Taking as his starting-point the television images of the famine, he asks whether they represent either an 'instance of the promiscuous voyeurism a visual culture makes possible', or perhaps a 'hopeful example of the internationalization of conscience'. At the outset of his discussion, Ignatieff applauds the impact the TV coverage of the famine had on western charity and on European governments, especially over the issue of surplus grain.[9] Without such television exposure, he argues, thousands more Ethiopians would have died. At the same time he points to the accusations that were levelled against TV news broadcasters that they had ignored food shortages until they acquired the 'epic visual appeal of famine', and also the criticism that the story would disappear from the bulletins when the 'focus upon horror shifts elsewhere in the world'. This of course is a process which continuously unfolds before our eyes: Rwanda is replaced on the screen by Bosnia-Herzegovina which is then displaced by the horrors of Chechnia. As Ignatieff puts it, the 'medium's gaze is brief, intense, and promiscuous', and the 'shelf life of the moral causes it makes its own is brutally short'. Quite simply, news bulletins are market-places in which images of horror compete against each other for precious space.

While praising the role television has played in the breakdown of the barriers of citizenship, religion, race and geography, Ignatieff laments the manner in which it makes us 'voyeurs of the suffering of others, tourists amidst their landscapes of anguish'. While television brings us face to face with their fate, it none the less obscures the distances – social, economic, moral – between us.

Ignatieff acutely observes that though a number of societies have sought to restrict the traffic in images of degrading sexuality, few, however, have attempted to 'restrict the commerce in images of human suffering'. The *form* news broadcasting takes is central to the problem.

> The time disciplines of the news genre militate against the minimum moral requirement of engagement with another person's suffering: that one spends time with them, time to learn, to suffer with, to pierce the carapace of self-absorption and estrangement that separates us from the moral worlds of others.[10]

When short bulletins of suffering are enjoined by quite different news items, it makes it even more difficult for the viewer to engage morally with the issue. In the end, Ignatieff argues, the real subject of the news is the news itself: 'In this worship of itself, of its speed, its immense news-gathering resources, its capacity to beat the clock, the news turns realities like Ethiopia into ninety-second exercises in its own style of representation'.[11] In war zones the bravery of reporters and camera crews is regularly spoken of, and they are themselves festooned with awards – despite the fact they are only doing what they choose to do, and being paid handsomely while doing so; issues like famine are often seen through a day-in-the-life of, say, a British relief worker, as a way of 'personalizing' the issue – we may well ask, isn't the horror of an untimely death enough?; reporters crouch by the remains of buildings, hiding from the falling mortars: 'we can hear the Russian tanks coming', they utter – who precisely is the *we*, whose side are the reporters on? Presumably the 'victims' whose plight creates 'better pictures'. All of this is slickly packaged and subsequently tailed with the now almost obligatory light-hearted item.

Michael Ignatieff asks whether in this flow of television news which reduces 'all the world's horror to identical commodities', some sort of practice is possible by which *real* horror may be given special attention. He points to those sacred occasions of modern secular culture like the Royal Wedding of 1981 or the funeral of JFK, where television has devised its own rules, rituals and rhetoric to enfold viewers in a sense of the sacred importance of such moments: why, he asks, cannot we treat suffering with equal respect? If television can 'jettison its schedules and transform its discourse for the sake of a wedding or a funeral, then we can ask it to do the same for a famine in which millions of people are at risk'.[12]

A question we may ask is, are the broadcasters in their coverage of 'news' merely pandering to the ghoulish tendencies inherent in the viewer? The question is extremely difficult to answer: there is no doubt that strangers flock to the scenes of disasters, and that many scenes of violence and carnage are enthusiastically and vicariously consumed. However, a substantial number of viewers, when asked general questions about the news, talked of the inappropriateness of showing deaths of children and animals – especially at meal times – and in particular cited the case of the Lockerbie disaster: 'relatives were in tears and all the time the cameras were on them'.

David Morrison's research into the television coverage of the Gulf War confirmed such widely-held opinions. Very little of the death and injury that occurred – 150,000 Iraqi troops and civilians – was actually seen on television. It was partially reported, but simply not seen. Morrison argues that as the British viewer tended to accept the war in the Gulf as correct and just, the tolerance to accepting death and injury is, therefore, likely to have been very high. However, as very few pictures of death and injury were shown, that tolerance was never really tested. There is, therefore, no knowledge of what the response might have been had the viewer seen the 'full carnage on the road to Basra inflicted on the Iraqi troops as they fled Kuwait at the end of the war'. But Morrison claims that his research did discover that the viewer does *not* wish to be exposed to the visual horrors of war: they do not appear to want to be 'visually dragged into the charnel-house of events themselves'.[13]

News and Propaganda

The question of whether the viewer will in fact be vicariously dragged through the bones of the dead is of course a decision taken by the broadcaster. On certain occasions such decisions will be partially determined by their specific relations with the political masters of the day. Under certain circumstances news may well simply collapse into propaganda, while at other times it may appear somewhat libertarian in its effects.

Because of the independent television pictures reaching Russian citizens graphically showing the gap between government claims and the evidence of such television footage, Boris Yeltsin's adventures in Chechnia were in 1995 under close scrutiny. The Kremlin has no choice but to consider public opinion. Contrast this with the Balkan wars of the 1990s, in which 'television has been more important than history', nowhere more so than in Serbia where the state television is 'perhaps *the* key element' in the regime of President Slobodan Milosevic.[14] He first tried out his propaganda exercises in Kosovo in southern Serbia where Albanians outnumber Serbs nine to one. Television spread exaggerated and even fabricated tales of Albanian rapes of Serb women and Albanian theft of Serb lands. After the creation of the Albanian 'enemy', there followed the Croat and then the Bosnian. Milosevic, it was announced, would avenge the 'victimization' of his people. The media technique was not to create prejudice, but rather to feed the 'seed material' of bigotry and hatred which already existed. For example, in November 1991, a Serb photographer was interviewed at length after he allegedly found the chopped-up remains of 41 Serb children in Vukovar. The photographer retracted his fabricated story the following day, but the television, however, only reported the 'howls of world wide protest that greeted the initial revelation'.[15] Similarly, in 1992 Serb viewers were not shown the shocking CNN pictures of the Sarajevo siege or the ITN film of the north Bosnian camps full of emaciated Muslim prisoners.

Propaganda, thus, is characterized as much by *partial-* as well as *mis-* information. As Christopher Lasch has succinctly put it, the 'master propagandist' avoids obvious emotional appeals but rather strives for a tone that is 'consistent with the prosaic quality of modern life – a dry, bland matter-of-factness'. Partial truths, he adds, serve as more effective instruments of deception than outright lies. What matters is that the information presented should *sound* true: 'it sometimes becomes necessary to suppress information even when it reflects credit on the government, for no other reason than that the facts sound implausible'.[16]

Conspiracy theorists tend to see *all* news as propaganda, albeit hidden through complex and sophisticated guises. For instance the so-called 'political economy' perspective views news output as merely the result of the ruling directorate of the capital class dictating to editors and reporters what to say. At its extreme, this model is characterized by the notion of 'manufacturing consent', as termed by Edward Herman and Noam Chomsky, the view that the media 'serve to mobilize support for the special interests that dominate the state and private activity'.[17] In the realm of television of course, such a view drastically underestimates both the importance of the mundane, routine day-to-day journalistic practices which occur and the culture of journalistic autonomy. The idea may, however, have more credence with respect to the press where, in the classic model, a 'free market of ideas' exists, but certainly less so in the realm of broadcasting. Indeed, because there is *no* unlimited access to television and radio such concepts as 'neutrality', 'impartiality' and 'balance', take on a central importance within broadcasting.[18] Accordingly, the modes of organization and control of the broadcasting institutions in Britain have theoretically been devised in an attempt to insulate them from external influence by separating their management and income from governmental or commercial pressures.

None the less, it is apparent that, in certain circumstances and on particular occasions, such institutions are not strictly impartial or neutral. This is evident, for example, in the way that the tenor of foreign media coverage of Northern Ireland is so strikingly different from that of the domestic broadcasting of the BBC or ITV.[19] Similarly the Falklands–Malvinas conflict of 1982 provides a quite recent example of the potential for governmental and broadcasting aims to *converge*. At the time of the conflict, the Director-General of the BBC recognized that the Corporation would come under pressure to 'conform to the national interest'. He duly accepted that there was legitimacy in this situation although he expressed his uncertainty as to what precisely the 'national interest' was. Clearly, he argued, the 'BBC should be careful not to do anything to imperil military operations or diplomatic negotiations, but none the less it should report accurately and faithfully the arguments arising within British society at all levels'.[20] This, in practice did not happen, as it is clear that both main broadcasters kept close to official sources in their coverage of the conflict.

Part of the reason why journalists identified themselves with the military units to which they were attached and whose behaviour they reported, was purely for reasons of personal, physical and psychological survival. Although subsequent convergence between the aims and values of the military and the government on the one side, and broadcasters on the other, was not only confined to the stressful conditions of combat. For example, following the Argentinean government's surrender, retrospective broadcasts of the campaign omitted to show (the available) harrowing pictures of blown-off limbs and severely burnt faces. This decision was taken by the broadcasters themselves but warmly applauded by the military, who were pleased the more unpleasant (and potentially unpalatable) visuals were not shown.[21] Despite all of this the Conservative government of the day was highly critical of the BBC's coverage of the Falklands–Malvinas conflict, and in particular it was unhappy over what it saw as the Corporation's detached and, on occasions, neutral stance. In response to such criticisms the then Director-General of the BBC rejected the allegations, claiming that there was 'no one in the BBC who does not agree that the Argentineans committed aggression'. But added, importantly, that the conflict did not represent 'total war' and that 'one day we will be negotiating with the enemy so we must try to understand them'.[22]

In his review of the overall coverage of the conflict and the government's various responses to it, John Eldridge argues that what emerges is *not* a conspiracy theory of the media but rather the 'consequences of a professional set of practices which, while valuing the principle of independence, relies heavily upon official sources for its news'.[23] Richard Collins concurs with such a view using the metaphor of 'the bargain' as his particular explanatory device.[24]

In times of war (or in cases of national crisis), the governmental concern with broadcast news is not with questions of impartiality, but rather 'which side are you on?' At times of such a crisis, the viewer is conceptualized as *passive* with broadcasters able to gain an advantage. According to the Defence Committee on the handling of press and publication information during the Falklands–Malvinas conflict,

> Many principles supposedly regarded as sacred and absolute within the media, are applied in a less rigid and categorical way by the public as a whole when it is judging its Government's conduct of a war. In our judgement the public is, in general, *quite ready to tolerate being misled to some extent* if the enemy is also misled, thereby contributing to the success of the campaign. (emphasis added)[25]

Such sentiments do not appear to be particularly different from the misinformation perpetrated by Serbian state television in its pursuit of Balkan dominance. Perhaps Bernard Shaw was being less than ironic when he remarked that 'truth telling is not compatible with the defence of the realm'.

It is thus obvious that the autonomy of broadcasters is constantly under threat. Take the example of so-called 'peace broadcasting': 'if US psychological–warfare experts in the Gulf could drop 29 million leaflets on the Iraqis, could a few thousand tiny, cheap radios, tuned to a "Peace Frequency", be dropped over the war zone so that combatants could hear something other than their own side's lies?'[26] This argument suggests that what is required, not just by the US but by the UN (as a 'peacekeeper'), is a rapid reaction contingency force that can go anywhere, set up, and beam news to those cut off from it – and not just through radio, but television as well. But the question is, of course, *whose* news? Despite the seemingly worthy intentions behind such broadcasting, one supporter unwittingly exposes the weakness of the idea: 'we're going to see an epidemic of regional conflicts. It will bankrupt the hi-tech nations if they try to put all these down with military force. Why not use "smart weapons" for peace?'[27] It is thus peace *not* for peace's sake, but for the benefit of those nations liable to suffer. Whither autonomy?

News Values

Academic studies of how news organizations produce news material dates to the American studies of 'gatekeepers' in the early 1950s. David Manning White, for example, studied a wire-editor at a small Mid-Western newspaper. This editor's job was to decide which wire-service stories would run in the paper, and which would not. He made available to White all the copy he received, some of which he rejected together with those he selected to print. He carefully itemized the reasons for rejecting the stories he turned down: 'not enough space', or technical or professional reasons – 'dull writing', or political – 'it's pure propaganda'.[28] Subsequent studies found that other editors on different newspapers made decisions in a similar manner. Their judgements were less of a personal nature, more of simply doing the job, and of maintaining the 'values' of the newspaper (and its owners). Television journalists carry out similar functions as *they* determine which stories are 'news-worthy' and which are not. For example, in the case of overseas stories the same processes are at work, the only difference being that the chain of gatekeepers is lengthier, stretching from, say, the camera crew of an international news film agency in New Delhi, by way of the agency's editorial staff, to gatekeepers in headquarters of the BBC or ITN. An incident in India, in Africa or anywhere else in the Third World, has to be exceedingly remarkable before it is judged 'interesting' or 'important', which invariably means either that a 'high degree of human suffering is involved or else that the interests of the developed world are directly threatened'.[29]

Before looking at such 'news values' it is, given the public's reliance on television news for their knowledge of the world, worth spelling out the *implications* of such gatekeeping behaviour.

Take the random example of ITN's *News at Ten* on 1 December 1994. An 'ordinary' day in news terms: no prime ministerial resignations, no royal weddings, and no serial killers arrested. The bulletin led with the story of the sinking of the *Achille Lauro* in the Horn of Africa. It was followed by an item on the IRA ceasefire; the Labour Party leader's decision to send his son to a grant-maintained school; Tory road-plans; NATO officials in Bosnia-Herzegovina; the murder of a child; an item on the so-called obesity gene; the conflict in Chechnia; job losses; TV licences; ten years after Bhopal; the 'last chance' for a footballer-cum-cocaine-user; and the Queen's visit to Manchester.

In total some 13 items of varying significance and indeed geography. Just under half of them could be termed 'world news'. But compare, for a moment, the stories contained in *The Guardian*[30] of the same day. Like *News at Ten*, the lead story was the sinking of the *Achille Lauro*, followed by job losses at H.M. Customs and Excise; rate rises; a rapist arrested; MP alleges Japanese fraud; Sinn Fein spurn talks; missing charity worker found near Rwanda–Zaire border; the Yemen refuse a safe haven for Saudi men currently in UK asylum; M11 protests; cot death group formed; 'Clause 4 only helps Tories', claims Labour's leader; gay demonstration names ten bishops; bank slated in survey; Britain banning more refugees; NHS market 'driving London's skin disease care to collapse'; NATO talks over Bosnia-Herzegovina; conflict in Chechnia; Mexico's poor; South African dams;

'Shi'ite succession puts Islam in turmoil', and many more reports, features
and stories.

The greatly enlarged view of the world that emerges from such a cursory
look at such newspaper content is plain to see. A simple comparison of
wordage too, is instructive. An average edition of *The Guardian* – the broadsheet section only, not the review pages – might contain almost 100 stories,
one-fifth of which will be foreign. Total wordage would be around 42,050
words, together with the illustrative photographs spread throughout the
paper. An average *News at Ten,* on the other hand, will consist of about 4,500
scripted words plus the visuals and voice-overs. It is of course unclear as to
the precise informational value of such pictures, especially as the aim is
to create emotional impact. The average number of stories on a *News at Ten*
bulletin might be between 10 and 14.

But *The Guardian's* own gatekeeping also keeps out stories which are
nevertheless available should the reporters and editors feel so inclined, or
able to do so. In the case of 'world news', the following are simply a few of
the *conflicts* untouched by *The Guardian* at that precise time, let alone television's *News at Ten*: in Afghanistan, especially in Kabul; Algeria, where
hundreds were dying weekly in the conflict between Islamic groups and
government forces; continued fighting in Angola despite the ceasefire;
continued violence in the Congo's Brazzaville; instability in Kashmir;
threats of further air and missile strikes by the Iraqis against the National
Liberation Army, part of the Iranian Resistance movement based in Iraq;
increasing fears that rebel Hutu militia-men have been rearmed and are
being retrained to re-enter Rwanda from camps in Zaire; fighting on the
border between Afghanistan and Tajikistan, between Tajik rebels and
Russian forces. Additionally, there were numerous other on-going conflicts
in such places as the Somali Republic, Sudan and Cambodia.[31]

Pierre Sorlin traces the history of the news, in the western world, to the
dramatic socio-technological changes which took place between
the sixteenth and seventeenth centuries. The vast expansion of goods that
subsequently appeared was accompanied by a desire to know about what
was happening beyond the small circle in which people lived their lives.
This, Sorlin argues, was linked to the 'needs of trade', and in time such
curiosity was intensified by the increasing availability of such information.
The subsequent development of the press and broadcasting has, Sorlin
argues, been more than simply a matter of gaining information about the
world: 'it has been an aspect of a move from one kind of society to a
profoundly different one'.[32] The supply of news, he believes, has become as
necessary as the supply of food or fuel, and is organized and distributed in
much the same way. In other words, as we have become eager for information and news, such news has been transformed into a commodity,
something that can be bought or sold.

In more recent times one of the important landmarks for an understanding of television news was the introduction in 1967 of *News at Ten* into

the ITV schedule. Previous to this initiative commercial television had experienced difficulty in persuading critics of its seriousness. This all changed with the introduction of *News at Ten* (and later with the emergence of Channel 4), which became so popular with viewers that the total evening schedule was built around it. Quite soon afterwards the 'news' became less of a bulletin and more an ' integrated programme of reporter packages, capable of delivering large audiences in peaktime'.[33] Technological innovations followed as did the increase in broadcasting hours which allowed for the growth in news programmes. TV increasingly came to be seen as the prime source of news for the majority of the population.

Colin Seymour-Ure suggests that there is no reason to imagine that people in 1980, or 1945, say, were interested in different things than we are today. Indeed, as he remarks, 'sex, crime and sport were the staples of the nineteenth century'.[34] A continuity is certainly evident in the tabloid coverage of 'news' but television news has unquestionably systematically created a window on the *world*. But, as we have seen, the extent to which the world is embraced depends on those news *values* which select and then construct 'news'.

Some of these values have already been alluded to, in particular the importance of 'events', as opposed to on-going processes. Such events have a greater chance of making 'news' if they are clear, unusual, unexpected or unpredictable; if they are able to adhere to television's time cycle – 'the movements of certain key actors are followed almost minute by minute, not because they are doing anything remarkable but because they have a keen sense of the sequence of deadlines';[35] if they involve recognizable or well-known people or places; if they exhibit negative implications ('bad' news is preferable to 'good' news); if a certain volume is reached (the number of dead casualties, the number of killings, the rate at which inflation has risen); if the event is home-based rather than foreign – 'the newsroom rule of thumb that one British, American, or European life is worth – in news value – a hundred Asian or African lives';[36] if it is recent – yesterday's famine is no longer 'news'; and crucially if pictures of such events are available, which can fit easily into short time-segments. An additional value, more likely to be seen on ITV than BBC or Channel 4 broadcasts, is the idea that some news ought to be good news, that broadcasts should 'discharge a certain function of good cheer in a cheerless world'.[37]

But most important – and pernicious, the critics would argue – is the imposition of time constraints. If news *is* so important, why is it given such little space in the schedule? Is it because of the costs incurred, or the limitations involved in getting the necessary volume of pictures to match the commentaries, or is it because the audience, ironically, *actually* has an ambivalent attitude towards TV news? They watch the news, but perhaps out of a sense of duty and habit as well as out of concern; too much news in the schedule would have them, perhaps quickly reaching for their remote. The consequence of the time allocated to the news, both in overall terms within its place in the schedules and within the packaged bulletin itself, is evident as Ignatieff observes:

> The promiscuity of the nightly news – the jostling together of tornadoes in Pennsylvania, gunmen in Beirut, striking teachers in Manchester, a royal outing in Suffolk, and infant heart surgery in a Californian hospital – is dictated by the time constraints of the medium.[38]

What, we may well ask, is the viewer expected to deduce from such a bizarre jumble of events, incidents and people?

A number of researchers have consistently shown that on the major news programmes the items shown follow an implicit hierarchy of relative importance. The Glasgow Media Group, for example, shows how this 'agenda' is presented as the 'natural, self-explanatory and common-sensible way to see things'.[39] Such an agenda reflects the news values itemized: unless consisting of disastrous implications, foreign news follows governmental utterances, and that royal stories have a higher-than-deserved ranking, while the past – yesterday's war – is demoted to a lower position in the running order. Of course such hierarchies do not operate on every bulletin, but rather are to be seen as general assumptions and practices.

More substantially the same Glasgow researchers show how the 'imagery of presentation' frames the situation, and in so doing endorses the way things are seen from the Establishment perspective: cabinet ministers are interviewed either with quiet voices in a resplendent room or study, while union spokespeople or activists air their views on the busy, crowded street. This is still true, notwithstanding the increase of more quarrelsome or dogged reporters; the rules remain basically intact.

From its earliest days the BBC (and subsequently commercial television), in its pursuit of 'balance' within the news, relied heavily on the role and stature of the presenter. Such newsreaders were well placed to take on such responsibility, especially after their performance in the Second World War where they were perceived to be the voice of authority and reason. Their presentational style has been described as a mix of 'aggressiveness, scepticism, irony, and detachment', as they speak for *us* against the interest groups they speak with.[40] Of course the presentational style differs somewhat between the more staid BBC, the allegedly middle ground of ITV, and the critically evaluative Channel 4. However, the fact remains that it is through the presenter that we are hurriedly led into and through the 'news of the day'.

The significance of the presenter, or anchor – often extremely well-paid for their autocue services and ability to appear emotionally restrained – is such that, inadvertently, it is the presenter that can become the subject of the audience's gaze, rather than the news itself. After all, they are the regular and recognizable feature of the programme and, besides, many viewers do not know the location of East Timor or the meaning of the Dow-Jones Index. Although such viewers may be but a minority, it has led some critics to argue that television news is not about information, but merely entertainment.

Contemporary news, such critics argue, is not raw information but rather fully structured 'stories', akin to those found in light-drama and entertainment. The story-telling forms are different from one another, and aimed at different audiences, but both may enact a similar depiction of the world. The similarities between, say, a news 'special' on the crack-cocaine war between the police and the dealers on the streets of South London, and a social-realist drama on the same subject, may be exceedingly close. And *both* may be received as either mere entertainment *or* as a stimulus to debate.[41]

Using the example of TV news in the USA, Neil Postman argues that Americans are in fact made ignorant by the process in which news is packaged as entertainment, therefore depriving them of a coherent and contextual understanding of the world. He views the world of news as one of 'fragments, where events stand alone, stripped of any connection to the past, or to the future, or to other events', where all assumptions of coherence have vanished.[42] Postman asks the question, 'what has music to do with the news?' He wonders why the programmes are topped and tailed with such triumphal and dramatic bursts of sound: 'if there were no music – as in the case when any television programme is interrupted for a news flash – viewers would expect something truly alarming, possibly life-altering'. But with the music framing the programme the viewer may rest assured that there is nothing to be greatly alarmed about. Postman adds that this perception of the news programme as a 'stylized dramatic performance' staged largely to entertain, is reinforced by the time constraints on stories. As he puts it, TV news has no intention of suggesting that any story has any implications, for that would require viewers 'to continue to think about it when it is done and therefore obstruct their attending to the next story that waits panting in the wings'.[43] The fact that news programmes will be followed or interrupted by commercials (or trailers, or quite different programmes), defuses their impact: the viewers know that however grave any fragment of news might appear, all has been returned to normal.

In support of his case that the news-as-entertainment format makes all reports of cruelty and death appear greatly exaggerated (or at least not to be taken seriously), Postman cites the case of the Iranian hostage crisis:

> Would it be an exaggeration to say that not one American in a hundred knows what language the Iranians speak? Or what the word 'Ayatollah' means or implies? Or knows any details of the tenets of Iranian religious beliefs? Or the main outlines of their political history? Or knows who the Shah was, and where he came from?[44]

We may well ask similar questions about the contours of the Balkans conflict, including questions concerning religious affiliations, regional identities and the precise nature of those charged with 'peacekeeping' activities. Or indeed other questions concerning the basic facts of the Chechnian conflict.

News Bias

It is self-evidently clear then, as Philip Schlesinger has put it, that the social function of the news is the 'construction of reality' for all those who were not present at such events.[45] Indeed, all news reporting implies a point of view, manifested through the selection of interviewees, the content and tone of the language used by reporters and presenters, and, of course, by virtue of the deceptive nature of the visuals involved; despite the sense suggested in 'seeing is believing', such matters as the placement of cameras do in fact matter. For example, in the visual reporting of a demonstration, it matters whether 'the camera' is looking over the heads of the police being stoned or over the heads of the demonstrators being baton-charged. This is not to say that other media filter or process 'events' less than television does; quite the opposite. But none the less the filtering and processing *does* take place.[46]

It was initially the work of the Glasgow Media Group that most recently raised the issue of *bias* (in contradiction to propaganda) in broadcast news. In particular their book *Bad News* raised the central issue of the 'unconscious editing' of many kinds that was taking place by many journalists and broadcasters. Richard Hoggart recalls debating the book with a 'distinguished television newsman', who could not see the point that was being made: 'he kept saying: but there is "the news" out there and we are giving it to you. It was graspable'. Hoggart makes the obvious point that there is no such thing as absolute objectivity, but rather there is the *'effort* at objectivity', which is assisted only when we are aware of our own inbuilt assumptions.[47] *Bad News* (and subsequently published studies of the Glasgow Media Group) examined the routines and practices which make up television 'news' and, in particular, looked at the treatment of issues which were socially or politically divisive. It is, of course, at such times that the inevitability of bias or a partial view is so visible. So what should we demand from such news, at such times? In a democracy, the only answer can be: reliable and accurate information. Bias is *not* the opposite of truth. The real issue is whether the 'range of biases represented is fair', and do they 'adequately reveal the range of points of view held by the public?'[48]

It is important to bear in mind that, as we have previously urged, audiences are not simply passive recipients of messages; they are, at most times, active and interpretative. In the case of television news, a question we may ask is what potential is there for the audience to produce their own meanings?

Michael Gurevtich points out that the 'raw visual footage', usually sent to broadcasters from news agencies, can legitimately be viewed as an 'open text', available for interpretation.[49] At such a level it is clear that many meanings may be made from the visual material, say, for example, showing huge crowds of people and police in Soweto. However, once picture-edited and packaged with an audio commentary, the viewer is more firmly in the grip of the broadcaster's definition of reality. This is not to say that such definitions are extremely biased or necessarily unfair; simply, to make the point that one act of meaning-making has already taken place. The chances are that the viewer – unless they were actually there – will likely concur with the version given on the screen.

However, it is also clear that when *we* make *our* meanings (interpretations) we do so from our own personal, ideological and subjective standpoints. And despite the fact that television news is a 'relatively legitimate provider of information about what has apparently occurred in the world', as audiences we have then to decide how this information relates to our expectations and values, and crucially whether 'the news account can be integrated into our beliefs or if it is to be dismissed as false, partial, or simply irrelevant'.[50]

A Brief Reading of the *News at Ten*

There are then numerous different readings possible of the news bulletins and of the individual items presented in such programmes. The *News at Ten* edition on 1 December 1994 was, for example, a normal, conventional bulletin. Nothing unusual or out of place. Technically competent. But of course within it we are able to highlight some features of the news values we have earlier discussed.

The running order of some 13 items is in line with an 'entertaining' format designed to bring moments of amusement and light relief amidst the gruesome horror stories. The format dominates potential content: if there happened to be 13 disasters on the actual day only a small number – perhaps one or two – would be reported.

Achille Lauro (survivors of fire aboard ship)
Talks with Sinn Fein
Labour leader's son goes to private school
Motorways
NATO foreign ministers (short item)
Murder in Peterborough (reported in a sombre manner)

End of Part One

Part two signalled by jolly headline about genes in 'mice and men'

Commercial break: wine, AMEX, RSPCA, National Lottery and Mercury phones.

Obesity gene
Chechnia
Job losses (short item)
TV licences (short item)
Bhopal (special report)
Footballer's cocaine habit
And Finally . . . The Queen in Manchester (light-hearted item)

The domestic political items are merely a number of soundbites tagged together with commentary; the focus of the Achille Lauro story centres on the plight of *British* survivors; the pseudo-science story of the obesity gene is a light-hearted item presented before the report from war-torn Chechnia; and the bulletin is rounded off with an account of flag-waving in Manchester at the Queen's visit. With the commercial break in the middle, the obligatory funny story and with the absence of any real detailed information this particular bulletin is standard fare. Two stories, however, typify the approach *televised* news invariably embraces.

The item on Chechnia tells us that it is a 'tiny, oil-rich republic with a violent reputation . . . and is a centre for smuggling'. Over the pictures of a number of soldiers the viewer is told that 'not surprisingly, *most* Chechens carry guns' (emphasis added). Most of the pictorial evidence is of Grozny airport and numbers of armed soldiers in and around the city.

Another more substantive version of the conflict could equally be told, but perhaps tends not to be by virtue of the lack of suitable *pictures*. Firstly, this 'tiny, oil-rich Republic' in fact is home to a mass of impoverished people, with the unemployment rate over the 50 per cent mark and with many families facing destitution. Most of *these* Chechens do *not* carry guns. Secondly, smuggling is only one of the criminal activities taking place. For example, some wealthy Chechens have established a multinational criminal network which includes illicit 'upperworld' investments in Germany and the USA, fashionable properties *in London* and a widespread network of car-thieving, drug-trafficking and money-laundering.

There *were* pictures of soldiers religiously calling to 'Allah', none the less the Islamic dimension was not specifically mentioned or discussed.

The second story, the 'special report' on the tenth anniversary of the Bhopal (India) disaster, concentrated on the appalling plight of the long-term victims. Again the item was picture-led, with scenes of sick and wheezing men, terminal cancer victims and people suffering from gross eye disorders. But such pictures are not *new*. They appeal to the emotions of the viewer, not to their powers of perception, evaluation and understanding. Union Carbide, the company responsible for the gas leak which caused such distress and suffering, was only mentioned in passing.

Another 'tenth anniversary' report could have painted a quite different picture. For instance, though admitting full 'moral responsibility' after the leak, Union Carbide has never been held legally responsible; that a Union

Carbide spokesman has described the company as one 'that looks to the future, having thrown off the traumas of the past'; that more than *half-a-million* Bhopal residents – half the city – have chronic illnesses; and that while under attack for the Bhopal disaster and other major disasters such as Seveso and the Rhine River spill, companies involved in chemical production continue to thrive in South East Asia, China, Latin America, and – despite Bhopal itself – India.[51] Such a version however would involve, for television, too much talk and too few pictures: hence it is unlikely to rate as news in this form and in this depth.

One of the problems *News at Ten* faces and, to a greater or lesser degree, other news organizations is that without providing a substantial *context* to the events reported, much of what is said is pretty meaningless. For example, unless a viewer had seen an earlier bulletin on Chechnia it would be unlikely that they would know precisely where it actually was, or what the conflict was about, or of the role of Islam in the conflict, of the international crime dimension, and indeed of the possible consequences.

However, the reassuring face of the presenter, the recognizable musical topping and tailing, and the obligatory light-hearted end-story demonstrates that it is only an ordinary kind of news evening. *Real news,* on the other hand, is presented minus music, and at awkward and unpredictable moments in the shape of short news flashes.

Local News

In respect of local news viewers questioned consistently, as they have done for the past decade, put newspapers significantly ahead of television as their source of *local* news. For example, in the 1994 survey 80 per cent named newspapers as one of their 'first-three' sources of local news, as opposed to 65 per cent who mentioned television. Similarly, among first-mentioned sources, newspapers were placed in the top spot with 42 per cent compared with 36 per cent who named television as the first source of local news. Interestingly, the strategy of 'talking to people' was still considered to be important in this respect, with over 30 per cent naming it as a major source of local news.

However, the most important point to be made regarding this issue is that the trend figures show a consistent increase in the reliance on television as a source for local news, accompanied at the same time by a steady decline in the relative importance of newspapers. The explanation for this change is undoubtedly the effect put into local news programming by the ITV companies, with some stations (like Anglia TV) splitting their regions into two identifiable and more localized geographical areas. Local news on television adheres to the same hierarchy of values that applies to national and world news, but with the difference that all of the stories are domestic. Interestingly enough, the longer local news bulletins sometimes allow a wider expression and range of voices, because many local issues *are*

Table 5.1　Sources of most local news: trends 1984–94 (selected years)

In percentages	'84	'88	'90	'91	'92	'93	'94
Newspapers	54	51	51	48	51	41	42
Television	18	23	21	25	24	34	36
Radio	13	12	10	13	11	12	12
Talking to people	11	10	12	11	11	11	9
Magazines	1	*	1	1	*	*	*
Teletext	n/a	n/a	n/a	n/a	n/a	n/a	*

Notes:　1　Don't knows are excluded.
　　　　　2　* Less than 0.5 per cent.
　　　　　3　Percentages based on 'first mentions' of each source.

concerned with matters of public participation and citizenship, but also by virtue of the need to fill in time. On a 'poor newsday', local news may well include an item about a one-legged dog being chased along Cromer pier.

Not surprisingly there appear to be gender differences in respect of watching local news on television. Although it is men who consistently claim an especial interest in news programming in general, the position is reversed when it comes to local news. Research suggests that many women express a liking for local news, especially as it has direct relevance to their daily lives. For example, if there is a spate of crimes in their own area, they feel they need to know about them, in order to protect their children. On the other hand, a number of men see no particular relevance of international (or even national) news to their personal and domestic lives.[52]

Trust in Television News

Quite apart from their reliance on it as a *source* of news, there is a degree of *trust* placed in televised news that is *not* attached to other media. Such sentiments appear to be held elsewhere in other countries too; for example, research in the USA has consistently found that television is believed to report events more accurately than newspapers, radio or magazines. This research has shown that on a number of measurement scales – honest, trustworthy, reliable, expert and substantive – television was judged significantly better than newspapers. Only on the matter of accuracy were newspapers judged slightly better, although both media were at the low end of the scale.[53]

Viewers in the 1994 survey were asked to evaluate broadcast and print news media in terms of five attributes, first, with regard to their provision of news of national and international significance, and secondly, with regard to local and regional news. Viewers were asked which medium they generally trusted to give 'the most complete' news coverage, 'the most accurate' news coverage, 'the most fair and unbiased' news coverage, 'to bring the news most quickly' and to give 'the clearest understanding of the events and issues'.

Turning first to perceptions of sources of national and international news, television scored the highest on all five attributes. It was rated as providing the most complete, most accurate, most fair and unbiased, quickest and clearest account of the news. Newspapers and radio competed for second position throughout. Radio was rated more highly than newspapers on four dimensions; it was considered as bringing the news more quickly and in a more fair and unbiased way, but also – for the first time compared to earlier surveys – more accurately and with a clearer understanding. Newspapers, however, were still perceived more often than radio as offering the most complete coverage of events.

Trends over time reveal that television has maintained its standing in every respect, though with a slight drop in the perception that it gave the quickest service. This decrease may be attributed to the perception of tele-text as being the fastest source of news by 7 per cent of respondents in 1994, having been added as an option for the first time in the survey. With respect

Table 5.2 Perceptions of sources of news concerning events of national and international significance

In percentages	Most Complete			Most Accurate			Most fair and unbiased			Quickest			Clearest understanding		
	'92	'93	'94	'92	'93	'94	'92	'93	'94	'92	'93	'94	'92	'93	'94
Television	75	78	75	77	76	76	71	72	71	76	78	72	76	79	78
Newspapers	13	13	15	9	10	9	9	7	7	3	3	3	10	11	7
Radio	8	8	8	9	10	11	11	14	12	18	19	17	9	9	9
Teletext	n/a	n/a	2	n/a	n/a	2	n/a	n/a	3	n/a	n/a	7	n/a	n/a	3
Magazines	*	*	*	*	1	*	1	1	1	8	8	8	1	1	8

Notes: 1 Don't knows excluded.
2 * Less than 0.5 per cent.

to news events of local and regional significance, television once again finished as the most highly rated news source, though the gap between tele-vision and newspapers on all dimensions was narrower than it had been for national and international news. Newspapers were rated higher than radio for completeness, accuracy, fairness and clarity of coverage, while radio once again scored more highly than newspapers in terms of the speed with which it was perceived to relay news of local and regional events. Trends over time show that television has maintained the improvements in its standing on all five dimensions shown in 1992. Indeed, there has been further improvement in the perception of it as offering clarity of under-standing. Newspapers, on the other hand, have changed little since 1993 except for a decline in the perception of them on issues of clarity, under-lining their slight loss of status as a respected regional and local news source. Radio showed a drop in the perception of it as the quickest source of local news, due to the introduction of teletext, and radio also suffered a reduction in perceptions on all other aspects of regional and local news coverage, significantly in the case of fairness and lack of bias, indicating some general erosion of its position since 1993.

Table 5.3 Perceptions of sources of news concerning events of local and regional significance

In percentages	Most complete			Most accurate			Most fair and unbiased			Quickest			Clearest understanding		
	'92	'93	'94	'92	'93	'94	'92	'93	'94	'92	'93	'94	'92	'93	'94
Television	46	49	497	48	53	53	50	54	55	56	60	60	55	58	61
Newspapers	36	34	33	32	24	25	27	20	21	16	10	10	27	21	18
Radio	15	16	15	15	19	17	15	19	15	24	27	24	14	17	16
Teletext	n/a	n/a	1	n/a	n/a	1	n/a	n/a	1	n/a	n/a	4	n/a	n/a	2

Notes: 1 Don't knows excluded.

Social Class and News Sources

Not surprisingly viewers from different social classes varied in their perceptions of major news sources. In a nutshell: in the context of national and international news supply, television was consistently more highly regarded by working-class viewers than it was by the middle classes. Such middle-class viewers rated radio and newspapers higher, more often than working-class viewers on all five evaluative dimensions: most complete, most accurate, most fair, quickest, and clearest understanding.

Similar class differences in news source preferences were found in the context of local and regional news, although for television in particular, these class differences were not as pronounced as they had been for national and international news. Television remained more often the preferred news source for working class viewers, while their middle class counterparts claimed more of a preference for radio and newspapers.

A solid diet of television news, in tandem with tabloid newspapers – a fare more likely than not to be enjoyed by the working classes rather than the middle classes – would not equip the citizen particularly well, especially in respect to their understanding of national and international news. As we have earlier shown, the broadsheet newspapers do, however, provide a greater range and discussion of such news events. Writing some 20 years ago Raymond Williams argued that the 'national television news bulletins provide more public news than all but a very few newspapers'. He added moreover, that such bulletins provide such news to a very wide public, 'in ways that would not happen if we had only a "minority" and a "popular" press'.[54] Twenty years on the importance of television news bulletins remains, while it is also true that the differences between the broadsheet and tabloid press have greatly increased. In the tabloid press the bend in reporting has been towards a steady increase in xenophobic editorializing, an obsession with the Royal family, increased sexism and the personalizing of all political issues. The language has become hypocritical and base. Often cruel. And the *staple* diet of the tabloid is of course television itself: previews and reviews of programmes, photographs and television celebrity-led articles. Soap stars make front-page headline news, not so Britain's record on the treatment of refugees. If each tabloid newspaper varies to the degree of xenophobia, sexism and racism it emphasizes, they all rely on television, however, for column inches and readers. This is perhaps one of the novel features of the 1980s and 1990s media environments: that the total information environment begins to mirror television.[55]

Many individuals appear to possess an almost insatiable appetite for personalized, sensationalized and often sordid news stories. As R. D. Laing has observed, people enjoy reading such material because it 'enables them to experience vicariously pleasurable feelings they are otherwise forbidden to discuss or imagine'.[56] As they do with television items too. It could be argued that there are indeed two nations: one knowledgeable and relatively well-informed, the other much less so. The immediate question is, then, whether the television news will further mimic the ethos of TV and move even closer to tabloid values. Steven Barnett cites research into the evolution of multi-channel television in the USA, and the general finding of such research that in the face of 'channel-hopping' broadcasters continue to respond with 'programming strategies of immediate attention-gaining pace, impact, brevity, the arresting, and the dramatic'. Such a strategy, he notes, directly impinges on news programming which is 'increasingly dominated by the tenets of good entertainment rather than good journalism'.[57] In the competitive media market-place of the UK (and the world) in the 1990s it is possible, Barnett argues, that an 'increased diet of salacious stories, crime stories, and showbiz stories will more effectively draw the crowds which a peak-time commercial broadcaster must maintain'.[58] The end result would inevitably be a further trivialization of the news and, possibly, force the BBC to alter its bulletins too. No longer would we, when watching news bulletins, ask the important question, 'says who?', rather we would wonder whether we actually cared.

But of course it need not be so. It is purely a matter of political will. News values and practices change over time. *Glasnost* altered (for how long?) the actual content of the Soviet news: reports of accidents, disasters and political protests became commonplace after years of being left unreported. Indeed, historical studies of the press elsewhere consistently reveal significantly different patterns of news gathering and news writing as practices changed over time.[59]

Television news *is* different. It is ensconced in an entertainment medium: it is picture-led, and operates only in short time-segments. Most importantly audience figures are never far from the minds of channel managers.

6

Television, Politics and Impartiality

The role that television now plays in the conduct of international relations is merely an extension onto the international level of the active participatory role that the media have always played in the lives of societies. But the dramatic expansion of the stage upon which television now performs this role – from a national/societal one into a global one – has endowed it with a qualitatively new and sharper edge. This is especially the case in times of social and political turmoil, of rapid and revolutionary social change, or in periods of international crises. The capacity of television, utilizing satellite technology, to tell the story of an event as *it happens*, simultaneously with its unfolding, can have direct consequences for the direction that the event might take. Some of the more memorable examples of this recently are television's coverage of the Gulf war, its reporting of revolutionary events in Eastern Europe in 1989, and the role played by television in the student uprising in Tiananmen Square in Beijing in 1988.

Michael Gurevitch (1991), 'The Globalization of Electronic Journalism'

It is inconceivable in the 1990s to imagine politics without spin-doctors, television opportunities and the televised debate. In this chapter we look at the long and gradual historical process which ultimately led to the current symbiotic relationship between the political process and particular genres of political television.

In the age of television there is simply nowhere to hide. Sooner or later the actions of a despot, the struggles of minorities, or the brutal truths of a bloody war are subjected to the electronic gaze. As the US marines recently escorted the UN peacekeeping force out of Mogadishu they were interviewed by television reporters and asked questions about the efficacy of their weapons. But such potentially revealing features are not the only aspects of television's involvement with the political process. At the same time as bringing political issues and decisions into the home, television has unquestionably created a superficial and somewhat trivialized notion of politics: politicians are increasingly judged by their appearance on the screen or by their ability to produce the obligatory soundbite. This degree of distortion is reinforced by the televised political interview, in which questions and limits are set beforehand and in which politicians are well briefed. Spontaneity disappears as does credibility, and it is hardly surprising that most politicians are considered to be somewhat untruthful. As the struggle for favourable media coverage becomes increasingly the key battleground in elections as well as in civil and industrial disputes, numerous groups and individuals 'play to the camera': reality is thus distorted. Ministers kiss even more babies, terrorists don balaclavas and wave flags, protesters lie down in front of lorries, and right-wing extremists disrupt sporting occasions in the full knowledge that millions all over the world will see their Nazi salutes on domestic television screens.

Much time and effort is expended in looking for cases of political bias on television, especially in news and other factual programmes. However, less thought is exercised over the longer term consequences of 'politics as media': it is fair to suggest that apart from such historic moments as the massacre in Tiananmen Square – captured on videotape – the average daily diet of political TV leads merely to disenchantment. One of the greatest effects of television may well be 'its ability to popularize new people or issues instantaneously by exposing them to a vast audience',[1] but the relentless over-exposure of domestic politics and politicians no doubt leads only to varying degrees of disinterest. Commencing with the well-honed and calculated soundbite, the predictability of questions asked and answers given, the insidious use of statistics and figures, and the affability between broadcaster and politician – 'that's a very good question, *David*' – all aspects of political coverage on television lead to a dulling of the senses, the feeling of *déjà vu*, of something tediously familiar: of something not really worth attending to.

The Personalization of Politics

In terms of mass audiences, their knowledge of and opinions about politics invariably emanate from television news, and programmes like *Question Time*, together with what they may cull from the tabloid press: all such media invariably reduce 'politics' to the utterances of parliamentary politicians, and usually those of ministerial or shadow rank. Rarely on mainstream television is politics truly presented as the art and science of government, rarely are such crucial matters as the precise (if changing) nature of the relationship between government and the global economy critically evaluated, and very rarely do alternative political voices have an opportunity to be heard, other than at unique moments of protest or crisis. It is fair to say that television almost reduces its representation of politics to the soundbites of a dozen or so men and women, all parliamentarians. Even specialist programmes like the BBC's *Newsnight*, which discusses politics in a much more discursive manner and occasionally adds extra voices to the debate, are still guided by the government/ opposition's agenda – *their* definition of the political situation.

Because mass audiences perceive politics invariably through television news programmes, the politics they actually do see has already been filtered by news values: politics as events, of soundbites and of attractive politicians. As Neil Postman puts it, 'you cannot do political philosophy on television. Its form works against the content'.[2] Peak-time television does not enjoy factual talk, especially political talk; it will however tolerate bloody, gruesome or unique footage, scandal or the soundbite. It will, also, encourage the studio argy-bargy, the shouting match, the insubstantial accusations, the outburst, as all such events are dramatic – if actually meaningless – and fit snugly into the prevailing format. The emergence of the image-maker in politics and the concomitant decline of the speech-writer is further evidence that television insists and demands a different kind of content from radio and broadsheet newspapers.

Political journalists working *in* television are likely to have to personalize both events and ideas. They seek to find individuals who may conveniently symbolize an issue and thereby make it easier to understand. And as television is a predominantly entertainment-based format it therefore follows that politics too will 'succeed' better if based on the same overreaching format. So a logical consequence of this tendency is, for example, that fitness for political leadership is considered and defined within the values of entertainment. Recent US history perhaps best exemplifies the point. In order to be currently elected American politicians must possess 'a sense of humour', they must be 'pragmatic enough to respond quickly to the pollster's instructions' and, above all, they must be 'likeable'.[3] Voters are fond of good-looking and attractive people. Indeed ex-president Richard Nixon, who once claimed an election defeat of his was caused by spiteful make-up men, suggested to Senator Edward Kennedy that if he were seriously to compete for the US Presidency he would offer him some simple but necessary advice: *lose weight*. Neil Postman summarizes the scenario as follows:

> Although the Constitution makes no mention of it, it would appear that fat people are now effectively excluded from running for high political office. Probably bald people as well. Almost certainly those whose looks are not significantly enhanced by the cosmetician's art.[4]

It would be comforting to believe that such considerations only apply to the USA, but clearly this is not the case. Indeed, as Greg Philo argues in relation to Labour's failure at the 1992 British general election, the prior collapse of the Conservative's economic programme *should* have been good news electorally for Labour. However, instead of 'using the media to establish key elements of popular understanding about what was going wrong and what should be done, they relied instead on the shallow science of imagistics'.[5] Indeed, if taken at all seriously, such contemporary imagistics would suggest that the Labour Party avoids candidates – especially for high-profile or leadership posts – with red hair, or with no hair, or those who speak with regional accents.

Given that much of their working lives – either in parliament itself or in the television studio – is spent under the media spotlight, one can only speculate as to the degree to which the motives of future politicians will be different from their predecessors. It is fair to say that even now there exists an almost symbiotic relationship between the majority of politicians and the media: both consciously and determinedly feed off each other. Such a relationship, however, does not of course particularly enhance the citizen's understanding of the political process, or indeed their own specific place within it.

Michael Young believes that many 'famous individuals' from earlier eras would have been perfectly suited to television. They were, he observes, good speakers but not good listeners. For most of them television would have been the ideal situation, where there is 'not the remotest danger of being interrupted and where they are on good terms with us without giving a thought to whether we are on good terms with them'.[6] Richard Sennett develops a similar argument and points out that the mass media infinitely heighten the knowledge people have of what transpires in society, but they 'infinitely inhibit the capacity of people to convert that knowledge into political action'.[7] As he puts it, we cannot meaningfully talk back to the TV set, only turn it off. Any gesture of response is, essentially, an invisible act. Audiences are unable to react to the politician on the screen as if they do so they will miss what he or she says next: 'you've got to be silent to be spoken to'. Sennett makes the interesting point that given both the absolute size of mass audiences as well as their quite diverse composition, the politician must address them in general and abstract terms, and avoid being particularly specific or concrete. Consequently, the attention tends to be towards the politician's personality, as well as a consideration of his possible motives. As Sennett observes, television's complete repression of the audience response creates the logic of interest in personality.

> In a darkened room, in silence, you watch actual people; this is no novel or entertainment which requires an effort of imagination on your part. But the reality of politics is boring – committees, hassles with bureaucrats, and the like. To understand these hassles would make active interpretative demands on the audience. This real life you tune out; you want to know 'what kind of person' makes things happen.[8]

This one-way form of communication somewhat blurs the fact that politicians are in fact mandated to *serve* their constituents and voters; instead, they tend to speak at their audiences as if it were they – the voters – who were reliant on them, the politicians. When politicians have no other real aim other than to sell their personality (and leadership) to the public, they deprive themselves of intelligible standards by which to define the goals of specific policies or properly to evaluate success or failure.[9]

In summary: since television implies that we vote for personalities and not parties we can no longer vote for a candidate because we like the party but not the person. Consequently, as Rees observes, the very people who 'rely most on television to form their political views tend to be the least politically sophisticated in society'.[10]

Politics and Television – a Brief History

In his discussion of political broadcasting Colin Seymour-Ure reminds us that 'we are rapidly losing the capacity to imagine what general elections were like before TV'.[11] Until 1959 there was no radio or television coverage of the elections, simply bulletins as to the likely weather on actual polling days. This so-called 'Trappist' policy had one exception – the in-dependently-produced party election broadcasts. In 1959, at ITV's initiative, this all changed with an extensive and in-depth television coverage. This, Seymour-Ure asserts, was arguably the single most impor-tant moment in the history of political broadcasting. Up until then broadcasters had followed the politicians in terms of media values. Broadcasters proceeded to make their own judgements about the relative worth of issues and personalities. All parties were encouraged to earn their coverage: 'politics began to adapt to broadcasting, as politicians became keener to use it'.[12] Cameras were to be found at the Conservative's Annual Conference, and politicians increasingly became regular visitors to the TV studios.

Three quite different political events of 1958, all covered by television, ushered in this watershed year of 1959. Firstly, there was the real live State Opening of Parliament. This was indeed a political risk, as it was thought that the uninitiated viewer might well erroneously believe that the Queen necessarily agreed with the government of the day's programme of legis-lation. Secondly, came the first CND Easter march to Aldermaston. Significantly, the following years saw the route reversed: from Aldermaston to Trafalgar Square, as it was decided that the Square was a venue which was more media-friendly with its more attractive visual potential. As Seymour-Ure notes, the televising of the march was immensely useful both to the broadcasters and CND. The reasons being that it was sustained over several days in the 'dead news period' of a bank holiday, that it consisted of 'ordinary' people together with a smattering of social and political elites – Bertrand Russell and Michael Foot, to name but two – and because it climaxed in spectacle and oratory at the 'greatest public space of the capital'.[13] The third important event was the coverage of the

Rochdale by-election in March of 1958, which set a precedent for this kind of so-called political broadcasting.

The introduction of current-affairs magazine programmes like the BBC's *Tonight*, also increased the amount of on-screen 'political broadcasting' and significantly, began to develop a new style of interviewing: essentially more journalistic, less reverential. TV's own political arenas – documentaries and current-affairs programmes – quickly began to be seen by politicians as useful platforms for their speeches and other acts of self-promotion. The coverage of general elections too began to change over the following two decades, and saw leaders and candidates arranging the actual venue and the timing of their utterances to suit the broadcaster's schedules. Style too was affected: for example, in 1966 Edward Heath commented that television coverage 'made his jokes stale more quickly', while at the same time his major opponent Harold Wilson commented that in order for him 'to make repartee with hecklers effective on TV', he had to repeat a comment 'before demolishing it'.[14]

The less-revential interviewing style introduced on some programmes like *Tonight*, subsequently took a quantum leap with the introduction of political satires, like *That Was The Week That Was* and *Not Only But Also* (and later developed, quite uniquely in the mid-1980s, through the puppets of *Spitting Image*). Politicians had great difficulty in condemning these shows, of course, for if they did so they would fall foul of accusations of pomposity. Exactly the point the satirists were trying to make.

The second half of the 1960s saw Harold Wilson installed as, what was termed, the 'first TV prime minister'. Although earlier prime ministers like Anthony Eden and Harold Macmillan were certainly sensitive to television's potential, Heath visibly suffered on the screen while Wilson systematically embraced it: 'talking quite frequently and informally in interview programmes, strengthening the Yorkshire accent, using pipe not cigar on screen'.[15]

Significantly, television coverage of politics became increasingly focused almost solely on party leaders, not least because of the limited availability of cameras and other technical resources. The extent of this constricted perspective cannot be over emphasized: in 1966 and 1970 more than half of all TV news coverage went exclusively on Wilson and Heath. An early hint of trends that were to follow. Indeed, in 1987, almost half of all mentions of the Conservative Party in the news on TV (and BBC Radio 4) were simply of Prime Minister Thatcher.

Harold Wilson paid attention not only to his performances however, he also steadfastly refused interviews he wished not to partake of or found other ways of manipulating broadcasters. None the less the die was cast: all subsequent prime minsters would have to be 'TV prime ministers'.

From that time onwards the prevailing trends have steadily increased, culminating with the televising of Parliament in 1989, following the pattern set by the transmissions from the House of Lords which commenced in 1985.

Parliamentary candidates and especially, leaders, come to be chosen in part on the grounds of their telegenic qualities. Alec Douglas-Home was an early casualty, as his cadaverous appearance, his slow delivery of words and his aristocratic persona were seen to be unsuitable for the small domestic screen. By 1994 the relatively inexperienced Tony Blair was elected to lead the Labour Party, not least in part because of his telegenic qualities. Indeed, as early as the mid-1970s it was no longer shocking to say that television coverage was the campaign, no longer simply a visual record of actual political events.

Over time another new genre was introduced into political broadcasting; namely, the dramatic reconstructions of recent political events: the Falklands–Malvinas conflict, the Suez Crisis, the Guildford Four, to name but three examples. In these programmes complex and sensitive matters of truth and fiction became controversial and contested issues.

More pragmatically by the 1990s permanent interview rooms had been established close to the House of Commons; camera crews and journalists would accompany prime ministers on diplomatic journeys; interviewer and interviewee would be on first-name terms; and politicians began to appear in pop videos, dramas, sit-coms and panel games.

The 'Thatcher decade' up to 1990 reflected, in a number of ways, the extent to which broadcasting and political events had become inextricably interwoven. Advertising agencies, market researchers and personal groomers were all employed by politicians in an attempt to use media coverage for their own personal and political advantage. Acutely aware of television's preference of pictures over words Thatcher herself provided 'good pictures' as when she herself was seen in Ulster in a red beret and flak jacket, and in the Falklands soon after victory, demonstrating her 'concern and commitment'.

This of course is not to suggest that political broadcasting is a totally denuded activity. For although there are immeasurably more media opportunities available to manipulative politicians, these openings are potentially available to opponents too and it is still true that the constant gaze of television puts all such performances under extreme scrutiny. And while there can exist an uneasy cosiness between broadcaster and politician, the unexpected *does* occur and a few interviewers do retain a healthy independent and critical spirit. At the same time within news and current affairs programming, however, politicians – in symbiosis with broadcasters – have developed their own solutions to television's editing process: the soundbite.

The role of Prime Minister – or, more correctly, the job description – has changed dramatically in response to the rise of political broadcasting: there has been a significant increase in the prime minister's role as opinion leader or mobilizer and as a consequence a pulling back from their natural parliamentary base. Not only does the televised Prime Minister's Question Time resemble a press conference (with the members of the House asking the journalists' questions) but, increasingly, it is clear that the career path leading to the premiership has of necessity changed: communication and telegenic skills take precedent over both party loyalty and experience, and certainly intelligence.

Truth and Bias

When Ron Ziegler, President Richard Nixon's press secretary, admitted that his preliminary statements on Watergate had become 'inoperative' it was assumed that he was groping for a euphemistic way of saying that he had lied. What he meant, however, was that his earlier statements were no longer believable. It was not their falsity but their inability to command assent that rendered them 'inoperative'. The question of 'whether they were true or not was beside the point'.[16] This incident is but one example of the manner in which at particular times the mass media renders the categories of truth and falsehood somewhat problematic. As Christopher Lasch has put it, 'truth has given way to credibility, facts to statements that sound authoritative without conveying any authoritative information'.[17] Certainly in an era when politicians readily admit to being 'economical with the *actualité*', it indeed becomes increasingly difficult to discern truth from credibility.

In any televised political debate what is the viewer expected to deduce from an exchange in which a minister claims that unemployment stands at two-and-a-half million, a figure immediately rejected by his opponent who instead posits the total of three million? There is no way the viewer can check the facts, or decide between the two competing statistics. The options available to the viewer are: simply to remain loyal to his favoured politician (or party); make a judgement of which one is more credible or authoritative – that is, who 'looks' and 'sounds' credible; or simply to pay little attention to such minutiae, or become (further) desensitized by such political broadcasting.

If it were not an issue of such importance it would be somewhat comic. Consider, for example, the role that television currently plays in the conduct of international relations. Michael Gurevitch carefully itemizes a number of ways in which the presence of television cameras may well affect international events.[18] To begin with, as we have earlier seen, television simply defines some events as newsworthy and others much less so. In so doing television may well create a global audience for such events: wars, acts of terrorism, political violence, revolution and uprisings are the most obvious examples, with the television world closely watching Bosnia, the Gulf, Chechnia, Tiananmen Square and Romania. Significantly the publicity subsequently enjoyed by such global media exposure clearly influences the behaviour of all those involved. For example, in 1989 the call for mass demonstrations in Prague's Wenceslas Square, enthusiastically publicized by the television cameras, was held to be responsible for recruiting even more demonstrators and that it had accelerated political change. Global television also assumes a major role in the construction and shaping of world public opinion. Such global television is, of course, in a monopolistic position to do just that: if CNN reports that 'the world is outraged by Yeltsin's attack on Grozny', who is in a position to disagree? Such global public opinion – 'the *world* is outraged . . . ' – is *wholly* a media construction. No one polls 'the world' for opinion.

Television also acts as a 'go-between', as a channel of communication, especially in those cases in which hostilities tend to preclude direct contacts. As Gurevitch observes, one of the 'more celebrated examples of television's capacity to open up such channels of communication is the role imputed to US television in bringing about the visit by the Egyptian President, Anwar Sadat to Jerusalem'.[19] In this example, the news people who mediated between the two sides created a channel of communication where no other *public* one previously existed. More recently there has been the case of 'tele-plomacy' in the Gulf. One critic of the American television coverage talked of the scramble by television reports to interview Saddam Hussein, the Iraqi President, in the course of which the 'interviewers slid, almost impercep-tibly, into the roles of advocates, as if representing their own government, and negotiators, exploring with their interviewee avenues for resolving the crisis'.[20] The role journalists occasionally play as go-betweens in such crises inevitably compromises their journalistic 'values'. Indeed, such journalists in the Gulf were obviously aware that they were being used by Iraq to present the Iraqi view of hostilities – indeed CNN's Baghdad correspon-dent was labelled an Iraqi sympathizer – but also that they became advocates for their own side. In addition to such issues of manipulation, control and impartiality, it remains an open question as to the actual effi-cacy of such involvement. Is diplomacy helped or hindered by making public such private negotiations, especially when translated into crude and simplistic television language? Television's participation in international events further blurs the line between 'social reality' and 'media reality': the more distant the event from the television audience, the 'more likely it is that the reality of the event on television will be the only "reality"'.[21]

The central thesis of Neil Postman's *Amusing Ourselves to Death* is that the best items on television are its *junk* programmes. Conversely, he argues that television is at its 'most trivial and, therefore, most dangerous when its aspi-rations are high, when it presents itself as a carrier of important cultural conversations'.[22] Postman believes that television's conversations promote incoherence and triviality, and, therefore, the phrase 'serious television' is in fact a contradiction in terms. Accordingly, television only speaks in the voice of entertainment, and, indeed, we have already alluded to the pre-eminence of the soundbite, the flagrant use of statistics and the rise of the televisual personality in political programming. But consider for a moment those political discussions which are allowed to develop beyond the 90-second segment. Shows like *Question Time* are classic toned-down studio argy-bargys, while the attempt to adhere to principles of 'balance' renders programmes like the BBC's *Newsnight* somewhat bland and awash with interviewees. Of such shows we may well ask the question, do we see or hear assumptions being truly scrutinized, explanations substantively offered, complex definitions given, or points of view extensively elaborated? No. Within the televised debate,

> It is very nearly impermissible to say, 'Let me think about that' or 'I don't know' or 'what do you mean when you say . . . ?' or 'from what sources does your information come?' This type of discourse not only slows down the tempo of the show but creates the impression of uncertainty or lack of finish. It tends to reveal people in the act of *thinking* . . . [and] . . . thinking does not play well on television . . . There is not much to see in it.[23]

Television is our culture's 'principal mode of knowing about itself',[24] therefore how it stages the world becomes the major model for how the world is 'properly' to be staged. One implication is that seeing, not reading, becomes the basis for believing. Accordingly, the aesthetic of naturalism appears to give factual programmes a believability they may not in fact deserve. The belief that the camera 'cannot lie' authenticates the audio-commentary that accompanies the pictures. But, as we know, a picture is able to carry a number of quite different and often contradictory readings. A television picture of employees outside a hospital may suggest to an active trade unionist that they are pickets, disgruntled employees engaged in a protest with which the viewer sympathizes. But other readings could well include the labels 'trouble-makers' and 'disruptive elements' being applied to the same people! On such occasions the broadcaster will actually encourage us as to what to think, by fixing their words to the picture. We, the viewers, are expected to accept that the word does indeed fit the image.[25]

Modern culture's store of information, ideas and complete ways of knowing are increasingly given form by television, and no longer by the printed word. One consequence of this is that newspapers themselves begin to look like television screens, as is evident from a cursory look at the tabloid press. It is, therefore, hardly surprising that television is now the home of politics and politicians.

Impartiality – the Audience's View

One of the core requirements placed upon broadcasters is that they should observe 'due impartiality' in their coverage of political and industrial matters. In respect of ITV, the Broadcasting Act 1990 requires the ITC to do all that it can to ensure that every service it licenses complies with the requirements to ensure 'that any news given (in whatever form) in its programmes is presented with due accuracy and impartiality' and 'that due impartiality is preserved on the part of the person providing the service as respects matters of political and industrial controversy or relating to current public policy'.[26] Of course the growth of cable and satellite channels will greatly increase the ITC's work load: 'instead of keeping an eye on a single news-gathering organisation with a long tradition of professional and objective reporting, the ITC will be responsible for monitoring at least one other 24 hour channel whose owner and managers are not renowned for their lack of partisanship in the print media'.[27]

An inherent problem in all of this lies in the fact that there exists no ideal way in which to investigate the existence or direction of political bias on television. One method would be to analyse the actual content of programmes and measuring, for example, how much time is allocated to different points of view. Another approach would be to elicit public opinion on the fairness or otherwise of television's coverage.

However, the matter of bias is extremely complex. For a start different individuals 'read' television news (and other programmes) in quite different ways. Where one viewer sees bias, another sees impartiality, or a different bias. On other occasions a broadcaster's 'intentions' are equally matched by a viewer's interpretation. But the most difficult aspect of the issue is the fact that television – so deeply embedded in national culture – has *already* itself defined much of the political terrain. If politics is seen to be the politics of the government and its parliamentary opposition, the viewer may well be unaware that the broadcaster is biased by excluding, say, a fringe group of activists protesting over a particular issue.

Perceived Impartiality by Programme Type

The ITC's 1994 survey, as in previous years, sought out public opinion on a number of questions concerned with the issue of impartiality. Such questions about impartiality were formulated in a number of ways. First, a set of questions was asked of all viewers which dealt with perceptions of the fairness and unbiased nature of television coverage on the four major terrestrial channels given to groups, interests and events within five categories of programming: news, current affairs, drama (series, plays and films), entertainment (comedy, quiz, variety and chat shows), and drama-documentaries. Viewers who believed that television exhibited favouritism towards or discriminated against any particular groups, interests or events, were asked as to the precise nature of this bias. Further questions were then asked about the fair and unbiased nature of news and current-affairs programmes on satellite and cable channels. Secondly, in widening the scope of the survey, another question addressed perceptions of the treatment by television news and current affairs programmes of a wide range of groups: ethnic minorities; the disabled; religious groups; management in industry; workers/employees; major service industries such as water, gas and electricity; health service employees such as doctors and nurses; educational services and teachers; government departments and ministries; and the police force. Finally, a customary set of core questions was asked which dealt with public perceptions of television's treatment of different political parties. With respect to each major television channel – including for some viewers, cable and satellite channels – viewers were asked if they thought the channel favoured any political party and if so, which one and why.

Viewers were asked, for each of six programme types, if they thought the major terrestrial broadcast channels, in general, provided a fair and un-biased view of the world or whether they favoured particular groups, issues or events. In response, the majority of viewers thought that mainstream broadcast television provided fair and unbiased coverage of groups, issues and events in all six programme types – news, current affairs, drama, enter-tainment, documentaries and drama-documentaries. Although it may be noted that such confidence has nevertheless exhibited a steady, if small, decline since 1984.

Averaged across all programme types, around one in six viewers thought that some groups, interests or events received favourable coverage whilst others were discriminated against. This opinion was most frequently mentioned in relation to news (31 per cent) and current affairs (34 per cent) programming. Not surprisingly, entertainment programming was least often perceived to contain any biased material (22 per cent).

Opinions regarding impartiality in different programme types included some variations according to viewers' stated degree of interest in politics, and which party they tended to vote for. This was most likely to be true in respect of perceptions of impartiality on news and current-affairs programmes. Thus viewers who said they were very or fairly interested in politics were less likely than viewers who had little or no interest in politics to rate television as fair and unbiased. A similar division of opinions occurred with regard to current affairs programmes. Politically interested viewers were more likely to perceive bias in current-affairs programmes than were those with little or no political interest. None of these findings are in any sense surprising: those who are politically conscious or committed will quite simply tend to be more knowledgeable about and attentive to current-affairs and political programming.

Party support amongst viewers proved to be a sensitive discriminator of opinions about impartiality. Generally Labour and Lib-Dem supporters were more likely to perceive factual programmes as fair and unbiased than were Conservative supporters. The significant statistic is that one-third of such Tory supporters believed the news and current affairs programmes to be biased. A number of groups, interests and events were seen by a small proportion of viewers to have been given unfair television coverage. Most of the items named, however, were endorsed by only tiny proportions of these respondents. *Favourable* coverage in the news on the main four broad-cast channels was thought to occur most often with respect to coverage of 'political parties in general', 'the Conservatives', and the 'govern-ment/party in power'. Further probing about who or what had been

Table 6.1   Perceived impartiality of different programme types and party support/voting intention on the main four broadcast channels

In percentages	Party likely to receive support		
	Conservative	Labour	Liberal Democrats
News			
Fair/Unbiased	62	71	73
Favouritism/Discrimination	33	20	20
Current Affairs			
Fair/Unbiased	66	67	69
Favouritism/Discrimination	26	20	21
Drama			
Fair/Unbiased	73	74	74
Favouritism/Discrimination	11	10	7
Entertainment			
Fair/Unbiased	82	80	77
Favouritism/Discrimination	10	6	10
Drama-documentaries			
Fair/Unbiased	74	75	75
Favouritism/Discrimination	18	11	13
Documentaries			
Fair/Unbiased	75	73	74
Favouritism/Discrimination	18	14	15

discriminated against on television news gave rise to replies such as 'political parties' (7 per cent), the 'royal family' (5 per cent), 'black people/ethnic minorities' (4 per cent) and other more general observations that programmes have 'biased reporting' (7 per cent), or 'put across their own opinion/views' (5 per cent). Similar views were also expressed in respect to current-affairs programmes.

It cannot be emphasized enough that such questions invariably produce an extremely wide range of opinions: each viewer brings to their reply their own reading of a programme and their own personal prejudices. For example, while a number of viewers believed that current affairs programmes 'favoured ethnic minorities', other viewers spoke of the 'omission of coloured people' in respect of the very same programmes. Other viewers are knowledgeable enough to realize that, in their words, 'producers generally are biased and have their own views which are put over'.

Of those viewers in multi-channel households the great majority believed that the news and current-affairs coverage on non-terrestrial channels tended to be fair and unbiased, and, indeed, very few of such viewers talked of *any* biased coverage. As the majority of viewing on these channels is entertainment-based or sport, again this finding is no great surprise.

Those small minority of viewers who claimed there was bias in drama and entertainment programming mentioned specifically the favouritism towards the rich and the excessive programming of soaps, while, conversely, discrimination was mentioned specifically in relation to black people, ethnic minorities, the disabled and 'ordinary people'. Certainly the 'rich' feature extensively in many dramas and soaps are a predominant genre, and clearly the disabled and black people are under-represented in drama and entertainment (consider the rare examples of *Desmonds* and *The Cosby Show* . . .). But the suggestion that there is a lack of 'ordinary people' represented on television is somewhat harder to understand. For instance soaps themselves are totally populated by such 'characters', while the growth of so-called 'people shows' in entertainment programming in the 1990s has been quite substantial. Such shows being cheaper to produce and which pander to many people's desire to appear on television. Perhaps that is why a small minority of viewers commented that entertainment programming was 'an insult to people's intelligence'.

Among those viewers who believed that drama-documentaries were biased, their main complaint was what they saw as discrimination against black people or ethnic minorities, and also in the unnecessary sensational-izing of a story, or of only showing one viewpoint. Those viewers who saw bias in documentaries also mentioned one-sided views, and also the use of biased reporting and the sensationalizing of reports. Such tendencies will invariably increase as the entertainment ethos spreads even more in factual programming.

In a follow-up question on drama-documentaries, viewers were asked if they felt that such dramatizations and reconstructions of real events typically provided an *accurate* account. The response was in fact generally favourable, with the majority of all viewers replying that they thought drama-documentaries were very (13 per cent) or fairly (57 per cent) accurate, with few viewers replying that they were not very (5 per cent) or not at all (1 per cent) accurate. Such findings are, in a sense, quite alarming because, how precisely would the viewer know whether or not a re-construction was accurate? How could they possibly know? Indeed, those viewers who stated an opinion that drama-documentaries were accurate were subsequently asked to say why they thought so, and their answers – though perhaps heartfelt – were, to a degree, naïve: 'they would have to be', 'they could not possibly depict something unless sure that it was accurate', 'they seemed or felt accurate', 'a lot of careful research goes into them', and the opinion that 'they have to be accurate or somebody would have complained'. Despite such an expression of faith in the broadcasters, viewers *do* complain, though probably not the last one quoted.

Among the small minority of viewers (7 per cent) who believed drama-documentaries gave inaccurate accounts of reality, the major explanation given was that in order to attract viewers such programmes *had* to sensationalize events. Other viewers pointed to the fact that the programme-makers could not possibly know all the facts and achieve 100 per cent accuracy while others argued that what was shown was simply a producer or writer's own point of view. What such viewers clearly forgot, or refused to acknowledge, is that such programmes are *drama-documentaries*, works of partial fiction.

Docu-dramas are a *genre* destined to grow, as there appears to be an insatiable desire on the part both of producers and – they would claim – viewers to see the creation of 'dramas' from true-life tragedies. In this process stories are ripped from the headlines and re-told in an aesthetic similar to movies-for-TV. Child-abuse stories, date-rape trials, cult and 'brainwashing' tales, and 'false-memory syndrome' cases are already in pre-production. If the family or friends of those involved in such true-life tragedies are hurt by the inevitable inaccuracies or distressed by the memories gratuitously recalled, *too bad*. Questions of ethics are ignored in the relentless search for high-ratings programmes.

Perceived Impartiality Towards Different Groups

Viewers were shown a list of 16 groups, and for each were asked to state whether the news and current-affairs coverage on the four main terrestrial

Table 6.2   Perceived impartiality of news and current affairs programmes on the four main broadcast TV channels towards different groups

In percentages	Fair towards	Biased in favour	Biased against
Women	77	7	12
Religious groups	76	7	14
Ordinary workers/employees	74	5	17
Major services in industries (e.g., gas, electricity, water)	72	14	9
Education service employees	71	9	15
Management in industry	71	15	7
Ethnic minorities	71	13	12
Disabled people	70	5	21
Health Service employees (i.e., doctors, nurses)	70	11	16
Police Force	68	13	16
Social Services employees	68	9	18
Unemployed	66	6	25
Government departments and ministries	63	22	11
Trade unions	62	6	27
Single parents	60	9	27
Politicians	59	25	13
Average	69	11	16

channels was generally fair to them or not. The groups towards whom television was most often believed to be biased *in favour of* were politicians, government departments and ministries, management in industry, major service industries, the police and ethnic minorities. Television news and current-affairs programmes were most often seen as being biased *against* single parents, trade unions, the unemployed, the disabled, social services employees and ordinary workers/employees.

Of course, such beliefs were related to viewers' expressed degree of interest in politics. Thus, the most pronounced differences of opinion were found with regard to the television news and current-affairs coverage of management in industry, trade unions, government departments and ministries, politicians and social-service employees. In other words, the politically interested were generally less likely to view coverage as impartial than were the politically uninterested. Those who were *very* interested in politics were proportionately more likely than others to say that television news and current-affairs coverage was biased *in favour* of government departments and ministries, management in industry, major services and industries, and women. At the same time though, those viewers who claimed to be very interested in politics were also proportionately more likely than those with a lesser interest in politics to say that television news and current affairs *discriminated against* trade unions, social services employees, ordinary workers/employees and education service employees. In other words, the results confirm the somewhat obvious fact that viewers with a greater expressed degree of interest in politics were also more opinionated about television's news and current-affairs coverage of different groups, tending to see both greater bias in favour and against the different groups prompted, depending generally on their political persuasion. Truth, in other words, is in the eye of the beholder.

Impartiality in the Coverage of Political Parties

As we have argued, politicians and government simply cannot escape the influence of TV, nor do they wish to do so; but neither has television itself escaped from the legislative powers and interests of politicians and governments. Indeed, the establishment of the BBC was, at the time, a breathtakingly imaginative piece of social policy. Similarly, in the recent Thatcher government controversy over broadcasting incidents and policies was a frequent political issue. For example, broadcasters were blamed for favouring the miners in their lengthy strike with the Coal Board, the BBC was harangued over much of its Falklands coverage, and there was the thorny issue of the censorship of IRA voices on television (and radio). However, it is not an easy task in separating those political factors from other factors – social, economic and technological – that have collectively contributed to the making (and dismantling) of public-service broadcasting.

As Colin Seymour-Ure has persuasively argued, government policy covering media institutions from 1945 onwards was often '*indirect* in its motives but *direct* in its effect',[28] and was predominantly concerned with the organization of media, finance and technology. Successive British governments, he adds, expressed a 'hostility towards a single media industry or a single set of strategic national media'.[29] Instead,

> policies were generally uncoordinated, reactive, expediential, partial and indirect; a matter of broad objectives and attitudes ('freedom of the press', 'an independent British film industry', 'public service broadcasting') rather than of detailed programmes and plans. The whole thus added up to less than the sum of its parts.[30]

Given the pervasiveness of media institutions, however, numerous government departments have been involved in such processes, and as media organizations increasingly became 'conglomerate, the more likely they were to encounter government policy in one of its forms'.[31]

Up until the Thatcher decade of the 1980s governments tended to favour a policy of minimal legislation, a preference espoused by both Conservative and Labour governments. Although actual specific policies were quite different from the decisions the other party would have taken if it had been in office. For as Seymour-Ure notes, a 'Labour government of the mid-1950s would not have introduced ITV; nor would Channel 4 have taken exactly the same shape under a Labour government in the 1980s'. Nevertheless, he adds, when it was given the opportunity to do so in the 1960s and 1970s, Labour did *not* reconstruct the ITV system – 'not surprisingly, in view of ITV's popularity with Labour voters',[32] and neither did the Conservative government give the third channel to ITV in 1962, but rather opted to create BBC2.

In addition to 'non-doctrinaire' standpoints, subsequent government policies towards the media (in general) have been characterized by a discrimination between media that 'entertained' and those which 'informed'; therefore, 'sport, education and showbiz elements were able to carry all manner of political undertones without being subject to "balance"'.[33] Centrally, government media policy systematically failed to recognize the difference between the non-political and the non-partisan. Politics meant parliamentary (or party) politics. As Seymour-Ure observes, it was far easier in the 1970s and 1980s to make a radical political statement about such issues as Northern Ireland, race relations or unemployment in a television play than in factual programmes.[34]

The Thatcher government ultimately introduced a set of more interventionist policies towards the media, firstly with the enthusiastic introduction of cable and satellite policies, and then with the radical overhaul of broadcasting through the Broadcasting Act of 1990 which was substantially the most active policy intervention since the 1920s.

The main focus of attention in the ITC annual survey's measurement of perceived bias on television has traditionally centred on the major television channels treatment of the political parties. Each year viewers were asked if they believed that television had provided fair and unbiased coverage of all political parties or whether in fact some parties had received more favourable treatment than others. In such surveys ITV has consistently been regarded as less biased than BBC1 in its political-party coverage by a greater proportion of the viewers, although both channels are regarded as fair by overall majorities of viewers. In 1994, as in other years, only minorities of viewers in the survey perceived any bias towards political parties on the four terrestrial television channels. The 1994 survey found that ITV was the channel most widely perceived as not favouring any political party (69 per cent), followed by Channel 4 (68 per cent), BBC2 (62 per cent) and then BBC1 (52 per cent). BBC1 and BBC2 (29 per cent and 19 per cent respectively) were notably more likely than ITV and Channel 4 (14 per cent and 9 per cent) to be perceived by viewers as favouring a particular political party.

Viewers who could receive satellite and cable television channels were specifically asked if they believed there was any political-party favouritism on these channels. In respect of Sky News (71 per cent), other Sky channels (68 per cent) and CNN (63 per cent), the majority opinion among those viewers who said they received each channel was that such channels did *not* exhibit any political party bias. Indeed very few viewers indicated *any* perception of such bias, with the responses to satellite and cable channels being characterized by high levels of 'don't knows'. However, some comments regarding bias displayed the 'background knowledge' viewers always bring to their perceptions and opinions: 'CNN has an American bias. They don't have a fair-minded approach to the "enemies" of the USA', opined one such viewer.

Those viewers who claimed that a particular channel had demonstrated favouritism towards a political party, were asked to state which party this was. The trend seen in previous years towards detecting a *pro*-Conservative bias on both BBC channels was apparent again in 1994. Opinions of ITV exhibited a slight shift towards decreased perceptions of Conservative bias but a relatively stable perception of Labour bias. There continued to be an even split between these perceptions on ITV. On Channel 4, perceived pro-Conservative and Labour bias was also down slightly, but on balance it was believed that the channel favoured Labour. Looking at the following table it is obvious that during the General Election year of 1992 increased numbers of viewers were sensitive to pro-party bias across all the mainstream television channels, which has diminished now that the election has faded in people's memories.

Table 6.3   Viewers' perceptions of political bias on television

Which party favoured? (*in percentages*)	1984	1985	1986	1987	1988	1989	1990	1991	1992	1993	1994
ITV											
Conservative	6	6	4	8	9	8	7	6	8	7	5
Labour	8	8	6	8	7	9	6	6	8	7	7
Liberal Democrat	1	1	*	*	1	1	1	*	1	1	1
BBC1											
Conservative	20	22	18	24	22	27	22	18	24	23	22
Labour	3	4	5	*	4	9	6	10	7	5	6
Liberal Democrat	*	1	*	*	*	*	*	–	*	1	*
BBC2											
Conservative	11	11	10	12	13	16	12	11	14	14	16
Labour	1	2	2	2	1	4	3	6	3	3	3
Liberal Democrat	*	1	*	*	*	*	1	1	1	1	*
Channel 4											
Conservative	1	1	1	2	3	3	3	2	3	3	2
Labour	4	6	5	7	6	7	4	6	7	5	4
Liberal Democrat	1	1	*	1	1	1	1	1	1	1	2

Note: * Less than 0.5 per cent.

These trends concerning issues of bias have remained somewhat stable since the 1970s. For example, the IBA's comparable 1974 survey concluded that 'more people thought the BBC was biased than ITV' and were also 'more in agreement as to which direction the BBC lay', namely to the Conservative Party.[35] Similarly the IBA's 1984 survey found that the channel on which political favouritism was perceived most often was BBC1, and least often on Channel 4. The 1984 report continued to note that such political bias on BBC1 and 2 was most likely to be perceived as slightly favouring the Conservatives, while ITV, on the other hand, was more likely to be seen as slightly favouring the Labour Party.

Those viewers who in the 1994 survey alleged that particular channels had been biased towards certain political parties were subsequently asked to explain in more detail why they believed this to be the case. They expressed their opinions in their own words in response to open-ended questions. For example:

BBC1: they pander to Conservative Ministers in return to being able to run their stations as they please . . .
ITV: are happy to stir up the camp and give Labour a voice . . .

The most common explanation offered was simply that the channel in question had a 'leaning towards that party'. BBC channels were perceived more often than commercial channels as being 'government controlled'. Some viewers referred to a more generalized 'general feeling I get', or the 'impression given by programme content', an opinion which characterized perceptions of Channel 4 more than the other channels. Channel 4 was also thought to be more controversial or 'radical' than the other channels. It is worth understanding, however, that these opinions were expressed by a very small number of viewers.

A conundrum which has been regularly observed since the early surveys of two decades ago is why should so many viewers believe the BBC to be biased towards the Conservative Party? After all this is the channel which regularly grills ministers on *Newsnight* which allows them to embarrass themselves on *Question Time*, which eavesdrops on events in the Commons, which breaks scandals or damaging stories on the news, and which consistently produces documentaries and dramas which often show the government in a bad light. And while the BBC *has* at times deferred to governmental pressure – for example, the case of the prohibition of the transmission of the *Real Lives* documentary *State of the Union* – at other times it has steadfastly stood its ground. For instance, in 1988 it refused to make the changes, requested by the Defence Secretary, to *Tumbledown*, the first major Falklands drama.

One explanation as to why the BBC might appear so biased towards the Conservative Party is that the viewing public will 'generally perceive the nation's public broadcaster to be supporters of and in sympathy with the government of the day'.[36] The assumption being, of course, that a change of government will correspondingly induce a change of political sympathy in its so-called impartial reporting. However, earlier research demonstrated that even in the midst of a Labour government, the BBC was nevertheless perceived by nearly one in six viewers to favour the Conservative Party. It is not, therefore, the case that viewers consider the BBC to be synonymous with the government of the day, rather it is more likely, as Steven Barnett puts it, that the BBC is simply regarded as 'the Establishment' and, therefore, 'more in tune with the political psyche of the Conservative Party'.[37]

This belief that the BBC is more 'Establishment' than commercial television is, of course, only a misguided or superficial judgement. One of the reasons for this misplaced perception can be traced to the fact that viewers pay a licence fee for the services of the BBC, money they may well see as a form of taxation. Commercial television, on the other hand, may be seen to be a 'free' service (with cable and satellite channels being services they may *choose* to pay for). Of course such beliefs are deeply ill-informed. If viewers were aware of what the cost of ITV was to them in the price of consumer goods, as a result of the advertising budgets companies spend on commercials, perhaps they would look at the matter somewhat differently. Besides it could be argued that the *overall* tenor of commercial television is much more akin to Conservative values of acquisitiveness and competition, unlike the BBC, still half-heartedly clinging on to public-broadcasting values.

An evening of ITV can, at least in its less enlightening moments, appear to be an almost constant stream of quiz and game shows, imported US dramas and films, all interspersed with commercials ranging from National Lottery promotions, corporate ads, alcohol and foodstuffs, and for high-powered and expensive motor cars. In terms of programme content too, ITV has changed. No longer do documentary slots exist at 9 p.m. as they did as recently as 1987, while as we earlier noted unsuccessful attempts have been made to shunt the *News at Ten* out of the way to allow movies an uninterrupted slot. Such changes are precisely those a Labour government would theoretically disapprove of, believing not only in simple entertainment but rather in the values of public-service broadcasting. A system empowered to inform, as well as to entertain. Of course all of the aforementioned renders the claim that there is no longer something called 'channel loyalty' somewhat premature.

Despite the intentions of politicians, members of the audience are not easily fooled: they spot bias everywhere, and with ease. The close relationships that exist between television and politicians further erode conventional notions of 'truth'.

7

Offensive Television

From the doors of meat companies, the cigarette-wounded larynxes of over-weight men shouted utterances such as, 'We gotta hurry the fuck up and get those fuckin' boxes on that fuckin' truck or we're all gonna be fucked!' The language of 14th street is so dependent on the all-purpose word *fucking* that it can't really be called English; rather a separate dialect best referred to as 'Fuckinese'.

Edward Allen (1989), *Straight Through the Night*

Individual viewers do not always agree on issues of 'taste and decency' on television. Indeed, the issue of what constitutes offensive television and what does not is another conundrum, the matter often being conceived as one of irreconcilable subjective/individual differences. This chapter looks at the issue through the eyes of the viewers interviewed.

On the 13 November 1965, live on a late-night BBC satire programme, Kenneth Tynan uttered the word 'fuck'. It was the first time the word had ever been used on television. As Kathleen Tynan later remarked, the consequence of his actions was to 'set off an explosion, to produce a national fit of apoplexy'.[1] Forever after, she adds, Tynan was known as the 'Man who said fuck'. In a studio discussion about censorship he had been asked if he would allow – had censorship been abolished – a play in which sexual intercourse took place to be put on at the National Theatre: 'Oh I think so, certainly. I doubt if there are many rational people in this world to whom the word "fuck" is particularly diabolical or revolutionary or totally forbidden'.[2] Not surprisingly, however, the BBC's switchboard was jammed by virtue of the mass of calls from indignant viewers. Tynan's actions managed to eclipse all the other news of the day, including the Vietnam War and the Unilateral Declaration of Independence in Rhodesia. In the House of Commons four motions were set down, supported by 133

Labour and Tory backbenchers, attacking both Tynan and the BBC. Stanley Reynolds meanwhile, writing in *The Guardian*, wondered why 'that one simple word of four letters can provoke a greater reaction inside us than long and complex words like apartheid, rebellion, illegal, police state, and treason'.

Thirty years on from that historic moment there still would be annoyance if the word fuck was used in a studio discussion programme like, say, *Newsnight* or *Question Time*. Indeed, following the 1994 Channel 4 *Cutting Edge* documentary on the England football team manager, there was considerable unease expressed at his 38 uses of the word *fuck*. Such behaviour simply did not fit within the documentary format it occurred in. Conversely, hardly an eyebrow is raised after the television showing of a film like Martin Scorsese's *Goodfellas*, in which the characters speak an almost continuous form of 'fuckinese'. The context is all-important.

Any discussion of the issue of 'taste and decency' in broadcasting is hampered by innumerable problems. To begin with there is the fact that taste is such a subjective and personal characteristic. Witness Mary Warnock's frank recollections of her time spent viewing a Stanley Kubrick movie:

> I personally have a very low sex-and-violence threshold. I remember once going with Lady Plowden [Governor and Vice-Chairman of the BBC from 1970–75 and Chairman of the IBA from 1975–80] to see the bits of *A Clockwork Orange* that had been left out. We sat together most of the time with our eyes shut, and I felt, even so, so faint and ill at the end that I had to be escorted back to the IBA.[3]

In the early months of January 1995 Channel 4 was roundly accused of acting as 'purveyors of filth', when it broadcast a documentary, *Beyond Love*, which discussed the condition of *paraphilia*, an 'extreme sexual disorder' in which individuals seek stimulation through acts of necrophilia, auto-erotic asphyxiation and amputee-fetishism. At the very same time however the channel's offices were being picketed by a direct-action lesbian group, protesting against its decision to edit a 'lesbian kiss' from the pre-watershed edition of *Brookside*. So the channel was simultaneously criticized for being too explicit, yet not explicit enough. Proof enough of the 'moral and cultural divisions within British society', and a salutary reminder that 'notions of taste and decency are debatable concepts, not fixed moralities handed down from on high'.[4]

'Taste' is also socially determined. As Stuart Hood reminds us, there are, indeed, some societies in which public executions are filmed for television screening.[5] Consider also the case, across the Atlantic, of police officer Paul Broussard who, after killing his wife wished then to end his own life. As he sat opposite the Louisiana County courthouse with a gun aimed at his head, every family in the small town of Alexandria watched in tense fascination as local TV station KALB-TV fed them live pictures of his actions. When officer Broussard subsequently blew his brains out, viewers were still glued to their screens. As his body slumped to the ground, however, the cameras panned away from him.

This is so different from events in 1914 when the first night of *Pygmalion* caused a 'national scandal' as Mrs Patrick Campbell uttered the famous line 'Walk! Not *bloody* likely. I'm going in a taxi.' By the 1990s even Prince Charles was publicly complaining that English was taught 'so *bloody* badly' in schools. Now KALB-TV. What next? And when?

Offence and Acceptability: the Audience View

It is conventionally accepted that while the majority of viewers desire choice and diversity in programming, there are, however, limits to what is generally deemed to be acceptable material. Some programmes may be considered acceptable if scheduled at an appropriate time depending on their particular style and format.

Since the 1970s the ITC/IBA, in its annual surveys, has asked viewers a number of questions about issues of offence and acceptability. The core question has asked viewers whether they have seen or heard anything on television in the previous year which they found offensive.[6] In response to this question 60 per cent of viewers replied 'no', with 40 per cent saying 'yes'. Women were more likely than men to report having been offended by television. And progressively larger proportions of viewers reported having been personally offended by something on television with increased age. Conversely, the youngest viewers (16–24) were the least likely to express having taken offence at television. Professional and middle-class viewers were more likely than working class and unemployed viewers to have experienced personal offence. As the unemployed and working classes tend to watch a little more television than other classes, perhaps they tend to be more desensitized to offensive material than other viewers? Besides which, the middle classes are more used to making critiques and complaints about their cultural environment, including television. And we must not forget that mass/popular television is of course aimed specifically at the working classes, thus it is not surprising they find most of it *acceptable*.

Such findings are in keeping with long-standing trends, for example, the IBA's 1974 survey concluded that it was clear that 'women are more offended by some television material than men and that older people are more offended than younger people'.[7] None of this is at all surprising, and is entirely predictable. Older viewers have seen values and standards change over time and, therefore, are able to make comparisons; younger viewers merely wish to see an increase in risqué programming.

Those viewers who had satellite or cable channels in addition to the four major terrestrial channels were less likely to be offended than those who did not subscribe to such services. Again, not particularly surprising. Indeed, it is precisely for the somewhat risqué nature of some of the satellite programming that the service is purchased in the first place.

In 1994, as in all previous surveys, ITV and BBC1 rather than Channel 4 and BBC2 were named more often by those who said they had been offended by something on television as the source of such material. Of course as ITV and BBC1 are much more heavily viewed than the other two channels, this result is somewhat predictable. Similarly, ITV, in its turn, is watched by more viewers on average than is BBC1, likewise contributing towards any difference between these two channels in claims of offensive material being encountered.

Among those satellite-TV viewers who reported having been offended, the most common source was BBC1, followed by ITV and Channel 4, then BBC2, the Sky Movies Channel, followed by other satellite channels. In the case of cable viewers who claimed they had been offended the most common sources of offence were again ITV, BBC1, and Channel 4/S4C followed then by other cable satellite channels, BBC2 and then the Sky Movies Channel.

Table 7.1 Viewers' perceptions of offence on television

Have seen offensive material on: (in percentages)	1984	1985	1986	1987	1988	1989	1990	1991	1992	1993	1994
ITV	35	37	35	36	31	35	29	28	30	31	28
BBC1	30	33	31	31	29	31	27	25	25	26	27
BBC2	13	13	12	12	13	19	19	20	20	20	20
Channel 4	16	17	17	19	19	27	25	27	28	29	24
Sky Movie Channels	–	–	–	–	–	–	–	1	2	2	3
Other Cable/ Satellite channels	–	–	–	–	–	–	–	–	1	2	3

Looking at table 7.1 we cannot escape from the observation that although television has become – especially since the 1980s – more graphic in its portrayal of violence and sexual behaviour, the majority of audiences have either welcomed and enjoyed the changes or been cultured into accepting them. As ITV, for example, has progressively shown more violent films the percentage of offended audiences has correspondingly reduced. But it can also be seen that as Channel 4 and BBC 2 have increased *their* share of such programming, their audiences are only becoming slowly adjusted to such a change as witnessed by the rise of offended viewers.

Next, those viewers who claimed to have been offended, were then asked how often this had occurred. In the 1994 survey, around one in ten viewers claimed to have been offended by something seen on ITV, Channel 4 or BBC1 'at least once a week', with somewhat fewer making similar claims in respect of BBC2. Amongst satellite and cable viewers there was less perceived offence than amongst the overall sample across all channels. Offence was more often noted for ITV and BBC1 than for Channel 4/S4C, BBC2 or for either the Sky Movie Channel or other cable or satellite channels.

'Bad Language', Violence and Sex

Viewers were then asked a question about what kinds of things had offended them, and in keeping with long-standing trends they replied 'bad language', violence and sex. For all four main terrestrial channels, bad language was the most often mentioned cause of offence, followed closely by violence and then sex. In addition, a smaller but not insubstantial group of viewers – around one in twenty – mentioned offensive items which set a 'bad example to children'. Reported causes of offence on television in satellite and cable households suggested that the main causes of offence were the same as those among viewers in general; levels of complaint were, however, generally lower.

Differences of opinion about the causes of such offence emerged among viewers who had children in the household and those who did not. With regard to BBC1 and ITV, among viewers who had been offended, larger proportions of those with children at home than those without expressed concern about television setting a bad example to children. However, no such difference emerged in the case of either Channel 4 or BBC2. Interestingly, smaller proportions of those with children at home than those without, expressed concern about violence, sex or bad language, although these results should be treated with some caution by virtue of the survey size. The explanation would seem to lie in the older age-profile of those who are offended, but who no longer have children in the household. Or perhaps those without children at home have a somewhat 'romantic' view of children, seeing programmes as potentially more offensive than perhaps the children (or their parents) themselves do?

Viewers were then asked if they could remember anything offensive in different programme types. Five types were offered as probes: popular drama series; comedy, variety and chat shows; news and current affairs; drama-documentaries; and crime reconstruction programmes. In response to the question about 90 per cent of viewers claimed they had seen nothing offensive in any of these programme types, but those who did so, nominated – in descending order of importance – popular drama, comedy/variety/chat shows, and news and current affairs. Drama-documentaries and crime reconstructions were mentioned by even smaller minorities of viewers. For those who mentioned having been offended by popular drama, the most often named sources of offence were bad language and swearing (7 per cent of total sample), sex (4 per cent) and violence (4 per cent). In comedy/variety/chat shows, bad language (5 percent) was again the most often mentioned offender, followed by 'vulgarity, lavatory or smutty humour' (3 per cent), and 'going a bit far', or 'bad taste' (2 per cent).

'Bad Language'

It is unquestionably true that many viewers find bad language (especially swearing, more than blasphemy) offensive. Often, they will decry such language because of the potential it has to harm children who, they claim, are in need of protection. Perhaps children themselves, however, have somewhat different ideas as to such potential for harm:

> Girl (12): . . . they think their children have never heard a swear word before in their lives, and they're going to go out and start swearing immediately and its going to turn them into right little rebels . . . it's a load of rubbish really.

> Girl (11): I mean, like, you have people killing each other, before the watershed like *Ninja Turtles* and that's really violent, but you can't have swearing . . . but in real life what's going to hurt you more, if you swear at somebody or beat them up?

> Boy (11): . . . which are you more likely to see, somebody being killed in the street and raped and mugged and stamped to death, or hear somebody swearing? Yet they have people being killed before the watershed but you don't have swearing . . . [8]

Despite such 'streetwise' (world-weary?) acceptance of swearing it is, none the less, an issue which stirs emotions and produces firmly held attitudes.

Linguists Keith Allan and Kate Burridge view strong language – in the form of insults, epithets and expletives – as *poetic*. Swear words do not, in their view, suggest a diseased mind, but rather are the product of 'healthy, flourishing, superbly inventive, and subtle minds of ordinary people'.[9] Similarly, psychoanalyst Ariel Arango believes that 'dirty words' – those that refer to parts of the body, secretions, or behaviours that arouse sexual desire – are in fact terms which describe 'true and lewd sexuality', free from hypocrisy, euphemism or modesty. He argues that 'for the preservation of a healthy society, "dirty" words must have a legitimate place in our daily life', and, moreover, that such 'obscene words should enjoy full freedom on radio and television'.[10] If the purpose of the euphemism is to hide our animal natures, strong or offensive language (*a.k.a.* dysphemism) serves to illustrate such animal natures. Repression, argues Arango, serves no positive function whatsoever. It is unlikely that such a view would ever enjoy majority support. And it is not simply only in so-called 'civilized' societies like ours, that certain words are disapproved of. Indeed in all so-called 'primitive societies' there are taboos which make the utterance of certain words strictly forbidden: from Siberia to meridional India, from the Mongols of Tartaria to the Tuaregs of the Sahara, in the Nicobar Islands of Borneo, in Madagascar and Tasmania, and many cultures elsewhere.[11]

Research undertaken by the Broadcasting Standards Council (BSC)[12] sought the opinions of viewers over a number of matters surrounding the use of 'bad language', and many of their findings are broadly similar to those of the ITC's 1994 survey. In very *general* terms it is women and the elderly of both genders who are more likely to be offended than those viewers aged under 45. However, certain types of words offended some age groups more than others. For example, those of both genders in the 16–44 age group were considerably more offended by the use of the word 'nigger' than those in the older age group. Although the sample is small, the third column's findings are alarming: *fairly acceptable* terms of abuse include such words as Nigger, Wop, Darkie, Dago, Chink, Kraut, Frog and Jap.

Table 7.2   Acceptability of racist terms of abuse

In percentages	Not at all	Not very	Fairly	Very
Nigger	55	27	40	4
Wog	49	29	17	5
Coon	44	32	20	4
Paki	40	29	24	6
Wop	40	28	25	7
Yid	39	30	24	7
Darkie	39	30	24	7
Dago	34	30	31	5
Chink	32	32	29	7
Honky	27	33	32	8
Nip	30	27	35	8
Kraut	22	28	40	10
Frog	21	25	42	12
Jap	20	25	43	11
Mick	11	19	50	19
Taffy	11	15	52	21
Paddy	11	15	51	22
Jock	10	14	54	22

Source: BSC 1991 Annual Survey, Research International.
Note: The date have been repercentaged to exclude those who had not heard of the term or did not reply.

It is also clear from the findings of the BSC's research that younger men were found, on the whole, to be more comfortable with sexual words than younger women. For example, the word 'slag' was thought to be particularly offensive by women, but young males were twice as likely as any other group to consider the word acceptable. Similarly, words generally acknowledged by both genders of all ages to be strong – like 'fuck' and 'cocksucker' – were considered slightly less offensive by those in the 16–44 age group, especially among younger men.

Findings of the BSC research also predictably confirmed the fact that viewers disapproved of hearing certain words on television because of a sensitivity to the potential influence on others, especially children, and indeed a reluctance to cause offence to other people. In addition viewers made the point that when watching TV with others they disliked the embarrassment caused by some offensive words used.[13] Swearing on television was considered more acceptable if it was thought to be an 'integral'part of a programme – for example, in order to depict 'real life' more accurately – rather than when swear words were gratuitously employed. But some viewers believed that some producers – behind the veil of making TV more 'realistic' – were trying to push back the barriers of acceptability. This was of particular concern to those who believed there was already too much 'bad language' on contemporary television.

The producers of Channel 4's successful scouse soap *Brookside*, certainly believe in social realism. Although, it must of course be noted that if they truly wished it to be a 'real-life' soap the characters would constantly talk (which they tend not to) about politics and politicians, *television*, sexual behaviour, sports controversies and the sex lives of some of the members of the Royal family. None the less since its first transmission in 1982 the series has attempted to reflect the earthy language of working-class Liverpool, though in recent years somewhat less so. The producers of *Brookside* argue that swearing is an effective shock tactic, and that the use of the corrective expletive will either guarantee attention or alternatively end a discussion. They note that conventional US cinema uses this device consistently, as in 'shut the fuck up!' In defence of such swearing on television the producers, quite correctly, argue that unfortunately 'most of society's cultural arbiters belong to a minority cultural elite divorced from the population'.[14] Indeed, it is fair to say that what may well seem distasteful and shocking in the House of Lords may well be ordinary language on an inner-city council estate.

But the shock value of the expletive, however, must not be underestimated. For many television viewers one utterance of the word 'fuck', 'bastard' or 'shit' is quite sufficient in an hour's programming; for others, one such utterance is simply too much. From a programme-maker's point of view though, such words are *tools* (especially in drama) and are to be used 'sparingly and strategically' in order to achieve the desired effect.[15] Through overuse the words become irritating and tiresome or, worse still, almost ignored or forgotten. In Brophy and Partridge's *Songs and Slang of the British Soldier: 1914–1918*, they, interestingly, report a process in which the use of the word fuck by British soldiers was so common in its adjectival form that after a short time the ear refused to acknowledge it, and instead took in only the noun to which it was attached:

By adding -ing and -ingwell, an adjective and adverb were formed and thrown into every sentence. It became so common that an effective way for the soldier to express emotion was to omit this word. Thus if a sergeant said, 'Get your -ing rifles!' it was understood as a matter of routine. But if he said, 'Get your rifles!' there was an immediate implication of emergency and danger.[16]

In television comedy – with the exception of stand-up routines by so-called 'alternative comedians' – explicit language is usually kept to a minimum. Sit-coms, for example, are expected to be 'warm, good fun, undemanding and entertaining', and not too controversial. However, many well-known sit-coms of earlier decades did make controversial words and phrases fashionable: 'git' from *Steptoe and Son*, 'silly old moo' from *Till Death Us Do Part*, and 'naff off' from *Porridge*.[17]

It is in television drama and in particular films, however, that strong language arouses the passions of the viewer and occasionally the censor or regulator. Such movies as the previously mentioned *Goodfellas*, Brian De Palma's *Scarface*, David Mamet's *Homicide*, Martin Brest's *Midnight Run*, Scorsese's *Raging Bull* and Spike Lee's *Do the Right Thing* all contain dialogue replete with expletives. Indeed, the dialogue in the Spike Lee movie – a view of 24 hours in stiflingly hot Brooklyn – is littered with the television regulator's dreaded word, the one they term the 'Oedipal noun'.

The censorship of movies to be shown on TV is an issue of some controversy. Whereas a cinema viewer will, sitting comfortably in the dark, expect 90 minutes of 'mother-fucker this and mother-fucker that' – after all that's what they've paid for – the domestic television viewer is seen as in need of some protection, either in the form of advance warnings or through cutting the film. The television regulators find themselves in something of a dilemma: the television companies buy the movies because they know they attract good-sized audiences, but the regulators none the less need to cut and trim them, especially if they are scheduled earlier rather than later in the evening. This may sometimes result in the absurd over-use of the term 'frigging' or, increasingly, the term 'freaking', instead of the more appropriate 'fuck'. Sex scenes too face the regulator's knife if scheduled too early. Again the consequences may, at times, be dire: the central sex scene in Bob Rafelson's *The Postman Always Rings Twice* was incredulously removed, while Laurence Kasdan's *Body Heat* was tampered with to such an extent that the story no longer made *any* kind of sense. Taking the argument to extremes, one could argue that, say, the slashing by television regulators of *Body Heat* is akin to a curator tampering with Picasso's *Crucifixion* before giving it gallery space.

The matter is both complex but none the less centres around the simple fact that individuals radically disagree over such issues as what constitutes 'bad language' and how far 'the public' should be protected. For example, one broadcaster claims that as modern society remains low on 'religious belief and observance, then for most people the blasphemous forms of swearing will hold little significance'.[18] On the other hand, Colin Morris, another broadcaster, laments the ironic fact that the only 'present-day British citizens likely to feel strongly enough about blasphemy to cause a public stir are Muslims whose deity does not enjoy the law's protection'.[19] He adds that as broadcasting is a 'recent invention', nobody can be certain as to what the total impact of it might be upon the 'human psyche'. In other words, might not the beating down of one moral inhibition – the 'tolerance of bad language' – not encourage collapse at other points? Morris concludes that none of any broadcaster's claims override the 'elementary decencies of life', and that the handling of such issues as blasphemy is a 'supreme test of the broadcaster's maturity of judgement', both as a professional *and* as a human being: 'even in an open, plural society, there is something to protect – the sacred, the intimate, the fragile, the dangerous and the forbidden'.[20]

Many viewers might well agree with such a belief, but others conversely believe strongly in no censorship and the right to self-expression irrespective of convention, tradition or, indeed, others' wishes. The regulator and censor has somehow to steer the ship between the two opposing elements.

Sex and Violence

On news and current affairs programmes the principal sources of offence named by viewers in the survey were – all at *only* 1 per cent – war coverage in Bosnia, biased reporting, violence, 'starving children or famine in Africa', Rwanda, and 'too much detail or explicitness'. Similarly, in regard to drama-documentaries the items which, again at a rate of merely 1 percent, received the most mentions were violence, 'bad language', sex and too much explicit detail. Finally, in crime-reconstruction programmes, the most often named sources of offence were the portrayal of violence, the potential encouragement of copycat crimes, bad language and of the reconstructions being too realistic or too explicit – all views again expressed at a ratio of only 1 per cent.

Viewers were then asked to pin-point specific programmes they could remember in the year of 1994 which contained unacceptable levels of violence, sex or 'bad language'. *Recall* of unacceptable levels of such offence were significantly lower amongst satellite (27 per cent, 22 per cent and 17 per cent respectively) and cable viewers (26 per cent, 21 per cent and 17 per cent respectively), but were a little different amongst terrestrial-only viewers (34 per cent, 29 per cent and 23 per cent respectively) who still of course comprise the majority of the overall sample. In keeping with the BBC's research, cited earlier, in all three cases such *recall* was more common amongst women than men, and also higher amongst the professional and middle classes, and the older (65 plus) age groups. Those viewers who did recall any programme with unacceptable levels of bad language, violence or sex/nudity were then asked which channel this had occurred on.

Responses for each of the three types of content generally focused on ITV, followed by Channel 4 and BBC1, and finally BBC2. Only a small minority mentioned any of the satellite or cable channels, due to the still relatively low penetration of satellite and cable television amongst the overall sample.

Within this broad pattern, BBC1 was mentioned more than Channel 4 in relation to violence. Amongst satellite viewers, on the other hand, the main sources were typically the satellite film channels, followed by Channel 4, BBC1, ITV and BBC2, and then by other satellite channels and finally MTV or the Music Channel. The only exceptions to this pattern were, firstly, that ITV was named as a source of unacceptable violence more often than either Channel 4 or BBC1, and second, that ITV was named more often as a source of unacceptable sources of sex/nudity than BBC1. Amongst cable viewers the main sources of offence were typically ITV followed by BBC1, Channel 4, the cable film channels, BBC2 and then other cable channels, and finally MTV or the Music Channel. Again the main exception to this pattern was that the cable film channels were named as a source of unacceptable violence more often than Channel 4, and that Channel 4 was named equally often as a source of unacceptable levels of sex/nudity as BBC1 was.

Finally, those viewers who had recalled any programme with unacceptable levels of bad language, violence or sex and nudity, were also asked what the actual programme was. In most cases films were mentioned, though there were some differences in emphasis. In the case of violence, for example, the main sources were, firstly, 'films', then police stories or other specified programmes including series like *The Bill*, *Cracker*, *Between the Lines* and *Taggart* or individual films like *Mad Max*, *Lethal Weapon*, *Terminator* and *Die Hard*.

In the case of sex and nudity, films in general were the most commonly stated source of unacceptable levels seen on television, together with unspecified plays and dramas as well as specific mentions of TV series like *Common as Muck* and *Margi Clark – Good Sex Guide*. Unacceptable levels of bad language were reported mostly from films, plays and dramas and from individual series like *Common as Muck* and *Billy Connolly*.

But while it is 'offensive language' that continues to preoccupy viewers – as is evident from IBA and BBC surveys from the 1970s onwards – the regulatory bodies themselves focus their attention more to issues of screen violence and, to a lesser extent, screen sex.

Violence on British television screens has undoubtedly increased over the decades, partly by virtue of the increasing importation of Hollywood movies for domestic television broadcast. Almost all Hollywood movies are violent in one way or another, including many aimed specifically at children. In *Home Alone*, for instance, the character played by Macaulay Culkin spends his lonely hours rigging up booby traps in order to punish *brutally* his enemies, the potential burglars. And nearly all Hollywood films portray a *death* of some sort. However, the fact remains that Hollywood studios are producing such films because that is what the audience in the USA wants: unlike in Britain where movie-goers are split fairly evenly between men and women, the majority of film-watchers in the USA are young men aged between 16 and 24. Such a film as Oliver Stone's *Natural Born Killers*, with its hip soundtrack and technical brilliance, is aimed precisely at such young men. But home-grown dramas too, including a number of soaps, have steadily increased their quota of violence. The question of whether such programming simply reflects 'reality', or helps actually to create it, is essentially unanswerable. However, what is undoubtedly true is that the level of screen violence now considered acceptable and legitimate has been raised from what it previously was. Similarly, it surely must be true that viewers have, inevitably, become partially desensitized to such screen violence or indeed cultured into an acceptance of it.

None the less, like televised 'bad language', the issue of screen violence is fraught with definitional problems. For one viewer (or interest group) the issue may revolve around the quantity involved – for example, how many deaths per hour – while other viewers may concentrate on the aesthetic involved or the motive/context of violence, or whether the violent behaviour is counterbalanced by on-screen 'pro-social' behaviour.

In an attempt to grapple with particular aspects of the problem in 1994 the ITC monitored four weeks of screen violence on television – ITV, Channel 4, Sky Movies, and The Movie Channel.[21] In classifying programmes for violence, ITC monitors noted the amount and type of violence portrayed, the time it occurred, and the extent to which the violent act could be judged as 'justifiable'. Their definition of violence was loose and wide-ranging, and included the following elements: physical aggression between two or more people; self-inflicted harm shown on the screen; vandalism against property; physical cruelty to animals; verbalized threats made by one person against another; pictures showing victims and the aftermath of violence, where the hurt or harm done is clearly shown.

The ITC's summary findings in respect of ITV and Channel 4 were that in 93 per cent of *all* programmes there contained either no violence at all or only minor violence, but within dramas (as opposed to factual or entertainment programming) almost 70 per cent contained violence, the great majority of which was of a weak or somewhat minor nature. On Channel 4, 74 per cent of drama contained violence, again predominately of a minor nature. Such violence was judged to be 'almost completely justifiable', and none of the programmes monitored were considered to be in breach of the requirements of the ITC Programme Code. The small amount of strong graphic violence found on ITV was scheduled 'appropriately late in the evening' and was justified within the context of the programmes. Of course it may well be true that post-watershed scheduling protects many children, but it may well also be true that the impressionable of *all ages* are watching at later hours.

Over the period of the ITC's monitoring exercise 100 films were viewed on the Sky Movies Channel and The Movie Channel. Of these films 67 per cent contained no violence or only minor violence. Of those remaining the great majority were rated as containing many incidents of strong violence, while a couple of films actually contained a few incidents of strong graphic violence. The violent content on both channels was found to be generally justifiable, and again, none of the films (or trailers) monitored were deemed to be in breach of the ITC Code.

Despite the obvious limitations of such snap-shot research, it undoubtedly paints a picture we may recognize. And given the high degree of such elements as physical assault, use of a weapon, asphyxiation, malicious intent and arson in overall screen violence, we must surely conclude that viewers either have become habituated to such material, or that they even desire such vicarious violence.

Screen Sex

It was as recent as 1978 that the BBC removed a four-letter word, together with shots of Gemma Craven's nipples and a full-frontal nude male shot from Dennis Potter's *Pennies from Heaven*. But conventions change over time and those concerned with screen sex are no exception. For example, Channel 4's *Eurotrash* series has recently (in 1995) featured items including a rubber-clad woman writhing while wired to a computerized 'sex machine'; a man having his pubic hair shaved off; and an item featuring an obese man lying naked and blindfolded on a bed in a Vienna shopping precinct while begging passers-by to have sex with him. As television playwright Alan Plater has argued, the problem for writers, programme-makers and law-makers alike, is 'that life never keeps still'. In recalling his own broadcasting career, Plater notes that 'even ten years ago it would have been impossible to use the word "condom" in the dialogue of a television play', whereas today it is 'more or less compulsory'.[22] Quite so, as in, for example, Alan Clarke's bad taste movie *Rita, Sue and Bob Too* (1986) which was broadcast on Channel 4 in 1995 in which condoms and talk of condoms feature significantly in the first few minutes.

As in the case of screen violence, screen sex too divides audiences and critics in respect of its appropriateness on mainstream television. Recently, one critic has accused the 'clodhopping barbarians of the BBC' of turning Edith Wharton's novel *The Buccaneers* into a 'kind of adult sex-comic' by inserting a rape scene and by portraying one of the main characters as 'a homosexual'. Writing under the headline 'Just why is TV so obsessed with sex?', Paul Johnson said he would have preferred the BBC to have explained its behaviour honestly: 'we are under pressure from the Government over our ratings. The Wharton story is good but we think we could attract a few more viewers by hyping up the sex angles'.[23]

In fact, on the basis of available statistical evidence, it appears that a considerable majority of viewers have come to accept sex on the small screen. In fact *most* of what is called 'television sex' is actually pretty innocuous stuff: partial nudity, extensive foreplay, occasional writhing bodies together with considerable innuendo. Indeed, perhaps the number of complaints would be even further reduced if it were not for the *familial* context of much of television viewing. For it could well be that a portrayal of sex, which each individual family member might find somewhat bland or innocuous *if seen alone*, only becomes embarrassing when viewed together. Such embarrassment is obviously more likely to be caused with children around, particularly when children 'approach, or reach puberty'. However, some research has suggested that such embarrassment is likely to be a 'two-way' process with children admitting (somewhat reluctantly) to 'discomfort when watching sex scenes on television while their parents were also there'.[24] It is a reasonable question to ask that even if a parent is aware of their children's sexual knowledge, do they really wish to experience vicariously such sexual scenes in their company? And do children wish to be reminded that their parents once had or indeed still have sex lives?

Cate Haste points to the significance of the generation divide in such matters of changing sexual values. As she argues, on 'almost all the main moral shifts – pre-marital sex, cohabitation, freedom of expression or censorship – the over-50s take a more conservative attitude'.[25] Unlike those raised in the 1960s, the over-50s were brought up in an era when sex was private, and the 'public code was one of restraint bordering on taboo'. But as sex is now a central issue in public debate, broadcasters will invariably reflect that in their programming. AIDS, for instance, has generated fierce debate about issues of sexual morality and also promoted an increase in homophobia, and similarly, cases of sexual abuse (and 'false-memory syndrome') have also fuelled discussion about sexuality.

Gay and lesbian life-styles have been to the fore in the pushing back of the boundaries surrounding the depiction of sexual behaviour on television. In the social realist soaps of *Brookside* and *EastEnders* (and even the social-rustic *Emmerdale*), strong lesbian story-lines have been features which have, not surprisingly, resulted in a number of complaints. Obviously it will take a considerable time for such life-styles to be fully represented, incorporated and ultimately consciously accepted by viewers of popular television. Research suggests that gay and lesbian hopes for the 'normalization' of their life-styles to be seen on television actually amounts to the twin demands that, firstly, their sexual behaviour is fully represented on screen but that, secondly, they also occupy 'character roles' where their sexuality does not affect their performance. Of course, the only way in which television can possibly 'normalize' such life-styles is to show such characters as 'mundane rather than special'. Such portrayals may, however, disappoint those who believe such characterizations should pointedly focus on the injustices and ill-treatment many gays and lesbians face.[26]

Viewers – other than those of the older age groups – who *do* complain about small-screen sex tend, generally speaking, to be women. Once again this is hardly surprising given that screen sex in movies, to cite the major example, is more likely to degrade women than men. Predictably enough, in addition to those special interest groups who have for decades actively campaigned against pornography on television, it has been feminists who have highlighted the issue. Again both critics and audiences are divided on the issue.

The dictionary definition of pornography states that the exhibition of sexual activity in films (and on television) intended to stimulate erotic rather than aesthetic or emotional feelings is *pornographic*. This would lead us, therefore, to conclude that much of contemporary film and television programming is, indeed, pornographic. There is no doubt that many viewers are *sexually aroused* while watching *Baywatch*, the movie *Blue Velvet* or say, a Sharon Stone movie, and the *intentions* behind such productions are unlikely to be solely artistic or purely aesthetic. However, the actual definition of pornography used in discussions of screen sex is the one which differentiates *erotica* from pornography. Despite the numerous complexities involved in such vocabulary, Gloria Steinem none the less expresses the difference between the two well when she argues that

> one could simply say that erotica is about sexuality, but pornography is about power and sex-as-weapon – in the same way we have come to understand that rape is about violence, and not really about sexuality at all.[27]

Depictions of non-pornographic sex will be of *shared* pleasure, and not examples of force or of unequal power or coercion. The underlying message of pornographic sex, however, is of the presence of violence, dominance and conquest. It is, as Steinem puts it, sex being used to 'reinforce some inequality, or to create one, or to tell us that pain and humiliation (ours or someone else's) are really the same as pleasure'.[28] If we are to experience *anything* from such depictions, we must invariably identify with either conqueror or victim.

Clearly the majority of television screen sex is *not* pornographic: graphic, joyous and *explicit* sex between consenting adults may well be deeply erotic, but it is not pornographic. Other programming may well be pornographic, and either 'soft' or hard porn. This is certainly true in the case of a number of the films on some of the satellite channels.

Sex on the screen is sometimes viewed by children of all ages, sometimes with parental permission, but sometimes not. It is, however, important to remember that soft porn is a central element of the popular culture which mainstream television is simply a part of. Consider the simple example of topless 'page three' (or 'page five') girls in tabloid newspapers. These photographs are depictions of women which objectify them, and which consequently turn them into objects for the delectation of male fantasy. And, worryingly, this may well be a case of first look, and then touch.

Of course, although it is obviously true that viewers may become sexually aroused by what they see on the screen – indeed, some viewers use screen images for precisely that purpose – the question of what the exposure of screen sex *leads to* remains stubbornly unanswered. The two traditional models of explanation are simply inadequate to the task. The 'catharsis' model asserts that strong erotic or pornographic images drain off tensions so that men will act less if they *see* more; if this model were accurate, then as the amount of pornography increased the rate of rape would be expected to decrease. But both, in fact, have been steadily increasing. The 'imitation' model, on the other hand, suggests that the viewer may simply wish to copy or imitate what they see on the screen. But this too is inadequate: 'it assumes that people are made of unimprinted wax and stamped with whatever messages role models present'.[29] But most of us do not, of course, to state the obvious example, turn out precisely like our parents in the ways they intended us to do.

Alan Plater expresses the opinion that sex has its place in every writer's spectrum, and 'crucially so in programmes like *The Singing Detective*, marginally in *GBH*, classically in *I Claudius*, rustically in *Trinity Tales*, conspicuously but significantly absent in *Inspector Morse*'.[30] He believes that such examples of screen sex bear witness to the dramatists' task of *refracting* reality: they are television writers who offer a unique vision of the world, building on those universal themes which govern all such work – birth, love, death, war, work, and, 'inevitably and properly, sex'.[31] What is worrisome for Plater, however, is the uncertain future:

> there is no evidence, scientific or anecdotal, that sexually repressed citizens, needing to sustain their masturbatory fantasies scan the pages of *Radio Times* in search of the latest work by Dennis Potter. The sad truth . . . is that such people go to their corner shop to buy a pornographic magazine or rent a dirty video; and sooner rather than later they will have satellite channels beaming in blue movies twenty-four hours a day. That is the logical conclusion of deregulated, market-driven television: at the end of the line is a warehouse full of cheap movies doing the dirty on sex, and doing it violently.[32]

And of course tabloid newspaper editors have long since learned that in a highly competitive climate, the mixture of sex and scandal sells newspapers. Perhaps television programming will follow suit; indeed, perhaps on some marginal channels it already has.

Even if all pornographic or violent sexual activity was counterbalanced on-screen with pro-social imagery of forceful explanations of why sexual violence is unacceptable, this would not necessarily prevent an individual viewer making his or her own interpretations. As a consequence of the anti-pornographer campaigns to ban *all* such imagery from the screen, the more libertarian view is for free expression in the name and defence of art. Perhaps caution and the 'middle way' is the most appropriate strategy;

especially considering that much of the nastiest and excessive cases of screen sex are not so much works of art, but formulaic *commercial* products made for profit.

Since the partial deregulation of French television, the race to capture large audiences has quickened, and the regulators have found themselves fully occupied. Attempting to tread a fine line between the 'rights of the freedom to communicate versus the protection of children and teenagers',[33] is precisely what British regulators too will have to engage in. Whether in multi-set and multi-channel households such a strategy is potentially effective or possible is another question difficult to answer.

Homo Committicus

Unlike in previous surveys the 1994 survey asked viewers if they had ever switched off the television or switched to another channel because of unacceptable levels of violence, sex and nudity, or bad language. Of those viewers who recalled incidents of such levels of violence or bad language, close to two-thirds *claimed* to have switched the television off or changed channel, while of those who recalled incidences of unacceptable sex or nudity, an even higher figure of over three-quarters claimed to have switched off or changed channel. Not surprisingly, in all cases a greater proportion of terrestrial-only viewers switched off or changed channels, than did cable or satellite viewers.

Historically, the British are famed for such qualities as the ability to form orderly queues, an almost obsessive love of pets (at the expense perhaps of children?) and a somewhat reserved disposition. Unlike other cultures, ours is not one in which we complain easily. Certainly in comparison to Americans such a statement is clearly true. Perhaps this is not surprising given the post-war welfare statism in which as a society we were given so much for free: why should we therefore complain? How could we be so ungrateful? But since the 1980s and with the extension of market principles into public life, the art of complaining has become a more accepted practice. None the less, complaining about television programmes appears to be an extremely difficult or problematic thing to do, especially as overall it appears to be such a good-value system of entertainment. Besides which it does not appear obvious that any such complaint would change anything. Moreover, complaining about, say, a sex scene on the previous evening's drama is a bit like bemoaning that the bus didn't stop – and as it won't come along again, why bother. Furthermore, as Barrington Moore perceptively reminds us, 'Homo Committicus, to coin an appropriate barbarism, is not the only species of homo sapiens', and, he adds, a very 'precious part of human freedom is that *not* to make decisions'.[34] Or to complain.

Obviously the number of *reported* complaints about television and television programmes is only *one* measure of the public's experience, attitudes and feelings about such matters. None the less, enough people complain to provide a substantial amount of work for both the ITC and the BBC's Programme Complaints Unit. This latter unit was set up in 1994 to investigate 'serious' complaints (the term being defined by the BBC themselves). In fact in its first report[35] it was revealed that 590 complaints were investigated, half of which concerned matters of taste and standards (including bad language, sex and violence), while the other half consisted mainly of issues of fairness and accuracy. Of the 590 complaints, 102 were, ultimately, wholly or partly upheld.

On such matters of taste the BBC's report argues that the volume of complaints speaks of a 'sense among some viewers and listeners that the loosening of restraints (in language, in sexual matters, in the way once-taboo topics are broached) is bad for society, particularly the young'.[36] The report adds that the main focus for such complaints has been so-called 'alternative comedy', which one section of viewers actively dislikes, while younger adults now accept such comedy as mainstream. In their judgement the BBC, quite fairly, states that it 'caters for the range of legitimate tastes, and the range is so wide that this will mean broadcasting material which is unacceptable to some'.[37] Similarly, the report notes that the majority of complaints about drama concerned soaps broadcast before the watershed, and the fear was expressed that younger viewers were being prematurely exposed to adult affairs, or even were being influenced to adopt amoral attitudes. However, the BBC concludes its report by arguing that the fact remains that 'very large numbers of families watch without complaint'.[38]

If a viewer does not accept the BBC's Programme Complaints Unit's decision, it is possible for them to appeal subsequently to the BBC Governor's Programme Complaints Appeals Committee. For example, one complainant had argued that an episode of *EastEnders* which contained scenes of violence – including an attempted rape and gun attack by a 'psychopathic maniac' – was unsuitable for pre-watershed programming. However, the complaint was not upheld. The complainant pursued the matter and the Appeals Committee duly met, but agreed with the Complaints Unit's judgement: '*EastEnders* is a long-established popular drama with a large regular following, [and] that the episode was part of a continuing storyline which regular viewers would have been familiar with and that an announcement alerting viewers to a "violent confrontation" in the course of the episode was broadcast immediately before transmission'.[39]

The range of issues that viewers complain about is impressively wide: for example, on *World Cup Grandstand*, a viewer complained that a commentator had made a remark which appeared to condone a foul by an Irish player, while another viewer complained that on the *Summer Holiday* programme a reference that a village in Turkey had been left empty since the 1922 Independence War was completely inaccurate, as Turkey had never fought such a war.

However, as the BBC's report stated many complainants claim to be concerned for the welfare of younger viewers, and not just in connection with alternative comedy programmes or drama serials or soaps. An interesting case in point involved BBC's *The Paul Daniels Magic Show*, in which the magician's assistant appeared to be cremated on stage. This illusion was the finale of the programme, and as such the assistant did not reappear at the end. A number of viewers complained that this was too macabre, and, indeed, frightening for the children who were watching. The BBC concurred with this view.

Finally, given the increase on all mainstream channels of so-called 'true-life dramas' (docu-dramas), a complaint about the *Screen Two* film *Criminal* is perhaps instructive. A prison officer at Armley Prison argued that *Criminal* (based on the true story of 'Simon', a young offender who committed suicide while on remand) showed prison officers 'turning a blind eye' while Simon was viciously assaulted by other prisoners. This, he claimed, was unfair to the officers concerned who had *not* been callous or indifferent to such assaults on prisoners, though they had, indeed, failed to prevent Simon's death. The BBC's Complaints Unit, in response to the complainant, argued that though the film had 'generally stuck very faithfully to the record', some 'licence had been taken with the facts: there was nothing in the record to suggest that this incident had taken place'.[40]

In 1994 the ITC received 3,065 complaints from viewers, itemized in the following table 7.3. As is evident from the statistics the greatest number of complaints arise in the categories 'other taste and decency', 'other unfairness', 'scheduling' and 'miscellaneous'. These cover a very wide range of both programmes and issues. For example, complaints included: the

Table 7.3 Total number of complaints made to the ITC, by category for 1994

	News/Factual			Fiction/Entertainment			Total	%
	ITV	C4	Cable and Satellite	ITV	C4	Cable and Satellite		
Accuracy	80	13	1	20	1	–	= 115	4
Impartiality	33	24	2	–	1	–	= 60	2
Sexual portrayal	2	3	–	87	19	2	= 113	44
Language	9	19	–	52	28	4	= 112	3
Violence	8	8	1	139	27	4	= 187	6
Other taste and decency	168	82	5	360	135	13	= 763	25
Other unfairness	124	182	–	50	7	–	= 364	12
Racial offence	45	5	–	34	7	–	= 91	3
Religious offence	10	31	–	26	32	1	= 100	3
Scheduling	185	16	–	220	40	2	= 465	15
Regionality	11	–	–	–	–	–	= 11	1
Miscellaneous	267	67	18	256	56	11	= 684	22
	942	452	28	1253	353	37	3065	

Source: ITC (1995a), p. 14.

increase of innuendo on *Blind Date*, a puppy shown walking over a cattle grid, the modelling of a coat with a beaver fur collar, the scheduling of trailers before the watershed, the late running of news bulletins because of football coverage, the use of wide-angle picture format and the cutting or slashing of feature films. The unusual number of complaints of 'other unfairness' is largely accounted for by the Channel 4 *Without Walls* programme on Mother Teresa, to be discussed.

Despite the long-term trend data which suggests that viewers claim that they worry more about 'bad language' than sex or violence, this is not translated into actual numbers of complaints. Obviously, this is partly explained by those complainants who are members of special interest groups, who tend to campaign more vigorously about the level of sex and violence on television, rather than 'bad language'.

In 1994 the ITC in its *pro-active*, as opposed to its *reactive* role, drew attention to numerous breaches of its Programme and Sponsorship Codes. The rules of such codes are specifically designed to ensure that there is a clear distinction between the editorial content of a programme and paid advertising or sponsor messages. These rules had been broken by two broadcasters. Similarly, it also chastized an ITV company for allowing a movie with an 'extended hanging sequence' to be transmitted at mid-afternoon. On the other hand, in its *reactive* role, the ITC responded to many complaints about an episode of *Cracker* which opened at 21.01 hours with an explicit scene of sexual intercourse between a schoolgirl and a middle-aged man. It upheld such complaints, and found that though the sex was not graphic it *was* too early and was not consistent with the requirement that the transition away from family-viewing standards after 9 p.m. was intended to be a gradual and progressive one.

The Two Catholics

The ITC's judgements, whether pro-active or in response to complainants, are based squarely on their various codes of practice. This obviously leads to a commendable degree of impartiality in judgements, in theory, and also provides useful guidelines for programme-makers themselves. It can, however, lead to anomalies or conundrums. Take the case of Channel 4's two programmes broadcast in 1994 about Mother Teresa and Pope John Paul II.

Many viewers (134) complained about the *Without Walls* arts programme, *Hell's Angel: Mother Teresa*, arguing that Christopher Hitchens' opinions were 'offensive and unfair' to Mother Teresa. In response to such viewers the ITC said it 'understood the distaste which many Roman Catholics' felt at the 'style of the programme and the choice of words at various points'.[41] Nevertheless, as the programme was part of a long-running series of '*personal view* features', it was not in breach of the ITC Code. Consequently the complaints were not upheld. On the other hand, the ITC did uphold the twenty complaints made about a *Witness* programme *The Pope's Divisions*, in which ex-nun Karen Armstrong argued that Pope John Paul II was a religious fundamentalist whose authoritarian style alienated many Catholics world-wide. Channel 4 was asked to explain how the programme could be reconciled with Section 9.4 of the Programme Code which requires that every attempt be made to ensure that programmes about religion are *accurate* and *fair*. In its defence of the programme, Channel 4 argued that *Witness* was a series about personal belief, that Karen Armstrong's opinions were transparent, and that the film was not about Catholicism as such but the current Pope's interpretation of it. However, the ITC found that the programme was at that time unique in the *Witness* strand in being a presenter-led polemic which at no stage was challenged or tested by any other viewpoint.

In fact both programmes were polemical rants against prominent Catholics, but one was broadcast within an arts strand devoted to such a format and style, while the other programme was commissioned by the channel's Religion and Talks Department.

In her own defence presenter/writer Karen Armstrong argued that the principle of 'fairness', was quite simply, an 'imprecise and subjective term, which can easily be exploited by any religious group that seeks to censor the media'.[42] Indeed, it appears doubtful that Jesus himself would have been allowed to broadcast in the 1990s, given that his message was deemed to be offensive by most of his contemporaries. Armstrong pointed to the original remit of Channel 4 which gave it special responsibility to represent views not aired elsewhere in the media, and to put forward the opinions of those who found it difficult to criticize the institution to which they belong. Arguing against the ITC Armstrong claimed that her programme was in fact welcomed by one Catholic group called Catholics For A Changing Church which, she claimed, challenged the right of the Catholic Media Office – which had *organized* the complaints to the ITC – to speak for all Catholics in Britain. The ITC chose to ignore this group in its judgement. Finally, she pointed to the very subjective nature of religion, much of which, historically, has often appeared shocking and offensive. Some of its worst excesses, however, have occurred when protest has been silenced by acts of persecution and inquisition.

> We are living at a time of increasing religious intolerance, when extremists call loudly for censorship. It would seem that in this climate, a responsible broadcaster should occasionally support those who object to this type of repression.[43]

The ITC judgements concerning these two particular programmes highlight both the complexities and responsibilities of regulation and censorship that are encountered by the ITC and other regulatory bodies. It is no easy task.

8

Children, Regulation and the 'Effects' of Television

The bureaucratization of ageing produces many abrupt qualitative leaps from quantitative changes . . . In Britain, after five birthdays have passed, children are whisked away from home and forced into an enormous building full of strangers; after twelve more, pulled out of the building and into the unemployment queue or a job; and after so many more, put out of a job for good. The criterion is not developmental age in biological or any other terms but simply chronological age.

Michael Young (1988), *The Metronomic Society*

No issue concerning television energizes individuals (and interested parties or pressure groups) as much as that of the potential *effect* television has on children, the vulnerable and impressionable, and, in particular, television's role in the creation of violence. This chapter examines the tradition of 'effects research' and also considers how viewers believe television should be regulated in order to protect those who may well be moulded by the experience.

In the 1994 ITC survey, when viewers were asked who they would complain to about a television programme, should they wish to do so, almost one in five were unable to respond to the question. However, four institutions *were* mentioned by at least one in ten viewers, namely the Broadcasting Complaints Commission (20 per cent), the Independent Broadcasting Authority (16 per cent), the British Broadcasting Corporation (11 per cent) and the Advertising Standards Authority (10 per cent). The ITC itself was mentioned by just 7 per cent of viewers. Nearly all of them, however, claimed to have actually *never* complained about a television programme. Amongst the small minority who had done so (3 per cent), such complaints had been addressed to the British Broadcasting

Corporation, the ITV Companies, the Broadcasting Complaints Commission or the Independent Broadcasting Authority. Again the ITC was mentioned by just one viewer. Of those who *had* complained the main causes of complaint were bad language, a change in programming to that advertised and 'bad manners'. Also mentioned were inaccurate programmes, sex on the screen, setting a bad example to children and 'disrespect or intrusion'. Over half of those who had complained said they had been unsatisfied with the way the complaint was handled, while just over one-third claimed to be satisfied.

The same set of questions was then asked about *commercials* broadcast on independent television. The Advertising Standards Authority was mentioned by over four in ten viewers as the organization they would complain to, followed by the 'company who was advertising' the product, and finally the Independent Broadcasting Authority and the ITC. Once again, however, a significant minority of viewers (24 per cent) was unable to name *any* organization they would complain to.

Just four viewers out of the entire sample (1000+) claimed ever to have complained about a commercial, three of whom approached the Independent Broadcasting Authority. The offences reported in these cases were of bad language and the setting of a 'bad example' to children. Two out of the four viewers claimed they were satisfied with the way their complaint had been dealt with.

That so few viewers complained about commercials bears witness to the way in which such annoying breaks in programming have come to be widely accepted.[1] At such breaks viewers are likely to engage in domestic tasks, enjoy the commercials, or simply zap them. Given the prevalence of this latter strategy, it is perhaps worth wondering why advertisers bother with television at all.

In the early 1950s one of the reasons commercial television was met with suspicion was because of the fear that there would be direct influence by advertisers on actual programme content. Such opposition to commercial television increased at the news that the American television coverage of the 1953 Coronation had been 'punctuated by ads featuring a chimpanzee, J Fred Muggs'.[2] What was considered to be particularly offensive was the studio 'interview' with the chimp (during the communion service) in which he was asked 'Do they have coronations where you come from?' It was, therefore, no surprise that after the inception of ITV, tight controls were created over the number, duration, placing and content of commercials.

In the early years of commercial television the commercials were conventionally and straightforwardly produced. The first one ever to grace the screens – on 22 September 1955 at 20.12 p.m. – was for Gibbs SR toothpaste: the tube of toothpaste was embedded in a block of ice, a woman vigorously brushed her teeth and the voice-over claimed it was 'tingling fresh. It's fresh as ice. *It's Gibbs SR toothpaste*'. The following year saw the introduction of British chimpanzees to the art of selling and promotion, with the broadcasting of the first episodes of a long-running campaign for Brooke Bond tea. And within a couple of years there was the start of advertising's first soap opera, starring Katie and her Oxo family, which ultimately was to run for some 18 years.

Since that time advertisers have continued to spend increasingly enormous sums of money on the production of commercials, which has resulted in a sophisticated genre, refined and developed to the extent that many viewers will casually claim that the commercials 'are the best things on the telly'. Certainly the 1980s witnessed the development of finely-crafted commercials-as-short-stories, which resulted in making Hollywood directors out of their creators. Indeed, critic D.J. Enright, for example, has claimed that the commercials for Hamlet cigars 'have as much entertainment value as anything else in television', and he marvels at the Andrex commercial in which the 'winsome puppy unwinding a toilet roll' is a 'brilliant piece of euphemizing' which 'puts the condom campaign to shame'.[3]

However, even something as innocuous as the 1958 Oxo family commercial ran into trouble: some viewers complained that when Katie arrived home and started making gravy she did not first wash her hands, and there was disapproval of her husband mopping up his gravy with his bread.[4]

None the less, the evidence – particularly that concerning the extensive zapping by the remote control device – suggests that commercials are only inattentively viewed. So why do advertisers persist with this expensive strategy? Barwise and Ehrenberg interestingly argue that the reason why advertisers spend so much money (and effort) is because advertising is a 'fairly weak force'. As evidence of this they cite the fact that consumers seldom buy any of the hundreds of brands or services that feature in television commercials. Rather advertising is, they claim, merely a defensive strategy aimed at keeping an existing market share. What it sometimes *does* achieve, however, is to create awareness and interest in a new brand or reawaken awareness in established brands.[5]

Psychologists Condry and Scheibe, after analysing several thousand commercials, claimed that in over half of them the supposed outcome of 'product possession or use' was happiness and social recognition. They found that in over three-quarters of television commercials there was the implicit or, indeed, explicit promise of feeling better or of enhanced social esteem as a consequence of purchasing particular products.[6] In a similar vein commercials have also been called the 'electronic icon of our time, appealing to hope and fear, promising miracles', and of 'selling the unnecessary, creating emotionally charged values to make the unneeded seem necessary'.[7] And in her review of the 'values' of television commercials Peg Slinger disapprovingly concludes that they create a 'world of mirrors in which we get new images of ourselves that fit well the purpose of the system'.[8] The question of whether advertising creates false needs and unattainable models of behaviour is one which is extremely difficult to answer. There is no doubt that some commercials are 'unrealistic' both in terms of what qualities a product may bring to the purchaser's life, and in the on-screen portrayal of those people using such products. For instance, women who use deodorants are always svelte, those women who try out shampoo are invariably blessed with long silky hair, while those actors in toothpaste commercials are very rarely in need for any orthodontic treatment. However, we cannot assume that *all* viewers are naïve enough to believe that product purchase necessarily leads to a personally desired state of happiness or a radical change in life.

For many years advertising agencies have been roundly criticized for perpetuating sexual stereotypes – women represented as merely 'vagina-on-legs' – and of misrepresenting family life by perpetuating the outdated statistic and image of a two-adult-two-children-happy-home. In 1991, however, agency Abbott Mead Vickers' BBDO decided to use a more contemporary family situation in their campaign to promote the gravy Bisto. The 'stories' of the commercials focused on a young boy, Neil, whose parents had recently separated. Preliminary research by the agency had suggested that viewers would appreciate the 'reality of the scripts', providing that Neil was not portrayed as a 'sad little boy' and as long as neither parent was portrayed as 'a baddie'.[9] Research prior to transmission then indicated that viewers would indeed identify with the stories and it was suggested to the agency that it was the viewers' hope that Neil himself would lead his parents (Jim and Helen) to a reconciliation. This theme is illustrated in one of the 30-second commercials titled *Jim's Flat*.

PICTURE	SOUND
Neil is laying the table at Jim's flat.	*(Music Under)*
He looks over to the mantlepiece where there is photo of Jim, Helen and Neil together.	*Neil*: Dad, I think Mum would like come to dinner one day.
Jim is at the oven. He bends to take out a roast chicken. He pauses, hidden from Neil's view as he answers.	*Jim*: Think she would?
Neil looks over as Jim stands up and puts meat tray down.	*Neil*: I'll mention it – you know – casually.
Chicken is a little over-cooked and smoking. He flaps a tea-towel at it	*Jim*: Alright, but . . .

He steals a quick look at Neil and sees him looking across to mantlepiece again.	Here, look what I'm using today –
He picks up Bisto and empty jug.	Bisto *chicken* gravy.
	Neil: Who gave you that idea?
Neil beams with pleasure at the answer. We stay on his face.	*Jim*: Who d'you think?
	Neil: I'll ask her, then?
Dissolve to pack shot of Bisto Chicken gravy granules next to steaming jug. Then dissolve to a 3-pack.	
Super: *Bisto. It puts the ahh! into a meal.*	

Neil's preoccupation with his parents' separation is highlighted in another 30-second commercial called *Margaret's Opinion*, in which he discusses it with his grandmother.

PICTURE	SOUND
Margaret, Helen's mother, is closing up her newsagent's shop for the day.	
She is a friendly, bustling woman in her late fifties.	
Neil sits reading a woman's magazine from the display.	*Neil*: Gran, it says here that a lot of couples get back together
She walks through curtain at back of shop into her flat. Neil follows her.	*Margaret*: I'm sure they do, Neil.
	Neil: What do you think?
Margaret is making gravy in a pan at the kitchen counter. A roast stands cooling nearby	*Margaret*: I think I should get this Bisto gravy going – and you should lay the table before your Mum comes.
Neil lays table.	*Neil*: Course she might marry Ted.

Margaret: And I might start dating Jason Donovan.

Neil is delighted by her answer.
Dissolve to powder pack shot next
to steaming gravy boat.

MVO: Bisto. It puts the ahh! into a meal.

Super: *It puts the ahh! into a meal.*

Clearly these two examples are socially *realistic*, and are very different from the conventional 'advertising families' seen on television. Both commercials express the hopes that such children hold that their parents will reunite, and that they themselves may be instrumental in such a reconciliation. It could of course be argued that Neil's emotional frailty was actually exploited by the stories, or that such narratives would raise false hopes in those viewers in similar circumstances. Perhaps, though, it is more reasonable to describe them as realistic bitter-sweet accounts of contemporary family life. A few complaints did indeed follow the transmission of the commercials. Most of which argued that the commercials painted a picture of marital separation (and one-parent families) in much too desirable a light, that they were in effect picking away at the normal task of keeping a family together. Other complainants simply believed that the commercials were irresponsibly using unhappiness to sell a product.

The Bisto campaign did not play for very long; however, the agency, none the less, claimed it was successful while it lasted (although it felt it did not have a long enough time to *build*). The campaign was halted, not because of the complaints, but rather because the launch of rival Oxo's instant gravy meant Bisto had to switch to a more product-led campaign. Indeed one of the problems with such a ground-breaking campaign is that it is an open question as to whether viewers were interested in Bisto's qualities or rather simply saw the merits of marriage guidance, or perhaps merely reflected on their own family lives.

Regulation

The 1990 Broadcasting Act introduced a new framework of legislation in the UK, directly affecting commercial television. This fresh system of regulation was designed to provide an 'enabling framework' which would subsequently foster the market-led diversification and expansion of television channels. Despite these changes, the new legislation still retained many traditional consumer protection requirements and, for some channels, introduced a number of additional 'positive programming requirements' aimed at preserving programming quality and diversity. In the UK television system there are four regulatory bodies: the Independent Television Commission (ITC), which is able to take action *after* programmes have been transmitted. In the case of the ITV companies, the ITC can impose fines, shorten the duration of or even revoke their franchises. The ITC can also fine Channel 4 or sack its chairman, but cannot revoke its licence. The Broadcasting Standards Council's remit covers all broadcasters including Channel 4, ITV, BBC and satellite/cable channels, and investigates complaints from the public about programmes, but subsequently merely *reports* its findings. The Broadcasting Complaints Commission investigates allegations that particular individuals have been *wronged* by television. Consequently it may impose fines. The only power to vet a programme in advance (and ban it), however, lies with the BBC's Board of Governors. The last time they actually ordered a BBC programme not to be broadcast is believed to have been in 1971.

Viewers in the survey were asked how much regulation they thought there actually was on terrestrial channels. Almost half thought that there was either 'a great deal' or 'quite a lot' of regulation over the four main broadcast channels, while just under three in ten thought there was only 'a little' or 'none at all'. Amongst satellite or cable viewers, however, beliefs concerning regulation of the main four terrestrial channels were more pronounced, with well over half arguing there was 'a great deal' or 'quite a lot' of supervision or regulation of these channels and just over a quarter stating there was either 'little' supervision or 'none at all'. There was no significant difference in this case between the views of satellite and cable viewers.

Perceptions of 'a great deal' or 'quite a lot' of supervision or regulation of terrestrial channels were also more marked, not surprisingly, amongst 16–44-year-olds, while perceptions of little or no regulation was most marked amongst the 65-plus age group. Among the total sample of viewers,

Table 8.1 Perceptions of degree of regulation over television channels

	Four main channels		Satellite and cable channels	
In percentages	All viewers	Sat./cable viewers only	All viewers	Sat./cable viewers only
A great deal	8	12	2	5
Quite a lot	42	46	13	29
A little	26	24	21	34
None at all	3	2	7	9
It varies	9	8	4	10

the majority held no opinion concerning the degree of regulation over satellite and cable channels. Viewers who did express an opinion were generally less likely to think that there was excessive regulation than that there was too little, or none. However, satellite and cable viewers' opinions were rather different. Those who could actually receive such channels, not surprisingly, felt better informed about these channels, with the great majority expressing an opinion about them. They saw them as essentially less regulated than the main four terrestrial broadcast channels. However, both satellite and cable viewers did not see these channels as completely devoid of regulation. Indeed, over three in ten satellite and cable viewers claimed there was 'a great deal' or 'quite a lot' of supervision or regulation of satellite or cable channels. In addition they were far more likely to state that there was a 'great deal' or 'quite a lot' of supervision or regulation of these channels than was true of terrestrial-only viewers.

In respect of the four main terrestrial broadcast channels, just over one in two viewers believed that the amount of regulation over the channels was 'about right'. The opinion that there was too little regulation, however, clearly outweighed the view that there was too much. In the case of satellite and cable channels, more than one in two general viewers could offer no opinion. Among those who did however, the most widespread opinion was that the amount of regulation was about right. This view was closely followed by the sentiment expressed that there was too little regulation over these newer television services.

Most satellite and cable viewers in the survey argued that these additional non-terrestrial channels were regulated to about the right degree. Among those whose opinion differed from this general viewpoint, the greatest proportion felt that there was too little regulation, though a minority felt there was in fact too much.

Those viewers who believed that there was too much regulation of the four main broadcast channels were more often male and aged 16 to 20, while those who felt there was 'too little' were more often those viewers aged over 65 years of age. However, in respect of satellite and cable channels those viewers who felt there was too little regulation of these channels were more likely to be from the professional and middle classes.

What this myriad of findings clearly demonstrates is that satellite (and cable) television has quickly developed an image of an almost unfettered system of broadcasting, especially in the eyes of those who do not actually watch such channels. At the same time those younger viewers who subscribe to such channels wish them to be even less regulated: indeed, it is likely that one of the major motives for purchasing such channels is for more explicit and less censored movies. Though the same pieces of legislation which apply to terrestrial television – the 1990 Broadcasting Act and the European Directive of 1989 – apply to these new channels, there are significant differences in terms of the regulatory *spirit*.[10] For instance, because in the near future there is the possibility of an almost limitless number of satellite and cable channels, there is, consequently, no legislation providing for the direction and central nature of programmes transmitted. The ITC, as the regulatory body concerned, argues that it would be entirely counter-productive to insist that any of them provide education or news or any other particular sort of material.[11] It is therefore left to the various companies themselves to decide on their programming 'quality': the assumption being that those that fail to attract audiences because of 'poor' quality will, therefore, go out of business.

Unlike in the case of ITV, satellite or cable channels are allowed to be owned by religious groups who may well proselytize on screen. Another difference between terrestrial and satellite/cable channels relates specifically to the premium subscription film channels, whereby the watershed is assumed to be 8 p.m. rather than 9 p.m. so that consequently most '15' films can be shown at the earlier time. In addition, later on in the evening it is assumed that these channels can show 'adult' movies that would not be broadcast on terrestrial television. Thus the Adult Channel is able to broadcast 'mild pornography after midnight'.[12]

The European Directive on Trans-Frontier Broadcasting of 1989 required each country to regulate satellite services under its own jurisdiction, and any service considered acceptable in any EU country was to be deemed acceptable by other such countries. As the regulator in the *country of origin* the ITC cannot intervene in relation to the content of other European channels, even if they 'include bull-fighting at tea-time'.[13] The exception to this rule concerns the protection of minors. Each EU country has the right to make its own decisions on what 'level of pornography or gratuitous violence might seriously impair the physical, mental or moral development of minors'.[14] On such grounds the UK government took action against Red Hot Television and effectively put it out of business. Within the ITC there is the view that the standards (and regulations) applied to both television and film have always been stricter (and more rigorous) than those applied to the printed word:

> The apocryphal visitor from Mars, judging sex from what can be seen on British Television, would get a very curious impression. Even on an encrypted late-night service there will be no erections, no gynaecological detail, no penetration (unless the context is unequivocally educational) – and certainly nothing illegal or violent.[15]

In 1929, Edward Shortt as the President of the British Board of Film Censors, claimed that the Board was 'an instrument to mould the minds of the young and to create great and good and noble citizens for the future'. The system of television regulation similarly expresses a history both of optimism and a desire to protect the young. But approaching the millennium we face a conundrum. On the one hand, there exist many regulatory bodies (too many perhaps, or just too many with the initials 'B' – BSC, BBC, BCC?), numerous and complex codes of practice, in addition to the well-established internal systems of accountability operated by the broadcasters themselves. But on the other hand, the market-driven television of the future will increase the number of channels viewers may wish to choose to subscribe to, and these viewers may not wish for regulators to interfere with the programming they have decided to purchase. Additionally, there is the

potential for terrestrial broadcasters to be drawn into more direct competition with non-terrestrial television over, say, 'adult only' programming.
And at the same time the relentless challenge to taboo areas continues: it is
unquestionable that, as present trends indicate, increasingly there will be
more screen sex and violence offered up for viewer's delectation.

Embedded Persuasions

There is one growth area that *will* ensure some complex work for regulators in the future: namely the licensing of sponsorship arrangements and
the monitoring of other such forms of embedded persuasion.

The regulatory institutions of British broadcasting historically have
substantially protected viewers from those subliminal messages, those
'hidden persuasions' that Vance Packard so forcibly and famously wrote
about in 1957.[16] Since those early decades advertisers have, in addition to
'spot' advertising, created other techniques to promote their products and
corporate images. These techniques may be generically termed 'embedded
persuasions' – promotional messages integrated into the television
programmes themselves. In his comprehensive survey of such techniques
Graham Murdock enumerates five main strategies through which companies can theoretically promote themselves and their products: they can
supply goods and services to a programme-maker free or at a cheap cost in
return for an acknowledgement; also in return for an on-screen credit a
company may contribute towards the costs of making a single programme
or series; sponsorship proper, either in the form of sponsoring an actual
event which is subsequently televised, or by directly sponsoring a
programme; product placement, which involves paying to ensure that
a product appears as a 'logical part of the action in drama'[17], finally, there
are those programmes which actually are nothing more than advertisements for products as in some rock music shows, or which constitute an
extended promotion for a particular product range, like many cartoon
series.

From the 1950s onwards regulators were earnestly engaged in dealing
with cases of product promotion on commercial television which were *not*
simply cases of legitimate 'spot' advertising. For example, advertising
magazine programmes like *Shop in the South* or *On View*, in which a range
of goods would be displayed and talked about in a domestic setting, were
not technically in breach of the rule separating programming from
advertising as they were labelled 'advertising magazines' on screen. Critics
were, however, unimpressed with them, and pointed out that such
programmes were produced by the companies trying to sell their products
and not the ITV contractors themselves. Moreover, they were concerned
over the crucial matter of who held editorial control and the degree to which
companies could influence the programme-makers. This issue was subsequently taken up by the 1960 Pilkington Committee on Broadcasting,

which was originally established to evaluate the performance of both ITV and the BBC:

> The more interesting the magazines become – and . . . it is on their intrinsic interest that their place in programming is justified – the greater the likelihood that the viewer will, on another level of his mind, cease to realize that he is being sold something. We consider that . . . the distinction insisted on by the act – between the programme and the advertisement – is blurred.[18]

Such advertising magazine programmes were consequently banned and advertisers, in response, turned their attention to indirect sponsorship through sport and, thereby, into television advertising. As Seymour-Ure wryly observes, from the 1970s onwards cricket boundaries were ringed with advertising boards, grand-prix cars were festooned with stickers promoting cigarettes and other goods, while equestrians were likely to be riding mounts more often called 'Sanyo Music Centre or Everest Double Glazing than Fox-hunter or Dobbin'.[19]

At the same time as such sponsorship grew steadily in the 1970s and 1980s, disenchantment with 'spot' advertising itself set in: because of the cost of producing the commercials themselves, because of the likelihood of viewers zapping them, and with the demographics of the ITV viewers themselves – both older and poorer than desired. Sponsorship is deemed attractive, as it is relatively cheaper than spot advertising, is seen by the viewer to be integral to a (popular) programme and may have a very wide audience reach. Indeed, major televised sporting events, for example, are globally distributed.

With the ITC replacing the IBA following the statutes of the 1990 Broadcasting Act, a new and revised Code on Programme Sponsorship was drawn up. In the code product placement remains prohibited while enthusiastic sponsors are simply not 'permitted any influence on either the content or the scheduling of a programme'.[20] Potential sponsors reacted cautiously to these strictures with the exception of Croft Port's sponsorship of the drama series *Rumpole of the Bailey*, at a third of the cost of the 'equivalent exposure using conventional spot advertising'.[21] What has subsequently become evident is that it is drama *series* that are most attractive to sponsors: the characters of such series tend to be middle or working class, there is the clear opportunity to build audience loyalty, and there is the likelihood that such series are likely to be repeated. As Murdock observes, this state of affairs is potentially worrisome if, in future, prime-time drama productions seek sponsorship as a means of part-funding. Such a situation would of course also accelerate the trend towards drama *series* (and *serials*) and thereby reduce the likelihood of other television fiction.[22]

So where do these recent changes leave the issue of editorial content and the influence of sponsorship? As the above example of *Rumpole of the Bailey* suggests, the sponsor may well be in a position to exercise influence on the overall mix and style of programming by supporting some projects rather than others, perhaps by 'favouring works and performers who are already well established and shunning controversy and experiment'.[23] And although there is no suggestion of interference with day-to-day creative or production decisions, it is surely disingenuous for the ITC to allow, as it has done, a medical insurance company to sponsor ITV's highly popular prime-time medical-romance *Peak Practice*.

The strategy and technique of product placement is another issue that regulators of both the BBC and commercial television will increasingly have to face. The technique is already apparent on television through Hollywood movies. This strategy, with a long history originating in 1930s Hollywood, was intensified in the 1980s following its success in such movies as *ET*, when for example, the lovable alien was 'enticed from his hiding place by a trail of Reese's Pieces sweets, producing a 300 per cent increase in the brand's sales'.[24] Most Hollywood movies now have multiple product placements, with goods ranging from nappies (diapers), cigarettes, cola, cars and, of course, clothes. Consider, for example, the US telemovie, *Stalking Laura* (1993), directed by Michael Switzer, starring Brooke Shields and shown on UK terrestrial television in 1995. Diet Cola was mentioned/seen at least on three occasions. Two scenes merit description. Despite being shot, and barely conscious, Brooke Shields (Laura) manages to stagger along an office corridor happily to discover a conveniently placed cup of cola. More crass is the wonderful moment when the stalker – a maniac who has killed dozens of innocent bystanders – talks to the hostage negotiator and all he asks for is a 'cola with plenty of ice'.

Such a strategy is found almost everywhere. *The Duty Chemist* is a Spanish soap which plays on Antenna 3 and centres on the owner of a chemist shop in the old quarter of Madrid. Spanish pharmaceutical (and other) companies queue up to take the opportunity to place their real-life products on the shelves of the Cano Pharmacy.

A major advantage of such a strategy of product placements is that they have an 'extended life in space and time': movies move from a theatrical release, on to home video, to a cable or satellite transmission and then, finally, on to broadcast television. And because they are designed to be embedded into the movie's action, they are invariably difficult to cut. Similarly, it is almost impossible to excise promotional materials from programmes like rock shows built substantially around video clips as the programmes in effect *are* such commercials. As an MTV spokesperson has put it, clients are attracted to the channel 'because the high production ads merge seamlessly into the high production videos to sell a total "rock'n'roll youth lifestyle" in which all desires and wants can be satisfied by buying commodities'.[25]

The onerous task thus facing public service broadcasting (including the ITV system of the 1990s) is how to continue to keep broadcasting out of the hands of advertisers.[26] How to keep programme content free from commercial considerations.

Family Viewing Policy

One of the key areas of concern about television centres on the suitability or otherwise of programmes for children. Younger members of audiences are generally regarded as lacking the psychological maturity to cope with certain types of programming and, therefore, the argument goes, they should be protected from exposure to unsuitable content as far as it is possible. At the same time only one in three television households have children aged up to 15 years, therefore leaving a great majority occupied by adult viewers only. So in addition to the need to protect children there is also a need to cater for the tastes of the wider adult audience. For this reason mainstream broadcasters employ a 'Family Viewing Policy' which aims to create a balance between these two sets of interests. Thus up to 9 p.m. in the evening, no material may be shown which could be regarded as 'unsuitable for children'. After that time there is to be a *gradual* relaxation of the rule.

In the 1994 survey, when questioned, over 60 per cent of viewers expressed the opinion that the responsibility for ensuring that children did not watch 'unsuitable programmes' lay squarely with parents themselves. Smaller numbers – about 30 per cent – felt that this responsibility should be *shared* between parents and broadcasters, while a few viewers adopted the 'passive' view that this duty lay *solely* with the broadcasters. The majority of viewers believed strongly that parents should control the amount of viewing, and times and programmes watched. Equally it was felt by the great majority of viewers that such control should be reinforced both by parental example and by watching and discussing television *as a family*. There was relatively little support for the strategy of allowing children their total freedom to view. Rather the general view was that parents should encourage their children to watch television in somewhat limited amounts, and, additionally, that parental control should be gradually relaxed as children grow older.

In general terms opinions did not vary greatly between viewers who had children aged up to 15 years living with them and those who didn't, although there was a tendency for those *without* children to be a little more protective. This is hardly surprising, as parents know, all too well, of the strength of peer group pressure and the inability to fight it, of their children's sophisticated televisual literacy and of the consequences of disagreeable conflict over what to watch. As we have earlier suggested perhaps those without children at home simply romanticize 'childhood'.

Nine out of ten viewers questioned knew of the Family Viewing Policy and of the principle of the 'watershed', and the majority of them knew that it was set at 9 p.m.

Where a non-terrestrial channel is encrypted or only available to cable customers on payment of an additional fee, its availability to children will, therefore, be more restricted and parents may, in principle, thereby assume a greater degree of control over whether their children will be able to watch. Under these circumstances, the ITC's Programme Code permits the point at which parents may be expected to share responsibility for what is viewed to be shifted from 9 p.m. to as early as 8 p.m. depending on the nature of the actual programme concerned. Similarly the Code states that material of a more adult kind than would be acceptable at the same time on a more broadly available channel may be shown after 10 p.m. and before 5.30 a.m. This flexibility does not, however, extend to basic subscription channels.[27]

Only one in five viewers questioned said that they were aware that such a policy was operated by cable and satellite channels, although those with children at home were a little more aware of the policy. Similarly those viewers who subscribed to satellite or cable services were far more likely to be aware of the ITC's policy.

Viewers were then asked as to their thoughts on the timing of the watershed for both terrestrial and non-terrestrial channels. The 9 p.m. watershed on ITV, BBC and Channel 4/S4C was regarded by seven out of ten respondents as 'about right', while over one in five thought it was 'too early' and one in twenty thought it was 'too late'. Viewers with young children aged up to nine years old were more likely to agree that the 9 p.m. scheduling restriction was 'about right' than were respondents with older children aged 10 to 15 years, who were more likely than any others to say that it was too early.

These sentiments and expressed attitudes have remained more or less stable over the years with, for example, similar findings being reported in 1984.[28] Although ten years earlier in 1974 the comparable IBA survey reported that over half of the viewers questioned believed that programmes 'which children should not see' were shown at times when 'children might be watching'.[29] Since that time, of course, there has been the introduction of the Family Viewing Policy and, relatedly, there has been a slight relaxation in the views about what is and what is not suitable for children to watch.

Opinions concerning the two scheduling restriction times on cable and satellite television channels revealed a majority of all viewers saying that 8 p.m. and 10 p.m. were 'about right', with fewer than one in ten preferring the time of 9 p.m. One in five thought that 8 p.m. was too early, while very few viewers thought it was too late. The watershed at 10 p.m. was seen as either too late or too early by only a very small proportion of viewers. Viewers who could actually receive cable or satellite channels were far more likely to endorse both times as being right for the types of material associated with them compared with viewers with terrestrial broadcast channels only.

A number of satellite and cable channels possess the possibility of parental-control devices which allow subscribers to control which programmes are received, potentially giving parents additional control over their children's viewing. Almost three-quarters of all viewers were, however, unaware of these devices, although those with children at home were slightly more aware of their existence. Such awareness – almost one in two viewers – was greatly increased among those who actually subscribed to cable or satellite channels. Among this latter group four out of ten claimed to own such a device, although 80 per cent of them said they had never in fact used it.

A fundamental problem with such survey findings is that in such surveys parents have a tendency to express those opinions which they believe are expected by the interviewer. No parents wish to admit that they happily sit young children in front of *Total Recall*, *Silence of the Lambs* or a gruesome episode of *Cracker* munching merrily away on their crisps, while they themselves prepare dinner. Research has long suggested, for example, that while some parents may forbid their children from viewing certain 'adult' programmes, and set bedtime limits on viewing, or discursively talk with their children about television, others, however, do not do so.[30] As Gunter and Svennevig report, many parents claim to be concerned about their children's 'indiscriminate television watching and claim to exert some sort of control over it', but in practice they argue this appears 'less likely to be true'.[31] There will obviously and sadly be parents who are totally irresponsible and take little interest in their children's viewing, while other parents may well be somewhat over-protective.

Children are, however, extremely televisually literate, and only rarely can they be viewed as passive victims of the medium. Children's own accounts of their television viewing certainly adds an extra dimension to the aforementioned viewer's opinions about the Family Viewing Policy, and, indeed, throws light onto the role of television in children's lives.

Girl (10): If my dad says I'm not allowed to watch [it] I just wait 'till he's gone to bed and I watch it on the video in my room . . .[32]

Boy (11): On Saturday night I watched a bit of the *Buddha of Suburbia*, because my parents were out. We got a video out then . . . and also an Indian take-away. We ate it in front of *Gladiators*. Just me and my sister. Most things on Saturday nights are crap like *Catchphrase* and *Gladiators*.

Girl (11): . . . they just leave them in front of the telly. I think it [the watershed] should be earlier. But nine-year-olds and stuff they'll want to know about these things because people are going to be talking about them at school . . . it's just stupid if they're kept protected their entire lives 'cos they'll just grow up being scared to do anything because they won't know about anything . . . it's like not letting people walk in the dark, some people aren't allowed to walk in the dark, but when they grow up they're going to be too scared to.

This same young girl added that she thought the watershed was a bad idea, because apart from the good it does in protecting very young children, the fact is that 'different children cope with different things, and it's not really the age it's just the actual child'.

These pre-teenage viewers do not watch television in a vacuum but rather bring to the screen the knowledge which they develop in the course of their family and school lives.

> Girl (11): . . . the telly isn't there to be your parents. I think the parents some-times leave the telly to look after their children . . . it makes children grumpy . . . isn't there some kind of energy that comes out of television – fuzziness? – my mum's nursing magazine says that it can actually make your children grumpy watching it . . . they're bored but they don't know they're bored.

But they, none the less, firmly believe that there are lessons to be learned from the experience.

> Girl (11): I know my mum doesn't know a lot about drugs and stuff – some people's mums do but my mum doesn't, so she couldn't tell me about those things, and I can learn about these things from the telly . . . I know I could read a book, but that's boring.

And such youthful viewers understood perfectly well how easy it is for the television to become a surrogate parent, a third parent.

> Girl (12): . . . your parents don't talk to you about gay people like for ages, or about rape, 'cos they don't bother, because they know you'll learn from the telly, but I suppose if the telly wasn't there then they would.

It is of course an open question as to what the *precise* value is of children learning about, say, AIDS, drug use or sexual behaviour *directly* from tele-vision drama. Such information derived without a suitable context, or in insufficient detail is, perhaps, almost useless. None the less, most of these viewers held opinions as to how valuable television was in family life, es-pecially with young children around and when used sparingly.

> Girl (11): When my little brother comes home from school and he's totally worn out and mum needs to cook the tea she will put him in front of the telly for half an hour because he's too worn out to do anything active, and then when he's watched a couple of programmes, she says why don't you do some drawing or something . . .

Modern Childhood

A 1995 survey reported in the *Los Angeles Times* suggested that 'most children say that what they see on television' encourages them to show disrespect for their parents, to lie and engage in aggressive behaviour, and to 'take part in sexual activity too soon'.[33]

Whether it is actually television itself that is to blame for such behavioural changes is difficult – almost impossible – to say, but what certainly is true is that as the decades unfold the concept of 'childhood' itself continues to change. Nicholas Tucker laments that contemporary children eat similar food to adults, drink alcohol while in their early teens, and watch the same television programmes as adults.[34] Indeed, soaps like *Neighbours* and *Home and Away* are now conventionally transmitted in what was previously children's hour. As Marina Warner sensitively observes, the modern emphasis on sex differences, 'on learning masculinity and femininity', begins with the clothing of infants and has developed significantly since the 1920s. The portraits of the English aristocracy which showed children clothed as adults – with jewels and powdered wigs – were displaying the status of their families; 'but the little girl in the black dress, patent pumps, lipstick and earrings who was brought out in the finale of a recent Chanel collection was showing off her body, and looked like a travesty of the sex-free youth children are supposed to enjoy'.[35] Children's magazines are far more explicit than ever before and, most menacingly, advertisers sniff around them and view them primarily as consumers not *children*. Children see little less of each other after school – unless heavily parentally policed – and are more often than not kept indoors because of fears about molesters, traffic and other potential threats. The days of unsupervised games in the park are more or less over as are the mass visits to Saturday morning cinema: childhood has become a more private affair and less under community control.

Perhaps we should no longer speak of 'childhood' at all, rather simply view all children – as advertisers tend to – as a market segment. Besides which, now that children are able to theoretically 'divorce' their own parents, perhaps it is the adults who are in need of protection. Or perhaps we are indeed returning to the Middle Ages in which, as Philippe Ariès has argued, there was no such thing as childhood.[36] In his view children were merely small people, unprotected and severely treated.

In his book *Out of the Garden*, an illuminating case study of US television programmes built around toy ranges, Stephen Kline asserts that 'as we listen to children's conversations we can't help but notice that the market touches their lives more directly than ever before'.[37] Children's preferences in toys and computer games as well as their access to television, guides most of their free-time activities and these activities, he argues, are profoundly linked to their sense of happiness. By the time of graduation from high school the average American child would have spent over 20,000 hours watching television and only 11,000 hours in the classroom. More worrying, argues Kline, is that a child would have been exposed *each year* to about 20,000 commercials' messages (indeed, overall, American viewers watch a total of 3.5 million years of TV commercials per year).[38] Kline maintains that commercial television – both in the USA and the UK – has been given no sense of its cultural mandate or mission: that the cumulative weight of over 40 years of market-driven experimentation with programming has demonstrated that, increasingly, business interests, not cultural and artistic considerations, are the medium's priority.

Of central concern to Stephen Kline is the growth in children's fantasy programming, aimed at ensuring that children buy the toy characters they see on the screen. This form of embedded persuasion – the promotion of toys within the programmes themselves – is far more effective than spot advertising. And, of course, the UK is not exempt from this practice. The Controller of Children's Programmes at ITV has recently argued that as 'advertisers want children because they have a large discretionary income', it would be no surprise if children's drama on ITV moved away from reality-based series and towards fantasy and adventure.[39] Indeed, in late 1994 the number one children's programme in the USA, Australia, and much of Europe including the UK, was *The Mighty Morphin Power Rangers*, a comic mix of fashion, martial arts, space adventures and monsters. In this blend of modern action and ancient sparring six high-school students have been recruited by a kind and powerful inter-dimensional being, Zordon. Their mission is to defend the earth against Rita Repulsa, a horned witch who lives on the moon and seeks to control the universe. Jason, Billy, Zack, Tommy, Kimberly and Trini have special powers to 'morph' into Spandex-clad super-heroes, drawing their power from the spirit of ancient dinosaurs.

The series has been highly successful and in the UK, GMTV have screened the first 60 episodes, with another 60 being available. And a *Power Rangers* movie was successfully released in the summer of 1995. The retail toy sales in the USA reached $450m while in the UK they have already reached £15m,[40] and in 1994 *Power Rangers* won the British Association of Toy Retailers award for 'toy of the year'. Similarly US publishers, Marvel, have invested £45m on the new *Spider-Man* cartoon series, one of which has already been bought by the BBC: the investment will be well worth it for the massive merchandising profits. This is perhaps, the shape of things to come.

Kline's disapproval is not of children's television *per se* which, he argues, *does* provide a distinctive and beneficial cultural product for young children's minds. Rather he is concerned when the product is devoid of moral purpose and provided solely for commercial reasons. It is not only the embedded persuasions of (toy) character-led series that influence children to be primarily consumers of course, but also the straightforward spot advertising that children watch. Research has consistently shown how parents feel harassed by children after their continual exposure to toy commercials,[41] especially over the Christmas period when almost three-quarters of all commercials aimed at children appear.[42] Perhaps it is now time to see Christmas merely as a seasonal consumption rite in which toys not only provide the emotional fuel but the central interpretation of spiritual experience for the child.

Older children, however, are not the problem. They are all too aware of the fallibility of commercials: that they are neither necessarily 'true' or that they will bring fulfilment and 'happiness'.

> Boy (10): The advert for 'old' Flash says it's rubbish and they show grime and everything, but then there is this 'new' Flash. But before the 'new' Flash came out they said the 'old' one was excellent.

But they are aware that younger children (as they themselves were once but soon forget) are inevitably more affected by such commercial messages:

> Girl (11): . . . adverts on TV for children's toys just make children want them. They go and nag their parents. The parents don't have the money to buy anything for them and they feel really guilty and they can't give them anything, and the children just harass and harass them, and the parents feel worse and worse.

Another child refers to her brother's delight in watching *The Mighty Morphin Power Rangers* on TV:

> Girl (12): He watches it with his friends, he's engrossed in it, then suddenly a fight happens, and he'll jump up and start kicking everyone and running around, doing Karate and yelling 'Power Rangers', then he'll sit down again, and he seems like he's in a trance . . .

Prior to Disney's 1950s *Mickey Mouse Club* children's television advertising in the USA totalled only about $1m per annum, and the product array was extremely narrow. But the *Club* was an enormous success, focusing as it did on the idea of peer culture. The *Club* included a peer group whose adventures and exploits provided the narrative link to the *pot-pourri* of the other animated and dramatic items. Most importantly the *Club* provided a first glimpse of an exclusively children's subculture created by television. As Kline puts it, advertisers could 'now direct their communication specifically at children – to explore new ways to shape children's wants and win their influence within the family circle'.[43] In due course television advertising rose quickly from about $25m a year in 1956 to approximately $750m by 1987.

In the various campaigns created to market toys on television the role of fantasy quickly emerged as an important dimension. Barbie was not in fact a baby doll but rather a fashion model: her identity was tied inextricably with the imagery of the glamour world of teenage fashion and romance. Thus, instead of finding a suitable television programme to sponsor, or patiently waiting for a popular series to survive a season in order to create spin-off characters, toy-makers decided to develop their *own* television characters and programme concepts. As, for example, in the early 1980s when Mattel produced *He-Man and the Masters of the Universe*. This series which 'brilliantly blended advanced technology, medieval magic and bulging muscles', came to define the 'basic thematic structures of most character narratives'.[44] In such series toy merchandisers renovated television's story-telling potential but, argues Kline, in the process they 'left behind the innocent garden world of literature for a cosmic battleground of mock-heroic adventure'.[45] The merchandisers no doubt did not give too much thought as to the impact they were having on children's culture, but were simply trying to promote their products with the most favoured narrative motifs. But what precisely is the impact of 'character-marketing' television series?

What concerns Kline is not, for example, the basic issue of the mimicking of violence, but rather the impact of such series on *play*. With this issue there is, as we would expect, contrary evidence and different interpretations as to its significance. A number of researchers believe that playing with character toys may beneficially encourage children to fantasize emotive scenes from television until they experience *in play* their control over those situations. Indeed, such researchers speculate that such imaginative play might even reduce the likelihood of aggressive responses to, say, violent programmes because children can express troublesome conflicted feelings through their fantasy life. Kline, however, strongly disagrees and in turn argues that although it is 'difficult to prove that kids are more isolated, consumer-conscious or less creative than they were, say, ten years ago, it is hard to deny evidence of an emergent pattern or "orthodoxy" of play being promoted through television':[46] such orthodoxy is created by the repeated exposure to television commercials and character-marketing series, as the child subsequently comes to accept the merchandiser's definitions of what the toy 'means'. In this respect television *narrows* the framework of play because the possibilities for *pretending* are confined to the actions and situations associated with the particular toys.

> Playing with these toys in part means playing with the identities – the technologies they use, the cars they drive, the magic powers they possess. But it rarely involves their subjectivity – the feelings, philosophies, wishes or hopes that these pretend characters experience. It is rare in our observations of these children at play to see them use these characters to express the inner experience of human desire and feeling in a simulated play situation.[47]

Character-marketing fantasy toys render it difficult for parents to guide their children's imaginative play or, indeed, make it relevant to their actual experience, especially as the television narratives strictly define the rules and outcomes of play. 'Moto can't fly, he's a motorcycle', 'Zordon isn't like that', 'Kimberley doesn't do that'. Character-marketing fantasy toys provide few opportunities for children in play to mesh their lived experience with their fantasies. As educationalist John Holt wrote, over 25 years ago, if we try to make children fantasize these fake fantasies like the ready-made ones of television we will, in time, drive out most of their true fantasies which actually help them make sense of their world: 'Children will have confronted stage fright, star flight, cosmic holocaust, beauty pageants and scheming witches in their daily play, but will rarely avail themselves of the chance to anticipate and rehearse for a new sibling, a dying parent or a runaway pet'.[48]

Kline concludes by arguing that playing with such 'television toys' cannot be described as a profoundly emotional activity, simply an energetic and pleasurable 'activity' that mingles fantasy with manipulating objects. He laments the way in which our culture has allowed manufacturers and marketers enormous powers to meddle in the key realms of children's culture – the peer group, fantasy, stories and play. Business and manufacturing interests trying to maximize their profits cannot be expected to be over-concerned about cultural values or social objectives: 'the marketplace will never inspire children with high ideals or positive images of the personality, provide stories which help them to adjust to life's tribulations or promote play activities that are most help to their maturation'.[49]

Cultural Discontinuities

It is frequently asserted that by virtue of the popularity of television, the CD-Rom and computers, the 'literature culture is disappearing', and, moreover, that children's tastes are changing in a quite profound way. Many cultural commentators mourn such changes. They describe the 'anti-language assumptions of our culture', and equally complain of the steady decline of intellectual and literacy skills.[50] But all this is *very* new, so modern perhaps that it is unwise to make such a judgement. Take the example of *writing* itself, which has been traceable in human societies for little more than 6,000 years and thus a short time given that the history of *Homo sapiens* now is thought to be about a quarter of a million years old.[51] Before such a literate culture there was oral society, in which cultural continuity was much more limited. Conversations did take things forward, but then constantly left behind what was simply to become forgotten noise.

On the other hand, literacy enabled the development of a new kind of thought and helped create entirely new relations between people. However, such a stupendous change was not without its costs for as Inglis reminds us, the 'important part of our lives to all of us is that lived in direct exchange with others: a book is no substitute for a body'.[52]

None the less, enigmatic story-telling, so central in oral culture, still survives and in such diverse places as Java, Ireland and Morocco there are still individuals who can tell stories for days on end without repeating themselves. Interestingly enough, the Nobel Prize-winning poet Octavio Paz, in response to the question 'will books disappear?', comments that poetry began as the spoken word and that 'television offers the possibility of returning to the oral form, as it combines words with images'.[53] For this to be at all possible though, television would need a variety of different audiences, not a homogeneous one; however, for Paz, the commercialization of words and messages will unfortunately lead to the one audience. The mass audience.

In the debate which could be paraphrased 'reading versus television in the lives of children', supporters of the written text argue that, unlike television, literature is a collaboration between author and reader with the latter reading at his or her own pace returning to previous pages at will if so desired, and to some degree controlling what is read. Faced with such an argument, perhaps television cannot offer a strong defence. But maybe it is more apposite to say that instead of replacing reading, television more than likely replaces non-reading.[54] On the evidence available the issue is, as always, complex and needs to be treated with extreme caution.

Until 1990 children's book sales grew steadily, but since that time there has been a slight decrease in such sales. On the question of the reading abilities of adults between the ages of 22 and 74 (in England and Wales) almost 40 per cent are said to be average, almost 30 per cent good, 20 very good and only 10 per cent poor or very poor. While statistics from the Department of Education demonstrate that the proportions of boys and girls who left school without a GCSE or equivalent has steadily declined since 1975, and indeed the proportion of adults in Britain with qualifications at above GCSE grades A–C has doubled since 1975.[55] Clearly if reading *is* being replaced by a television culture it does not appear to be having a deleterious effect on literacy or educational performance.

However, it is the computer and video game that have given rise to the cultural discontinuities of the 1980s and 1990s and sharpened the differences between generations. Intimately connected with television and viewing behaviour such consumer items have, in a remarkably short time, risen to prominence especially in *boys'* lives and have raised new fears in the minds of those not working or playing with them, or with little understanding of them.

The video and computer-games market is valued at something over $17 billion worldwide, with the UK market alone being estimated at $1 billion. Some children are quite insatiable in their pursuit of such activities: in the USA the Nintendo Fun Club alone receives over 120,000 telephone calls a week from game-hungry children. The market has exhibited quite astonishing growth, from almost a zero base in the mid-1980s it is now fore-cast to exceed $30 billion world-wide by 1998.[56]

While the 'gamers' (principally 10–15-year-old boys) are interested in novelty, better game content and playability, critics rather concern them-selves with issues over the violent content of many games. However, research suggests that most adults are less concerned with such issues of violence, and instead more concerned with the games' supposed addictive nature. In research carried out in 1993 almost half of the adults interviewed expressed concern over such addictive qualities, while a quarter believed the games were anti-social and discouraged conversation and a little over 10 per cent were concerned that they may encourage aggression or that there was too much violence in the games.[57]

At the beginning of the 1990s Nintendo, to name but one video-game system, was described in the following manner:

> ... like a '50s fantasy wedded with a '60s nightmare and '80s technology. It's about actually getting inside television and becoming one with it, being *of* it instead of outside looking in. Nintendo games call for good hand–eye co-ordination, and the capacity to handle myth, lore, a multitude of techniques, nuance, frustration, danger, betrayal, the fact that there's always somebody bigger and more powerful than you are, and the existential inevitability that – even if you kill the bad guys and save the girl – eventually you will die.[58]

Some research in the USA confirms the fears that the so-called 'addiction' to the game *does* lead to a distinct lack of conversation and social intercourse. One particular piece of research found that the 'gamers' rated video games higher than human companions as, unlike them, the games were more excit-ing and far more fun to be with. Indeed, they were an alternative form of companionship. Unlike television which helps create a common culture – most children know *EastEnders*, *Home and Away*, *Blind Date* and *Gladiators* – video games are profoundly individualist. In a vein similar to Kline's concerns about the limits of synthetic fantasy play, researchers posed the question as to the possible effect of the flat, two-dimensional, visual and externally supplied image, and of the lifeless florid colours of the screen on the development of childrens own *inner* capacity to bring to birth living, mobile, creative images of their own.[59] Only time may provide any clear answers. Interestingly enough, however, some recent research in the UK suggests that long hours playing video games do not necessarily transform children into withdrawn, anti-social and aggressive teenagers. This research, conducted into the lives of 13 and 14-year-old boys who played for long hours, argued that such boys expressed higher self-esteem and lower levels of aggression than those who didn't play, despite the violent content of most popular computer games. The researchers also found that such games were, overwhelmingly, a social activity, with teenage boys pre-ferring to play against each other than against the computer.[60]

The concern expressed over the violent content in particular games is that these games tend to feed into masculine fantasies of control, power and destruction. *Eat him, burn him, zap him*, is the message; not one of co-operation. Which is, of course, why boys play with such games. The fact that boys and girls have different cultural tastes is well known. For example, in the case of comics and magazines, between the age of seven and ten the most popular titles are read by about the same proportion of boys and girls. But by 11 onwards they have very different tastes indeed: boys will be reading *Sega Power* and *Gamesmaster* (as well as *Viz*), while girls will be turning the pages of *Smash Hits*, *Sky*, and *Just Seventeen*.[61] And, of course, much television aimed specifically at younger children is gendered: *Thundercats* for boys, *Barbie* for girls. Recent research carried out by Stephen Heppell on the ownership and use of home computers found, not surprisingly, that boys claimed greater ownership and use than did girls (interestingly, he also found that twice as many boys as girls said they hardly ever read books).[62]

But for many critics the particular problem with video games is, as we have seen, not simply that more boys than girls play with them but that the content of such games feeds masculine fantasies. And not merely the simple (but unacceptable) punishment of women, rather, as Marina Warner argued in her 1994 Reith Lectures, video games are 'scrupulous about current taboos: most of their heroes can't be seen to attack and murder as such'. As a result, other than the damsel in distress or the occasional female street-fighter (invariably as aggressive as the males), women have pretty much disappeared from the plots altogether. The effect of this absence of women from this 'all-engulfing imaginary world of boys is to intensify the sense of apartness, of alienation, of the deep oppositeness of the female sex'.[63] This can hardly be a healthy state of affairs, and must surely be sowing the seeds of future fear and loathing.

In his illuminating book on the life of Alan Turing, one of the pioneers of the computer revolution, David Bolter points to the profound limitations actually imposed by new technologies. At one level we may well be empowered, but on another we become quite ignorant of history and unaware of the natural world that surrounds us and maybe insensitive to deeper human motives.[64] Similar sentiments were, of course, expressed at the time of the birth of television.

Children and Television

It is perhaps true to suggest that the modern parent, juggling with jobs, time, 'family life', other people's opinions and social expectations, finds it somewhat hard to imagine what parents did with children before television came along to absorb three or four hours of their child's day. What has been erased from collective memory is the array of daily preoccupations, like talking and playing and working together, and being alone, that constituted family life before the advent of television. This is not to say that all children or families are happy with the reliance on television in everyday life.

> Girl (12): . . . we moved our telly into the other room, sort of like an experiment to see if we'd *go* into the other room – the other room was really uncomfortable, this one was really comfy and decorated – that one was really horrible and just a few chairs, and they put the telly in the uncomfortable room to see if we'd go in there or not – most of the nights I'd go into the comfy room and talk to my family and stuff . . .

No one surely doubts the potential value of television for children: it may provide them with common interests to share with their peers, may create discussion (and argument) within the family, may provide companionship, and it can entertain and inform them. Indeed, the television of the 1970s and 1980s successfully introduced children to environmental issues and in so doing spawned the generation that now follows Friends of the Earth, Greenpeace and other ecological movements.[65] Critics, on the other hand, point out that while print literacy excluded children from particular aspects of the adult world they should be spared from, television provides no such real barriers and accordingly exposes children to adult preoccupations. Of course it could be argued that keeping children ignorant of such things merely serves to stunt the growth of the child's own self-developed critical faculties.

Critics of television have even accused the broadly revered *Sesame Street* – which aims to teach children to read – of undermining intellectual and educational processes: '*Sesame Street* encourages children to love school only if school is like *Sesame Street*'.[66] Such critics argue that in 'television teaching' such notions as perplexity or exposition is destined to be a super-highway to low ratings: nothing will be taught on television that cannot both be visualized and placed in a theatrical context. Schools, they argue, simply aren't like that. Television educators, on the other hand, point to such programmes as *Barney and Friends* – featuring a six-foot bright purple Tyrannosaurus Rex with a plump green belly – which is enthusiastically watched by one in three pre-school children in the USA. The series, which is transmitted on GMTV and The Children's Channel in the UK, is considered educationally, ethically, ecologically and politically correct and, according to the Yale Family Television and Consultation Centre, each episode contains at least 98 different teaching elements.[67] It is, of course, difficult to know whether such young children are truly informed or merely amused by such series.

On contemporary television 'realistic' drama, especially soaps, adventure programmes, especially movies; and comedy programmes appear to be those most attractive to children. The popularity of *Neighbours*, especially for those aged between 9 and 15 years, is due both to its convenient scheduled transmission time, and the over-dramatization of the plots and the number of younger characters involved: truancy, teenage romance, school bullying, vandalism and drug-taking are all elements of the soap, but are wrapped up in an aesthetic which guarantees a speedy and comfortable resolution to every such issue.

Table 8.2   Top 20 programmes for children by TVR, Jan.–Dec. 1994*

Programmes	Channel	Day	Date	TVR	'000's	Channel Share in percentages
1 *Honey, I Shrunk The Kids*	ITV	Sun	09.01.94	40.6	3,868	82
2 *Gladiators Final*	ITV ·	Sat	17.12.94	37.7	3,602	76
3 *National Lottery Live*	BBC1	Sat	19.11.94	36.8	3,515	74
4 *Gladiators*	ITV	Sat	12..11.94	36.5	3,490	75
5 *Do It Yourself Mr Bean*	ITV	Mon	10.01.94	35.7	3,399	78
6 *Neighbours*	BBC1	Tue	23.03.94	35.5	3,383	79
7 *Ghostbusters II*	ITV	Sun	27.02.94	34.4	3,272	76
8 *Three Men & A Little Lady*	ITV	Sun	06.02.94	34.2	3,254	78
9 *EastEnders*	BBC1	Thu	27.10.94	33.4	3,189	88
10 *Uncle Buck*	BBC1	Mon	03.01.94	32.0	3,050	68
11 *Gladiators Celebrity Challenge*	ITV	Sat	24.12.94	31.1	2,974	62
12 *ET*	BBC1	Fri	01.04.94	31.1	2,961	69
13 *Turner and Hooch*	ITV	Sun	16.01.94	31.0	2,955	76
14 *Casualty*	BBC1	sat	19.11.94	30.5	2,919	75
15 *Back To School Mr Bean*	ITV	Tue	26.10.94	30.5	2,918	63
16 *EastEnders*	BBC1	Tue	25.10.94	29.8	2,847	86
17 *Mind The Baby Mr Bean*	ITV	Mon	25.04.94	29.3	2,790	68
18 *Vice Versa*	ITV	Sun	23.01.94	27.9	2,654	70
19 *Superman Film*	ITV	Sun	03.04.94	27.9	2,654	74
20 *Noel's House Party*	BBC1	Sat	15.01.94	27.8	2,649	64

Note: * Excluding multiple occurrences.
Source: Taylor Nelson AGB/BARB/AGB Television, 1995.

Children's viewing habits vary with the social class of the child's father. Those children from semi-skilled, unskilled and unemployed households tend to watch about five hours more television per week than those children from 'upper' and managerial households. Much of the difference is made up by the amount of time spent watching ITV by the first group of viewers.[68]

One of the many problems involved in any discussion of the relationship between children and television is that children differ considerably in their maturation. Some confident ten-year-olds appear more psychologically mature than an insecure thirteen-year-old; and a five-year-old may be more knowledgeable of 'the world' than an over-protected eight-year-old. Therefore we are only able to generalize. As with adult viewers children also *read* programmes subjectively: where some children may see irony in a programme, others may completely miss it; while one child is made fearful, another one may well laugh. Tastes differ widely too. However, one thing all children do with television is compare and contrast their own lives with those of the children, families and characters they see on the screen.

On the screen there have been subtle if not extensive changes since the mid-1980s. For example, although women still remain generally unfairly represented on television – they are offered fewer roles in drama, and are more likely to be asked to undress – and still remain subservient to their screen husbands in television families, changes are nevertheless taking place. Television tends to provide more images of middle-class than working-class families and, invariably, the husband and father figure is seen as responsible for the major decisions, financial or otherwise.[69] Any departure from this pattern tends to be restricted to comedy programmes especially sit-coms. Indeed, the central characters of *Roseanne* and *Grace Under Fire* are clear examples of powerful non-stereotypical women. But in other genres too changes are taking place, for instance, in the case of the resourceful female crimefighter of the *Prime Suspect* films, and of the BBC's *Chandler and Co.* Or consider the example of the beautifully-crafted *The New Adventures of Superman* which has managed successfully to translate the old macho super-hero into a new-mannish model. Clark Kent still possesses extraordinary powers but he is also a vulnerable and sensitive soul. More significantly, however, Lois Lane is thoroughly modern – extremely successful and determinedly independent. Similarly, both the female and male FBI investigators of *The X-Files*, Scully and Mulder, constantly express their acceptance of each other as equals. This is not to suggest that stereotypes have been erased from the television screen – consider, for a moment, the role of the bimbo hostess on Channel 4's supposedly postmodern *Don't Forget Your Toothbrush* – but it is apparent nevertheless that changes *are* taking place. No programme-maker in their right mind would consciously ignore the prominence and visibility of women in public life, or hide or debase them on the screen.

Programming aimed specifically at children – such programmes as *Blue Peter*, *Byker Grove*, *Grange Hill*, *Wizadora*, *The Geeks*, and *The Borrowers* – has changed considerably since the 1950s. Over the subsequent decades the Reithian notion of balance between edification and entertainment was progressively tilted in favour of the latter. And as early as the mid-1950s children were being perceived as consumers, not just passive viewers, and, indeed, were gently encouraged to buy Sooty puppets or *Muffin the Mule* merchandise.[70] By the late 1970s the introduction of Saturday morning magazine programmes like the *Multi-Coloured Swap Shop*, and later by such shows as ITV's *Motormouth* and the BBC's *Going Live*, children were no longer seen solely as active viewers but almost *exclusively* as consumers. On such programmes pop stars promote their singles and CDs as do their video clips, while celebrities talk about their forthcoming television series or movies. The idea of children's television as edification to all intents and purposes became redundant. The up-side to this state of affairs was that these contemporary programmes for the young 'take the *part of the child*', attempting to appropriate elements of their culture, compared with previous broadcasters who when addressing children, took the part of the parent, teacher or adult.[71] But there *is* another down-side too. As Stephen Wagg has pointed out, children's television – especially Saturday morning magazine programmes – troubles 'less and less to mediate the world to the child, or to impart knowledge or skills'. Instead, and in tandem with other media, television '*is* the world, and it happily discusses itself'.[72]

By the time children reach the age of six years of age, they are relatively sophisticated viewers; by nine even more so, and at eleven they are experts. In such views both irreverence and discrimination is expressed towards programming, as these extracts from the television diaries- of two 11-year-olds demonstrate.

> Girl (11): I then watched *EastEnders*. It was after Bianca's party and a bit funny. Pat is such a shit character. I then watched *Animal Hospital*. I wouldn't have bothered, but I couldn't be bothered to do my homework – Rolf Harris is just sooooo bad. I had to stop watching. Even bad enough to make me do my homework!

> Girl (11): 8.00, I watched a programme on Siamese twins – *Horizon*, was it? – it was brilliant. It was really moving and really interesting. 8.45 I watched the end of *Brookside*. I didn't really understand what was going on, but it was still quite exciting, especially when they dug up the body! (written for the author)

Given such a context television, thus, hardly appears as an heroic medium, instead an experience somewhat taken for granted. As one ten-year-old girl put it, 'when you come in, if there's nothing to do you just turn the telly on'. But she was also aware of its limitations: 'when I'm in and watching the telly it makes me feel really slobbish, you feel like you're wasting your life'. Another 11-year-old expressed a critical awareness of the dangers of living vicariously through television.

> Boy (11): . . . instead of sitting in front of the telly to find out things, they have to live the experience themselves. They could be out in the world getting a life rather than seeing it on the telly . . . a lot of people use the telly as an escape from real life . . .

It is now generally assumed that children are in many respects certainly 'much more active, sophisticated and critical viewers than is often assumed'. However, as David Buckingham has persuasively argued, in making such a claim there is a risk of replacing the conventional view of children 'as innocent and vulnerable with an equally sentimental view of them as "street-wise" and knowledgeable'.[73] Part of the problem for researchers is that many children claim – in a spirit of bravado – to have watched 'adult' material when, clearly, they have not. In Julian Wood's wide-ranging discussions with 14-year-old boys he recalls examples of such acts of bravado:

> All of Colin's friends said they had seen at least one of the *Nightmare on Elm Street* series (all of which are rated 18), though only two laid claim to more than three. However, the general consensus here was that Freddy Kruger was a 'wanker'. 'It's just for little kids, innit?' said Colin. 'All right when you're about ten or eleven', added Steve, as if this was decades ago rather than a few years ago.[74]

In Buckingham's own conversations with young children – all under ten years of age – many were keen to describe scenes from adult movies which they had not seen but had heard about or had seen the trailers. Interestingly enough 'the news' although considered by them to be adult viewing, was roundly reviled by most of such children. There was very little status attached to watching it, rather it was something that simply had to be endured.[75]

Children and the 'Effects' of Television

Beavis and Butt-Head, the cartoon which plays on MTV and Channel 4 was, in 1992, blamed for the death of a two-year-old child in Ohio who was killed in a fire started by her five-year-old brother, after he allegedly had watched the programme. Until that time the regular bouts of animal torture and pyrotechnics engaged in by the two cartoon characters had largely gone unnoticed by the critics. But following the Ohio incident the programme was variously called 'Sesame Street *for psychopaths*' and described as 'pure societal poison, glorifying losers, violence and criminality'. The alleged aim of the producers of the programme was to 'send up' children who mindlessly watched MTV and who were influenced by it, but critics argued that young children simply did not understand such 'satire'.[76]

In Britain the issue of the relationship between television and violence once again was discussed following the 1993 murder by two ten-year-old boys of a two-year-old child, Jamie Bulger. In particular, the press seized on the fact that a horror video *Child's Play 3* had been found in the home of one of the ten-year-old boys, although his father claimed his son had never actually seen it. The details of the actual murder were rewritten as a gruesome re-enactment of the film, and subsequently video shops across the UK hastily removed it from their shelves.

Historically the attention given to the potential harm of television viewing has generally outweighed that devoted to its potential benefits, despite the fact that it is the nation's (the world's?) favourite and best-loved leisure activity. None the less, the issue of the possible *effects* of television creates strong and partisan views among critics, researchers and members of the public alike. It is, however, a difficult issue either to conceptualize or research.

To begin with there is the tendency for critics to talk about the effects of television on *other* viewers, but rarely themselves. As Barwise and Ehrenberg observe, 'people rarely say that *they themselves* have been made, for instance, more violent, oversexed, materialistic, or radically intolerant by watching television programmes'.[77] Additionally, the questions often asked about such possible effects, but they were formulated with less than precision. For example, are we actually talking about intentional or unintentional effects, long-term or short-term consequences, of influence rather than effects, and of such alleged influence over a person's knowledge, attitudes, beliefs or behaviour? Richard Hoggart alludes to such complexity when he asserts that the 'gradual psychic changes are matched by changes in linguistic use', so that we never quite see ourselves as others see us – we actually alter the language to match. For example, through television we have perhaps gradually *in fact* become spiritual voyeurs, present at tragedy at the moment it happens yet incapable of being committed to it.[78]

On the other hand, there are those critics who believe that television does not deserve to have the complex and deep-rooted troubles of society – like family breakdown and high unemployment – laid squarely at its door. Others, meanwhile, point to the fact that viewers have the ability to discriminate between fictional screen violence and actual violence. For example, they can be riveted to a television story about a serial killer, deeply interested and intrigued by it yet feel utterly appalled at such real-life killers.

The issue is, of course, not new. In 1964 prominent psychologist Hans Eysenck claimed that the best way to destroy civilization was to pour out more and more violent fantasies through the media; while a television researcher suggested that televised Belfast street riots did more harm to young children than gun battles in Westerns – fictional violence could actually prove beneficial to some children, while 'realistic' violence was more likely to be copied; at the same time a police chief warned youngsters of the perils of imitating Kung Fu film star Bruce Lee; and it was reported that a police force believed that two missing servicemen's sons were acting out an episode from *Colditz*; enraged claims were expressed over the fact that children were reading half as many books as they were in 1938; and a headline asked the question, has 'the TV set had become the third parent in your child's life?' Similarly, 1984, a decade later, saw the 'violence' of *The A-Team* criticized as was the 'bad language' of *Till Death Us Do Part*; at the same time 43 families in the Devon village of Peter Tavy turned off their TV sets for an experimental week, and the 'IBA Chief' denied that 'TV caused violence'.

So, generally, the issue of the possible effects or influence of television is encapsulated in the issue of screen violence and its effect on children (and secondarily other potentially susceptible individuals). For many years researchers did not actually bother either to directly observe children watching television or even to talk with them. It must be remembered of course that it is by no means certain that what children *say* is what they actually *do*; none the less, conversations with children do amply demonstrate their sophisticated knowledge of the medium as well as the external world it reflects, refracts and possibly shapes.

> Girl (11): . . . people go on *Blind Date* for a laugh . . . they don't go on there to meet their ideal bloke or woman . . . they do it to get on telly . . . I sit there with my sister and take the piss . . . I notice the horny blokes and pretty women . . .

On the issue of whether television accurately reflects 'reality' there are differences in opinion.

> Girl (12): I watch *Brookside*. It's so realistic and it covers real-life issues, like with the body in the garden of the Jordaches . . .

> Boy (11): No it isn't. I mean, look, they've got one street, with only about six houses and they've got a cult, a murderer, a gay, a drug-dealer . . .

Regarding the issue of the representation of violence on television, one 11-year-old believed she knew what was 'realistic' and what wasn't.

> Girl (11): In loads of things if someone gets shot they just fall to the ground and die immediately. But when you're shot even if you're shot in the heart you don't die immediately 'cos you bleed to death . . . Like when the police officer in *Cracker* was stabbed, that was really realistic, when he crawled into the street and talked into his video . . .

When she was subsequently asked how she knew how people 'really died', the same girl replied that she had seen a 'programme about it on the telly'.

Two other 12-year-old girls also talked about a particular episode of *Cracker* and its impact on their thoughts.

> Girl (12): In *Cracker* when it was the one about rape and in the last episode he breaks into Fitz's house and tried to kill his wife . . . I went upstairs to go to bed afterwards and I am sure I saw someone and I got really freaked out . . .

> Girl (12): Yeah . . . I thought I was going to be raped.

Children can be eminently perceptive about television, as is exemplified by this particular ten-year-old when discussing screen violence.

Girl (10): If you're perfectly normal, watching a programme won't make you any different. Cartoons have been around forever, people get flattened and stuff and everyone knows that doesn't happen ... So people who do violence after watching TV are obviously twisted to do that.

The James Bulger case of 1993, however, reopened the debate on television *effects* and a well-publicized contribution was made by Elizabeth Newson in her discussion paper *Video Violence and the Protection of Children*[79] prepared for the parliamentarians of both Houses. The debates that took place at the time on the possible harmful effects of violent videos (and computer games) echoed, asserted Bazalgette and Buckingham, 'those which have been made throughout history in relation to successive "new" media such as theatre, the press, popular literature, cinema, radio and television'. This remark is, however, somewhat disingenuous: the situations are *never* quite the same and such a perspective can only lead to relativism.[80]

Newson argued that she believed that it had become absolutely clear that welfare professionals had underestimated the degree of brutality and sadism that film-makers were able and willing to portray, and that they further underestimated the degree to which many children regularly watch adult-only videos. She was particularly concerned that children (and indeed adults) were being repeatedly exposed to images of vicious cruelty in the context of *entertainment* and amusement which, thereby, tended to justify such acts of violence. Central to her argument, applicable to television viewing too, was that 'the principle that what is experienced vicariously will have *some* effect on *some* people' was well established, and that audiences differ in their stability, their susceptibility to influence and relative levels of immaturity. Elizabeth Newson then cites numerous research projects and papers – in their thousands – which all point to conclusions which assert that 'watching specific acts of violence on the media has resulted in mimicry by children and adolescents of behaviour that they would otherwise, literally, have found unimaginable'.[81] She concludes, unhappily, that as some parents clearly cannot be trusted to restrict their children's viewing habits, 'society' must, therefore, take on the necessary responsibility in protecting children from material through active censorship.

It is important to point out that it would be wrong to imagine that the issue of deleterious media effects is of concern only to the so-called anti-libertarian or reactionary elements of society. Critics from the left also express concern. Rosalind Miles, for example, begins her contribution to the debate in sympathy with the lone-parent mother snatching a rare night out, or the struggling couple desperately working overtime who, thankful for the TV, may none the less allow it to act in the role of an electronic babysitter. Notwithstanding such sympathy Miles none the less argues that the actual pernicious influence of video nasties on young children's minds will not be fully manifest for a generation or more to come: though she adds that even in the short term, 'anyone who has any knowledge of films like the *Tool Boy Murders* and *Bloody Thirst* can have little doubt that child viewers must be getting a sensation of some sort'. The model of the susceptible human mind Miles employs in her argument is not one of a simple cause-and-effect type; rather, she argues, 'images sink into the great quagmire of the unconscious where they work away unseen'. And it is precisely video-watching, rather than movie-going, that so unsettles Miles who quotes actress Catherine Deneuve in support of her argument: 'I am disturbed by the video revolution. The idea that someone can freeze a frame, rewind and play a scene over and over again unleashes the possibility of sexual perversions I do not even like to think about'.[82]

In an exhaustive survey[83] of the research on television effects David Gauntlett vainly attempts to put the issue to rest. Given the specificity of his concerns and the confidence with which he presents his argument, it is perhaps worthwhile to concentrate on Gauntlett's contribution to this area of research. He believes the issue is unnecessarily hyped, as what surveys actually show is that people accept the need that on certain occasions controversial or even offensive material may well be shown. He also contends that viewers also believe that it is their right to choose when they watch, what they watch and with whom (including, of course, their children). Again it is worth repeating that this directly touches on a human dilemma: whereas we consider that almost no serious violence in real life is justified, we none the less appear enthusiastically to enjoy watching such acts of violence on the screen. But this does not, of course, imply that we would wish to be involved with real-life violence.[84]

Gauntlett next turns to the conundrum faced by those investigating these issues that as television is so deeply embedded in the fabric of everyday life, it is, therefore, extremely difficult to know whether the medium presents viewers with new attitudes and behaviours or merely reflects those that already exist? He then makes the valid point that the assumption that different viewers will respond in the same way to programmes or videos is quite misplaced and, besides, he adds, when the TV set is switched on the audience is, as we already know, often inattentive to it.

In terms of television programme *content* Gauntlett argues that programmes rarely contain violent acts without at the same time pro-social ones, and indeed vice versa. Generally this appears to be a reasonable argument, except when certain movies play on television like, for example, *Goodfellas* or when such films as the following may be broadcast: *The Honeymoon Killers*, *Silence of the Lambs*, and the completely morally blank *Henry: Portrait of a Serial Killer* (and its 1967 precursor, *In Cold Blood*, based on Truman Capote's novel of the same name). None of these films (let alone the thousands which are available on video) express that moral balance which Gauntlett earlier describes.

One of the central problems in considering such an issue concerns the *definition* of violence: there is, as Gauntlett rightly asserts, not simply 'violence' on television, rather there are different ways of 'showing violent encounters' each with different meanings, intentions and motives. Interestingly, he notes that the possibility that the portrayal of violence on television may have the 'effect of turning viewers *against* violence in real life – not through "catharsis" but simply by showing its unpleasantness – is almost never considered', even though, he adds, there seems little reason for considering it 'less likely than the popular reverse hypothesis'. Gauntlett argues that only the crudest reading of television programmes could suggest 'that violence and killing is "celebrated", as is sometimes alleged'. In fact such acts are usually to be seen at least as unpleasant and painful. However, though it is possible as the ITC, for example, has clearly demonstrated, to describe and itemize aspects of behaviour and subsequently to measure such behaviour, the context of violence and the differential 'readings' of such violence are left open, but it is none the less an attempt at understanding.

Somewhat disingenuously Gauntlett claims that the best any research can possibly hope for is to establish *correlations* between, say, the TV viewing habits of certain children and aggressive behaviour, but we cannot expect any *causal relationships* to be discerned. But surely no social scientist would ever expect to find causal relationships in *any* aspect of human social behaviour, and certainly not in one so complicated as this. Put simply, social science is imprecise and qualitatively different from natural science: correlations, however, may well be instructive and meaningful. If it is imagined that the debate is to be settled only by the establishment of causal relationships we will be waiting a long time, maybe forever.

The argument that postulates that exposure to television portrayals of violence may 'desensitize' viewers to the unpleasantness of real-life violence is, argues Gauntlett, not supported by any 'methodologically sound research', neither is the argument that television turns children into mindless 'zombies' unable to discern the difference 'between television and the real world'.[85] Indeed, as we have already argued, children themselves make sophisticated judgements about the television programmes they watch. But it must be added that *not all* children are able to do so.

American research has shown – through extensive content analysis – that violence occurs much more often on television than in the real external world, and that this in turn leads heavy viewers 'of this distorted world' to become even more fearful of crime. Certainly some statistics suggest an imbalance between individual perceptions of crime and the actual figures. Indeed, a recent BBC survey found that viewers thought that more than a quarter of the population had been victims of violent crime in 1994, whereas the actual proportion was under 2 per cent.[86] And given the plethora of police and crime programmes on television (both fictional or otherwise), it is fair to say that such individual perceptions are to an extent *influenced* by the media. Obviously it is unlikely that viewing an occasional episode of, say, *Brookside*, will lead a viewer to believe that the world is full of murderers, drug-dealers and bodies buried underneath patios. However, it is certainly plausible to suggest that some heavy viewers, *over time*, after watching particular crime-related programmes, with little else to do with their time, and living in a crime-ridden environment, may well believe that the situation is worse than it actually is.

Gauntlett then considers the 'pro-social effects' of television, the positive influence on behaviour that television might create such as an increase in personal social skills and acts of altruism. The research on the issue is, not surprisingly, inconclusive. For example, longitudinal studies of *Sesame Street* have suggested that the programme has been effective in teaching social and intellectual skills and that viewers are positively influenced by the examples shown of friendship and social harmony. On the other hand, research on the phenomenally successful series *Roots* found that the declared aim of the series to increase racial tolerance was *not* achieved.[87]

Turning his attention to the effects of public information programming and in particular anti-smoking media campaigns in the USA, Gauntlett notes that the conclusions drawn from such campaigns suggested only 'modest effects'. Similarly in respect of the effects of television advertising, he concludes, given that in a capitalist society 'people expect to be sold things', one can only point to the modest effects of such commercials. He also, interestingly, points out the unintended effects created by television advertising, namely those young TV-literate viewers who consume commercials 'independently of the product being marketed'.[88] Assessing the degree of pro-social effects across a number of genres, including didactic teaching, informational campaigns and advertising, Gauntlett concludes that on the whole,

> deliberate efforts to cajole and persuade the public via television have met with what might be considered a remarkable lack of success. Since those who have worked in the field for years apparently find it so hard to produce minor but socially beneficial results, it becomes difficult not to think that the idea of negative effects accidentally 'slipping out' is equally unlikely.[89]

It has been suggested that while working-class individuals are more likely to point to socio-economic factors as being responsible for violent crime, the middle classes are prone to look for more individualistic explanations such as lack of discipline in the home or the effect of television on unsupervised minds. And for certain politicians such explanations invariably would be far more congenial than those which argued for political or economic change.

Film-maker Oliver Stone claims that the real reasons for violence are social: poverty, neglect and lack of family.[90] Ironically, however, his own movie *Natural Born Killers* – which reached UK cinemas complete with the 150 cuts insisted upon by the US censors and which is intended to show how television creates monstrous heroes only to shoot them down – is apparently being critically viewed as merely glamorizing the two murderous central characters. The film's mishmash of newsreel, documentary-style coverage and MTV-style editing evidently fails to convince both critics and viewers. But how can we evaluate the influence of poverty, neglect and lack of family on the causes of violence?

Michael Tracey pointedly asks the question 'who could question that the disaster of missing parental love will mark a child more than the flickering violence on a screen?'[91] Although hard to quantify there surely can be no doubt that since the increased rates of divorce, remarriage and the emergence of 'reconstituted families' in post-war UK, the emotional traumas that thousands of children are confronted with are profound. Feeling unloved, angry or cheated are potentially destructive emotions. This is not in any sense to be critical of, say, single-parent families, which are often far more positive units compared with dysfunctional families. Indeed, theorists from Freud to R.D. Laing have highlighted the frustrating and destructive lives individuals are often forced to live because of the nature of the traditional family.

There has unquestionably been a steady rise in the cases of real-life violence since the 1950s, notwithstanding the difficulty in interpreting any such statistics; indeed, we would have to be singularly perverse to deny the evidence of our eyes. But returning to the statistical evidence the rise in repeated offences of violence against the person in England and Wales has been from the rate of 100,000 in 1981, to 205,000 in 1993. Similarly, reported sexual offences have risen from a figure of 19,000 in 1981 to 31,000 in 1993 (of which cases of rape have risen from 1,000 to 4,000 in the corresponding period).[92] It seems highly unlikely that such a systematic rise of crime could be positively correlated to television viewers being exposed to screen violence. Consider also the rise in unemployment rates for the UK since the mid-1970s. Using the OECD/ILO concepts of unemployment, the numbers involved have risen from a figure approaching 5 per cent in 1976 to a current figure of approximately 10 per cent. In all age groups the rates are higher for men than women. In addition, a recent survey has suggested that Britain is more unequal now than at any time since the war.[93] Add to these figures another pair of statistics – firstly, according to the Child Poverty Action Group one third of all UK children are suffering from an unacceptably low standard of living, and secondly, that of the million jobs to be created by the year 2,000, 90 per cent will be for women (though there is publicly-funded child-care for only 2 per cent of under-threes)[94] – and it becomes apparent that the seeds have already been sown for widespread anger and frustration before one TV set has even been switched on. In a culture in which self-esteem and social worth are defined predominantly in materialistic terms, to deny individuals the opportunity to earn a living is therefore inviting trouble.

One final ingredient may be added. The cultural air which we all inhale – including the displaced, disadvantaged and frustrated among us – is *already* tainted with images of violence and the systematic debasement of women. Tabloid newspapers for instance are characterized by stories of success and greed, failure and misery, sexual innuendo and soft porn, and a lexicon of mistruths, sensationalism and spitefulness. Women also continue to be treated shabbily on film as in the 'bimboizing of women' as in Jennifer Jason Leigh's character in *Last Exit to Brooklyn* and *Miami Blues*, and of Victoria Abril in *Tie Me Up! Tie Me Down!* Advertisements continue to use partially-clad women for the delectation of men while, according to Marilyn French, rape or near rape is becoming 'as obligatory in violent films in the United States as it has long been in India'.[95] She believes that 'man's long-standing war against women' is taking on a new ferocity and a new urgency. The major arenas of contemporary culture – television, film, computer and video games, toys, print, and 'the street' – are all to be found within this overarching cultural climate. And they all feed off each other.

Researchers will *never* agree with each other as to the effects of television and its precise role in contributing to violence. Indeed, when asked about the conflicting interpretations of data one researcher commented that 'if you torture the data for long enough, in the end you are bound to get a confession'.[96] As we have earlier remarked television is so embedded in social life it is unlikely that we will ever be able to separate it from those other cultural, economic, social, emotional and subjective influences that equally contribute to violent behaviour. But it would surely be apposite to be cautious; especially if we constantly remember that it is not art that is being restricted by any censorship, but *commercial* practices. In the following passage D.J. Enright succinctly summarizes the interrelationship between violence and the television experience:

> The germ of sadism has to be there already, and in all of us excepting saints it is there already . . . television can foster sadistic behaviour by a slow erosion of the more decent, human qualities. Evil grows ordinary, it flickers away in your living-room as if it were a Christmas tree . . . We are influenceable creatures, even the most sturdily independent of us, and 'recorded history' records no vehicle of influence to approach television in respect of potency, relentlessness and ubiquitousness. Nothing, I believe, has *no* effect.[97]

9

Television's Uncertain Future

In general, we shall spend more time at home, as it becomes easier to communicate without having to meet other people – shopping through your television, attending video conferences. They say it will be easier than ever not to leave the house . . . Phillip K. Dick has described one result of this arrangement with technology. One of his characters is saved the trouble of a tourist trip to Mars by contracting the services of an agency which implants in his mind the memory of such a voyage. What point is there in making a real journey to Mars if you can enjoy the best memories of the trip without leaving home?

Tomás Delclós (1992), 'The Screen Comes of Age'

Only a hard-nosed futurologist would confidently predict what television in the year 2000 will look like – what the programmes will be like, who will own what, and whether or not the viewers will approve of the changes forced upon them. This chapter looks at this uncertain future. What, for example, will be the future of children's television?

Children's programmes are costly to make and invariably do not 'deliver' large audiences. Thus, there will always be a question-mark against their survival especially on commercial television. For the foreseeable future at least the BBC's traditional 'children's television mix' will continue, although as with ITV it will increasingly be aware of the competition emanating from specialist satellite children's channels. It is of course in such an environment that toy merchandisers, with huge amounts of money to spend, will be able further to enter children's television by sharing the costs of production with financially strapped broadcasters.

As the current century comes to a close, it is certain that viewers will continue to be mesmerized by the pure magnetism of TV. Animals too: 'in one experiment, some academics observed family goldfish kibbutzing on their keeper's TV viewing by consistently "swimming on the side of the tank nearest to the television set"'.[1] The omnipresence of television perhaps is best illustrated by the O.J. Simpson trial in the USA which kept Americans and some British viewers close to their TV sets. Not only did the television coverage result in the usual theatricality that comes from the presence of cameras, but additionally one of the key witnesses complained of being harassed by the television media and, thus, was allowed to give evidence on video tape!

In the UK, as a population we generally spend up to 20 hours a week watching television, time-shifted programmes and videos compared to four or so hours spent reading books.[2] It is not surprising, therefore, that from time to time guilt about such behaviour sets in – about the loss of 'time', and that there may be other more worthwhile things which we could be doing. Perhaps as a consequence we attempt to turn the television set off. Indeed, in March 1995 TV-Free America organized a national TV-Turnoff week. To compensate for the subsequent loss of *Roseanne, The Power Rangers, Oprah Winfrey* and other programmes, the organization recommended over 40 substitute activities. TV-Free America is an organization concerned about what it sees as the harmful effects of *excessive* viewing, especially on literacy and productivity. It highlights the statistic that calculates that Americans collectively watch 120 billion hours of television a year. Thus, it believes that the untapped potential for community work, 'thinking' or even talking to each other is enormous. Not everyone is convinced, however, that such a TV turn off would, say, result in 'reading Solzhenitsyn and going to Covent Garden or attending lectures on the Late Renaissance'.[3] Indeed, some critics doubt whether there was in fact *ever* a golden age of leisure *before* television, when families would happily converse and provide their own entertainment, whether through boardgames, music or bingo.

British television has created and ruined reputations, has transformed the economics of sporting stardom, produced pop stars as we now know them, and enabled the Royal family to acquire a more 'complex kind of superstardom'.[4] To concentrate exclusively on the effects of television on children or on the issue of media violence and its impact is, perhaps, to ignore its wider effects. On behalf of the culture it is firmly embedded within, television communicates a complicated set of values. However, the core value expressed – not surprising within a capitalist economy – concerns the propaganda of commodities. Popular television tells us that consumption is an intrinsic good and that happiness consists in obtaining material goods. Relatedly, the value of narcissism or of self-absorption, and of the immediate gratification of wants follow closely behind.[5]

Christopher Lasch argues that through the bombardment of images of glamour, of celebrity and of success, mass culture 'encourages the ordinary man to cultivate extraordinary tastes'.[6] Advertising and commercials are merely the most obvious symbols of such values: quiz shows conventionally trade in hope and greed, television presenters are invariably youthful, successful and wealthy, newsreaders are paid enormous sums of money for reading large print on autocues, while dramas trade on hopes and fears in the pursuit of success (and happiness). And, as we have argued earlier, many viewers live their own lives *vicariously* through the medium of television, perhaps hoping that they too can be fulfilled, beautiful and successful. Of course, television opens other windows too: on the sad plight of famine victims, merciless killings around the globe, and also of encouraging and positive accounts of heroism, altruism and the fine qualities and sensibilities of particular individuals.

As in most aspects of life there are two sides to television's influence. Consider the major cultural changes in British social life since the 1950s when television first became fully operational. On the positive side we have become a more multi-cultural nation, are more environmentally and economically aware, the rights of women and children have been duly recognized, there has been more freedom in marriage and family life and, compared to the pre-war period, there has been a remarkable growth in prosperity. At the same time, however, we witness in the 1990s the relentless growth of racism, acts of thoughtless (and conscious) waste and environmental damage, continued sexism and the recognition of widespread child abuse, escalating rates of divorce, and a rapidly growing divide between the rich and very poor. Can we ask the question, what precisely is television's role in all of these changes?

Television reflects and refracts changes in the external world, and rarely initiates any truly novel or innovative behaviour or practice. *Live Aid* and the accompanying news reports certainly accelerated immediate acts of charity, but it did not *create* such generous dispositions. In terms of television's content various programmes and strands – from *Blue Peter* to *World in Action* – have, for example, helped create environmental awareness if not actual action, but in other areas of social life the influence of television has been somewhat minimal. It may not perhaps directly contribute to inequalities of wealth and income, rather it merely enables the unemployed to take their minds off such inequalities. In the realms of gender and race, television's role is uncertain and ambiguous: positive representations of women and ethnic minorities are gradually emerging at the same time as sexist and racist imagery still lingers on. In politics, as we have earlier argued, television has entered into an almost symbiotic relationship with parliamentarians, faithfully relaying their messages while at the same time turning them into celebrities and persuading them to personalize politics.

In one area of social life television has ruthlessly endorsed and reinforced pre-existing societal trends. As it kneels at the altar of the chapel of youth, television ignores, misrepresents and is guilty of a disservice towards older individuals (and viewers). Television relies on youthful appearances, rapid modern talk, and targets those viewers whom, advertisers believe, are worth appealing to. Perhaps by the year 2000 it will be this long-standing prejudice of programme-makers which will be most under threat, for at that time long-standing demographic changes will become clearly visible.

Television and the 'Third Age'

When the doctor-theologian-musician-philosopher Albert Schweitzer was asked, at age 86, who would replace him as head of his jungle hospital at Lambaréné in Gabon, he remarked that he was always asked that question but that he still had much to do: 'I will never retire and am not yet dead. Please have a little reverence for *my* life'.[7]

In all cultures there are customs that mark or celebrate age. In a western, European society like ours, such customs are intimately connected with the precise *measurement* of age. People are constantly reminded of how young or, more likely, how old they have become. For many the consequence is existential anxiety: how much longer have I left to live? Maurice Halbwachs succinctly and autobiographically expresses such fears: 'I anxiously reflect on my age, expressed as the number of years lived and remaining . . . as if the years ahead of me shrank in proportion as the elapsed time of my life increased'.[8] Such concerns are illustrative of the fact that we live in an ageist society in which individuals are almost solely judged by age alone. The following description of the consequences of ageism by Michael Young and Tom Schuller is worth reproducing in full.

> People are publicly and privately humiliated on a million fold scale by reason of their age, not just deprived of work and money because they are the wrong age but shamed by being regarded by others as slow, rigid, unenterprising, incapable of innovation, intellectually decayed by reason of their age alone. Almost the worst of it is that the cruelty of others is internalised by those it is vented upon, so that they feel old and unworthy when they do not need to.[9]

Recent research has suggested that older viewers have a love–hate relationship with television, trying hard not to allow it to dominate their lives yet often keeping the set switched on simply for its company. Generally speaking they watch a lot of news programmes, daytime TV, quizzes, and claim they feel patronized by programmes made specially for them, for example BBC's *Primetime*.[10] Older viewers are, however, not the only group who feel patronized or indeed misrepresented by the medium. For example, over 15 per cent of the adult population of Britain have disabilities of one kind or another, yet only 0.5 per cent of characters in television drama are actually portrayed as having such disabilities. More importantly, the attitudes displayed towards such disabled characters within such programmes are also radically different to those shown towards able-bodied characters. On-screen disabled characters are much more likely to evoke sympathy, pity, sadness or fear, in contrast to able-bodied characters who are more likely than not to evoke respect or attraction.[11]

For some older viewers the characters on the television screen become substitutes for missing loved ones. Indeed, television may well compensate for feelings of loneliness or a lack of contact with others.[12] Television is of assistance to those older people with a lot of empty time on their hands and indeed they watch more television than any other group. For example, the average retired woman will spend over half her free time watching the box. Such older viewers tend to watch the same programmes as the mass of population – soaps, light entertainment and dramas – but additionally may consume a considerable amount of daytime television.

The precise timing and scheduling of television programmes provide a path through the empty hours ahead for many of these older viewers. For example, in their research Young and Schuller encountered many men for whom, like the following, 'the 12.30 news on TV was the crucial point in the day, a kind of axis on which it turned. He waited for it greedily, but would not switch the telly on until exactly 12.30'.[13] They add that many such viewers could well be the best informed people in the land digesting, as they did, almost all the news bulletins of the day. This of course may be unhappily compared to the no news of their own lengthy days. However, while many older people use programmes (and their scheduling) as one stepping-stone to another in order to get through the day, at the same time they suffer from lack of contrast. For in order to thrive, *all of us* need both routine and habit *and* variety or contrast. For many older viewers – especially given their reluctance or inability to subscribe to satellite or cable channels – daytime television is an all too predictable diet: the same faces, the same guests, the same issues, the same prizes, the same questions and the same predictable stories.

Apart from their heavy television diet and despite the amount of free time available to them, older people are less fully engaged in almost every social and cultural activity compared with the general population. As Eric Midwinter rightly argues this can only be partially explained by factors of low income, lack of company, ill-health or disability, or fear of the streets or lack of transport. More significant is the impact of those cultural values which paint older age as a time of withdrawal and decline and, sadly, older people may well act out this image of themselves.[14]

So how are older people actually represented on television? To begin with there are not too many of them visible on screen, especially in prime-time dramas or soaps. When they *do* grace the screen they tend to be characterized as either eccentric or crotchety. For example, in a survey of American television it was found that there was a general invisibility of older people on the screen, and when they *were* pictured they revealed 'rigidity, decline in intelligence, a decrease in productivity, a sexlessness, a major degree of decrepitude and utter dependence'.[15] Older people are thus seen to have failed to conquer nature and stay young and beautiful, have little or no labour-market value, and indeed have little or no future left. And when an older person achieves anything at all in the world it is reported with a gusto totally inappropriate to its merits. A phenomenon that the playwright Alan Bennett has scornfully referred to as the wonder expressed when an octogenarian succeeds in fastening her shoelace.

The genuinely innovative and creative programmes featuring older people are rare, indeed, and always an exception. *The Golden Girls*, with its focus of the agonies of sex for the over-60s is rare, as is the BBC's *Waiting for God*, a brilliant comedy which explores the existential issues surrounding impending death, while *One Foot in the Grave*, through its eccentric main character Victor Meldrew, draws an amusing picture of the consequences of long-term marriage. The BBC's *Last of the Summer Wine*, however, is all too ready to play 'the unattractive old woman and dirty old man' card, and as Midwinter observes, sadly underlines the 'amalgam of hilarity and revulsion with which sexuality in older age is regarded'.[16]

An ex-commissioning editor of Channel 4 suggests that the lack of older people on the screen is caused by the fact that with its roots in show-business, television is predominantly a 'young medium'. She adds, however, that Channel 4 itself did attempt to accommodate older people and that, she adds in all seriousness, the Channel's 'regular coverage of the House of Lords [added] a further dimension'.[17] Conversely, one of Channel 4's founding editors Naomi Sargant, however, agrees that television is 'more ageist than sexist' and adds that the medium was deeply cruel in the 'clarity of its pictures'. She suggests that behind all of this lies our inability or dislike of looking at images of old age, 'for in them we see our own future'.[18] Population historian Peter Laslett has coined the phrase the 'third age' in an attempt to replace the unsatisfactory concept of retirement. This 'third age' of life after work could well last for up to 20 or even 40 years – and with more people finishing work at 50 or 55, in Britain alone this would account for some ten million people. Laslett argues that the first age of our lives is concerned with dependence, socialization, immaturity and education, while the second phase is an era of independence, maturity, responsibility, earning and perhaps saving. The third age offers the *potential* for personal fulfilment.[19]

Why such 'third agers' will increasingly be important for the television programme-makers of the future is because of their sheer number and also their purchasing power. In fact by the year 2000 one-fifth of the UK population will be over 60 years of age, some 12 million or so in total. The proportion of a fifth is more significant than the simple arithmetic of the numbers, for the chief cause of this increased fraction which has trebled over the century, is the reduction in the population of younger people. By 2000 there will be an equal proportion of the over-60s, and the under-16s, approximately 12 million of each cohort.

It would be naïve to believe that all of these third agers of the future will be free-spending consumers; some will survive on welfare benefits alone. However, many will not rely solely on welfare; for example, the number of adults aged 55 and over who are in the social class category ABC1 (upper, middle and lower middle), and therefore likely to be economically comfortable, has risen from 4.35 million in 1975 to almost 6.5 million in 1995. In fact as a society we are as young as we are ever going to be again, and in future years there will be more older people and fewer younger ones. The really dramatic change that will be evident in the late 1990s is among the so-called 'younger old', the 50–60-year-olds. By the year 2000 there will be a 23 per cent increase in this age group. These over-50s are the same ones who in the 1960s were involved in the social and sexual changes that occurred. They will look at the world, and hence television, through the 'presbyopic eyes of fifty-year-olds' and will demand that it is changed for *their* benefit.[20] Television channels will be forced to feature this age group in their mainstream programming because their influence will possibly be much stronger than that of 'youthful' viewers.

One of the problems for the advertisers of the future is that the over-50s are less favourable to commercials than younger people tend to be. They resist 'enculturation', or in other words, such individuals do not like being told what to do or what to buy. Especially when they do not 'see themselves' represented in such commercials. Advertisers and broadcasters thus have much to learn if they wish to reach such people. Judie Lannon neatly summarizes the changes that are currently taking place in the mid-1990s: 'We are living through a period in which the centre of gravity of our society is shifting away from the preoccupations of youth: an unacknowledged quiet cultural revolution which will gradually become more dramatic'.[21]

Wall-to-Wall Movies?

Whether the varied tastes of future fifty-somethings will be met by the television of the late 1990s, or conversely whether or not quality children's television will survive, are difficult questions to answer because of the uncertain future. One thing *is* certain, however, namely that the overall television mix of programming will continue to be shaped by the importation of products from Europe, Australia and, most significantly, the USA.

Statistics of the 1993[22] overseas transactions of the BBC, ITV, Channel 4, satellite and cable companies showed that collectively they had sold £113m worth of programmes, almost half of which were sold to EU countries and almost 40 per cent to the USA. Obversely, £179m was paid to the USA for their programmes, out of a total expenditure of £228m. Thus for the year 1993 UK TV companies had a net deficit of £115m on overseas transactions. Comparable data from a decade earlier show that sales and acquisitions both totalled £90m.[23] So the growth in overseas acquisitions over the decade is evident, fuelled particularly by the newly-established satellite channels intent on purchasing US movies.

Some television genres and indeed particular programmes 'travel' better than other ones, and also countries vary widely in their appreciation of such programmes. Israel, for instance, has bought *One Foot In The Grave* from the

BBC, who have also managed to sell the police corruption series *Between The Lines* to Saudi Arabia and David Attenborough's *The Private Life of Plants* to numerous countries including China, Sweden and Italy. Such trade is valuable not only in terms of funding future productions, but also in making library material pay handsomely. But, as earlier remarked, the acceptance of foreign material both here and overseas varies widely. For example, *The Cosby Show* was a huge success almost everywhere except in the UK where it has consistently played to small audiences. Or take a market like Asia, which with its collection of discrete cultures differs widely in its appreciation of foreign programming. Hong Kong enjoys US programming while Taiwan tends not to. Indeed, a Singapore television executive remarked that although he had given viewers *Cheers* and *Northern Exposure*, they were both rejected. He believed 'local' (national) programmes would also be more popular than those imported.[24]

Many critics, often speaking on behalf of so-called underdeveloped nations, express their concern over the proliferation of the trade in television programmes especially the domination of US-originated material. Richard Hoggart, for example, has argued that the imported programmes have 'redefined the medium' so much that it is difficult for an African or an Asian or Arab to approach the medium's possibilities with his or her own different eyes or to persuade his own country's programme planners to accept new ways of seeing television's possibilities.[25] Of more general concern, however, is the fear of so-called 'media imperialism'. Indeed, as far as back as 1978 the Senegalese-born Director General of UNESCO announced that he was deeply concerned about the one-way flow of information and feared the 'effect of domination'.[26]

As television continues to colonize every corner of the globe, it influences all the cultures it impinges upon. And in most of these cultures what is on offer is entertainment rather than information. And *whatever* the mind of society or culture, audiences wish to be entertained – especially by all forms of drama and sports programming – rather than taught by the small screen. Consider the nations of India and China, those so-called 'emerging markets' which are enthusiastically coveted by western media moguls. In India, especially through the growth of satellite television, US sit-coms and dramas are beamed into all the major cities. Traditionalists fear that such programming will continue the growing westernization of Indian culture, though the educational benefits of satellite broadcasting, for example, must also be recognized: thousands of villagers have received health education programmes delivered by satellites since the early 1970s. However, the one-channel terrestrial system has already affected the Indian way of life. As the cheapest available entertainment for families, it has, for example, resulted in a decline in theatre and movie-going as well as visits to relatives and friends.[27] Similarly in remote Indian villages food is cooked earlier than it conventionally was, with 'great panic and anxiety' among women to cook it on time. As Neena Behl puts it, 'time is now defined for them by the clock,

not by the position of the sun in the sky'.[28] Similarly, the introduction of television into the homes of Chinese families may be the most important
cultural development in the People's Republic since the effective end of the
Cultural Revolution in the 1970s. People inhabit the streets less, sleep less,
read fewer novels and the attendance of live theatre – especially traditional
Chinese opera – has declined. Chinese women watch drama while men
watch sport, they also claim to be more interested in factual programmes
than women do. Significantly, such Chinese viewers do not always accept
the intended messages of the broadcaster: some viewers, for example, pay
more attention to the street scenes of foreign cities than to the audio political reporting that accompanies the pictures. Viewers continue to make of
television what they want for their own purposes.[29]

Indeed, the potential political and ideological consequences of such international broadcasting are deeply profound. Islamists, for instance, fear the
potency of messages being beamed into Muslim homes in countries as far
apart as Afghanistan, Iran, Algeria and Saudi Arabia. Such Islamists have
considered establishing their own satellite services but would of course face
stiff competition from the highly sophisticated broadcasters like BBC and
CNN. Whereas in the age of print an educated minority could control the
masses, 'insulating it from alternative versions of truth', in the video age
'no one is safe from Madonna or CNN'.[30] An alternative scenario is,
however, put forward by historian Akbar Ahmed who believes that the
proliferation of western values in Muslim countries – through the impact
of television and the VCR – *reinforces* the sense of Islamic identity. He
believes that many Muslim viewers perceive that the West offers little other
than sex and violence, which they believe must be rejected.[31] Obviously
both responses occur and will continue to do so: both the westernization
(especially among the young) of Islamic culture, and the entrenchment into
traditional values. With respect to the 'media imperialism' thesis it is wise
to be cautious: the domination of information flows does not directly translate into social power.

'Wall-to-wall *Dallas*' was the term employed by those who were fearful
that the gross importation of US television programming would irrevo-
cably damage host nations' cultural and artistic integrity. In the 1990s,
however, with the steady growth of cable and satellite channels the phrase
'wall-to-wall *movies*' holds far more resonance. Additionally, the map of
soap imports has changed, for while afternoon television broadcasts such
glossy material as *Knots Landing* it is the predominance of antipodean
programming that is so evident: *Home and Away*, *Neighbours*, *The Young
Doctors*, *Shortland Street*, and *A Country Practice*. For the UK broadcaster
these programmes are extremely inexpensive to purchase and, despite their
variable quality, appeal to both the very young and very much older
viewers.

Imported American programmes cannot simply be condemned in the
manner in which so many cultural critics have done so. *NYPD Blue*, *ER*,

Cheers, M*A*S*H, Taxi, Roseanne, Ellen, Frasier and *L.A. Law*, to name but a few, are programmes of innovation and quality that need to be listened to as well as merely looked at. Of course there is rubbish too, as there is in indigenous or home-grown programming.

This history of the condemnation of American television began in the 1950s especially at the advent of ITV. As Raymond Williams has rightly observed, many British working-class people 'welcomed the Americanised character of British commercial television; as an alternative to the somewhat stuffy BBC'.[32] ITV offered, in its early years, novel cultural forms based on elements of working-class and regional cultures – melodramas, irreverent presenters and non-standard accents – but also a substantial amount of American programming. This, argues David Morley, is precisely what the working-class audiences enjoyed and appreciated.[33] Such American material offered alternative life-style (and hope), unusual and quite often higher production values, and had an emphasis on adventure, action, fantasy and escapism.

The issue of whether national cultures and identities are threatened by a deluge of foreign programming is no longer such a straightforward proposition with Europe itself being a set of nations each with a rich diversity of cultures. Besides which, previous anxieties were predicated on an almost mythical 'England' – a rural arcadia – a land in need of vigorous protection. And, of course, there is the other assumption that all viewers will 'read' these programmes in one particular way which, of course, is false. Viewers, especially the youthful, interpret and assimilate American programming – as they do with other Americana – to suit their own purposes and in so doing, inadvertently perhaps, create their own sense of the USA.

In an attempt to stem the tide of such foreign programming, both commercial television and the BBC informally operate a quota (which used to be 14 per cent), which stipulates, therefore, that a considerable proportion of its programmes must be European in origin. Additionally, there are restrictions on the scheduling of imported programming in peak time and the number of feature films and repeats that are allowed to be shown. However, in the case of satellite and cable channels such a quota system (51 per cent or so of programming to be domestically produced) is inappropriate. For example, cable channels may be designed solely for ethnic audiences and consist mainly of foreign material, or they may be film channels which depend totally on Hollywood movies to maximize their audience. Additionally,there are numerous problems for such satellite and cable operators in obtaining programming from terrestrial television companies which, for example, may not wish to co-operate with them.[34]

Although the European Directive on Trans-Frontier Broadcasting 1989 stipulates that quotas must be achieved 'where practicable' this will invariably be widely interpreted especially in the future. As Richard Collins has pointed out, the internationally traded sector of the world television-programme market is dominated by the Anglophone world. An OECD estimate for 1980 was that of a world-traded volume of US $400m the US television programme exports accounted for US $350m, and the UK (second to the USA) accounted for US $22m.[35] The USA's domination is based – in addition to any possible aesthetic reason – on its home-market size and, relatedly, the size and wealth of the whole language community within which it operates. Because *within* a single language community composed of several distinct national markets the factor of home-market size is significant. For example, as Collins explains, within the Anglophone world the 'United States is advantaged relative to the UK, the UK relative to Ireland, and among German-language communities West Germany is advantaged relative to Switzerland'.[36] However, it is well-established that some language communities are more resistant to foreign material than others: there is less penetration of non-English-language programming into English-speaking markets than of English-language origin programming into non-English-speaking markets. This is by virtue of the fact that Anglophone producers benefit from their membership of the world's largest and wealthiest language community. Such a position enables such producers to produce high-quality material with high production values. Moreover, they additionally benefit from the status of English as the world's preferred second language, which means they may reach more viewers and that such material can be more easily dubbed or subtitled.

Table 9.1   A comparison of linguistic markets

Language	Native speakers (millions)	1981 GNP (US $ million)
English	409	4,230,375
Hindi/Urdu	352	209,023
Spanish	265	653,958
Arabic	163	328,547
Bengali	160	12,692
Portuguese	157	303,465
Malay/Indonesian	122	237,715
Japanese	121	1,198,861
French	110	812,179
German	101	1,017,528
Punjabi	69	29,575
Italian	62	502,306

Source: Wildman and Sinek (1988).

It seems more than likely that the trend of the USA's domination of the world market in television programming will steadily continue. Profits will be sought in new territories, especially in the 'emerging markets' of Asia. The UK will continue to sell its programmes overseas, but it is likely that the trend of Europe accepting US material more readily than the USA embracing European programming will not change to any substantial degree.[37] Unlike pop and rock music UK television programmes do not play so well across the Atlantic.

An Uncertain Future

In contemplating the possible future contours of the communications industries, including that of television, it is worth remembering the observation of French philosopher Simone Weil who remarked that 'the future is made of the same stuff as the present'. For example however much the so-called information superhighway (or *Infobahn*) is positively hyped and described in ever-decreasing esoteric terminology and perceived to be a development of truly revolutionary significance, it is essentially merely an extension of existing technologies. Most importantly, it remains, theoretically at least, under the surveillance and control of political will. This is not to suggest that the future shape or direction of such a motorway is easily predicted or mapped, far from it. Such superhighways – fibre-optic networks capable of carrying voice, data, still and moving pictures – will transform society, it is alleged, by granting people even greater access to both information and each other. In principle European politicians have agreed to allow market forces to determine the development of this global information superhighway: EU nations have already agreed to liberalize their telecommunications markets by 1998, although it is clear that the Americans (and Japanese) will now also have access to such markets.

The social consequences and costs of such technological, economic and corporate developments as the information superhighway have been barely considered. It is yet another example of what G. E. Moore in his 1903 *Principia Ethica* termed a 'naturalistic fallacy', that is, feasibility, which is a strategic concept, is elevated to the status of a normative concept, with the result that whatever technological reality indicates *we can do*, it is taken as implying that it *must be done*. As John Berger has succinctly argued, although modern technology is essential to the modern world, the danger is that 'the instantaneity of its techniques defines its aims', including 'the instant future'.[38] Very little substantive and sustained thought – particularly among the wider public – has gone into the implications involved, especially in relation to such issues as those of confidentiality and copyright and, most importantly, teleworking. The advantages of flexible hours will perhaps be countered by increasing isolation and the disappearance of trade unionism and with it the principle of collective protection. Workers' whole lives may be dominated by their employers 'speaking' to them constantly through the medium of computer screens.

Can we be certain that we wish to learn more about the world and be provided with more and more information? Is it not more accurate to suggest that individuals – other than confirmed techno-addicts – wish to receive relevant information when it is useful to them but that they do not want to be confronted with a window to *all* of humankind's knowledge?[39] Over forty years ago the writer, philosopher and occasional broadcaster Cyril Joad, remarked that there has never been 'an age in which useless knowledge was more important than in our own'.[40] It is plausible that by the year 2000 we will all be in danger of being deluged with information of little value which will make any really useful data and knowledge hard to locate.

Television itself is, theoretically speaking, simply one of a number of electronic sound and picture signals entering into the home. In some quarters television is deemed to be, increasingly, of less importance compared to the myriad other attractions available like the CD-ROM, computer networks and so-called interactive services. Despite the enormous technological changes lurking just over the horizon it is fair to suggest that our culture is *already* a media-saturated one. This has sometimes been termed the 'confetti era', in which all events, experiences, ideas and values are the same size and weight and float down upon us like cheap confetti,[41] but more usually it is referred to as postmodern culture. Dominic Strinati describes such media-saturated cultures as consisting of media screens and cultural surfaces:

> TVs, VDUs, videos, computers, computer games, personal stereos, ads, theme parks, shopping malls, 'fictitious capital' or credit, money as a set of figures on a luminous display screen . . . have become part and parcel of the trends towards postmodern popular culture. Postmodernism in this perspective is therefore an argument about the mass media taking over – a cultural invasion of our senses which knows no boundaries, only surfaces.[42]

Such postmodern popular culture is, it is said, a fragmented culture with no overall coherence. Within television viewing itself there is, it is argued, less and less coherence: viewers graze channels, skip commercials, see trailers for programmes and switch between and within different programmes.[43] To add to a sense of pervasiveness and/or confusion, commercials also feed off programmes at the same time as programmes feed off commercials, while newscasters appear on game shows, and quiz show contestants win TV sets or VCRs. And increasingly 'real people' play *themselves* in fictional narratives – cricketer Ian Botham plays Ian Botham in *Emmerdale*.

The major notion of postmodernism is that popular culture together with media images increasingly dominate our sense of reality, and the way we define ourselves and the world around us. Indeed so much so that we can no longer say that the media *reflect* a wider reality, but rather that such a reality *is* the media. Similarly, as Strinati further argues, it is equally difficult to distinguish the economy from popular culture, since consumption patterns are increasingly influenced by popular culture.[44]

The postmodern thesis clearly has a superficial ring of truth to it. The young in particular consume cultural symbols and artefacts and, in so doing, create their own quite distinctive identities. Similarly, much of the nation's talk emanates from what has been seen on television or the cinema screen, heard on the radio or the CD player, or read in the myriad of general or specialist publications available on every street corner. *However*, people's lives continue to be more readily defined by more solid features of everyday life: relationships with the State or an employer; family life and illness; personal illness or disability; experiences at school or within the peer group; sexual and romantic successes and disappointments; physical and mental changes and decay; parenthood and retirement; and hope, despair and death. These are the realities and features of everyday life which crucially assist us in our definitions of ourselves and of the world around us.

But this is not to deny the pervasiveness of television and other media. And which ever prediction or forecast turns out to be the most accurate it appears likely that the future will herald an explosion of television channels. There are, we are somewhat reliably informed by the 1995 Broadcasting Bill seven more terrestrial channels on their way which will mean, by 1998, a total of twelve land-based channels. Digital technology also may well be responsible for up to 700 channels in the next 15 years or so. The TV set of the twenty-first century will be alive with potential and possibilities: personalized TV channels, video on demand, home shopping, interactive multi-media activities and telecommunications services allowing us to communicate on-screen with friends or colleagues.

The traditional principles of public-service broadcasting are that television programmes should 'inform, educate and entertain'. Those particular words – and in that order of priority – were included in the BBC Charter and were passed on to ITV in similar form in 1955.[45] From its early transmissions the BBC conceived a well-considered mixture of 'high' and popular culture.

> They had gardening programmes alongside books (classics) at bedtime; they had avant-garde plays besides Shakespeare and Dorothy L. Sayers' detective stories; they had roaming microphones picking up British life on the road and in the street, and they had the great popular ceremonies of national sport: the Derby, the Cup Final, test matches.[46]

Television soon followed radio's example and began a tradition – allegedly envied world-wide – of providing factual programming, news, drama, light entertainment, adult and children's education, and sport. However, the public-broadcasting duopoly of the BBC and commercial television is now at an end. A broadcasting system already characterized by varying degrees of concentration, conglomeration and internationalization[47] is now primed for further growth. Defenders of the existing system believe that the expansion of broadcasting now rapidly taking place will – if successful – inevitably disperse audiences and take resources away from broadcast television, removing its protection, reducing its revenues (especially in the case of the BBC) and will ultimately lead to the break up of its institutions.[48] Rowland Jr. and Tracey, for example, assert that the character of the 'assault' on public-service broadcasting is apparent in the 'language of dialogue about the future of television'. That dialogue, they argue, speaks of the 'inevitability of change', 'consumer choice and sovereignty', and of the 'third age' of broadcasting. It is, they believe, a vocabulary driven by ideological fervour and the 'naked pursuit of new wealth at the expense of all other considerations and values'.[49] A future characterized by hundreds of channels means that genuine diversity of programming disappears; when there were only four channels available it was almost impossible *not* to view some factual and entertainment-based or dramatic programming if the set was simply left on. But with a so-called narrowcasting diet a viewer can actively choose to avoid any informative or educative programming whatsoever.

We may ask, why more terrestrial channels? Why create *hundreds* by the year 2000? It is a salutary exercise to consider the programming currently available in the mid-1990s. A UK viewer cabled or dished, with subscriptions to a couple of premium channels and, of course, with their normal access to terrestrial channels could, on any given day, consume a diet similar to the following:

> A twenty-four hour service. View *at least* forty movies totalling well over sixty hours of screen time. A daily diet of satellite or cable programming totalling over three hundred and thirty hours, plus in addition eighty-three hours of terrestrial material. Available on terrestrial television are: discussion programmes, news, soaps, quiz and game shows, crossword puzzles, animation, natural history for children, sit-coms, factual entertainment (*How do They do That?*), sport, movies, parliament, at least three cookery programmes, business, *Songs of Praise*, *Star Trek*, arts, drama, made-for-TV movies, chat shows, cartoons, travel documentary, daytime magazines, movie review, jazz, *L.A. Law* and *Ricki Lake* – 'Is plumpness a problem in the dating game? Katherine, a sylph-like model, says her friend Ketha (who weighs 190lbs) always gets the boys'. Satellite and Cable offerings include: enormous quantities of recycled terrestrial programming – *The Bill*, *Neighbours*, *When the Boat Comes in*, *Dallas*, *Dr. Who*, and cookery, psychology, *The Mighty Morphin Power Rangers*, *Peyton Place*, cartoons, NBA Basketball, Skiing, Aerobics, Tenpin Bowling, *Rivera Live!*, *Wagner: Götterdämmerung*, *The Quintessential Peggy Lee*, keep-fit, and a multitude of movies, including Orson Welles' *Touch of Evil*, *Hello Dolly*, the animated Hans Christian Anderson's *The Emperor's New Clothes*, *Carmen Jones*, *Pet Cemetery II*, *Vanishing Point* ('existential cult road movie'), and *Kingdom of the Spiders* – a fantasy horror about a host of deadly tarantulas which goes on the rampage in the Arizona desert.

All these programmes – and many, many more – were available on *one* day.[50] But in the future *hundreds* more channels are planned. Indeed, among technologists the race is on to produce the most efficient 'browsing aid' to help the viewer negotiate the 500 + channels which may one day be available. For example, the Bell Atlantic 'stargazer' system allows the viewer to use the remote control to 'wander around a shopping mall – a click on the video shop reveals film previews, a click on the pizza shop allows the viewer to order a take away'.[51]

According to Jay Blumler the model of America suggests that a regime of increased channels not only extends 'choice' but also redefines it, 'closing or narrowing doors on certain kinds of programmes': original television plays (which cannot be turned into marketable series); major documentaries; critical and controversial programming; TV feedback programmes; anything thoughtful and slow-paced; educative fare for children.[52] It is fair to say that, up until now, the effect on British public broadcasting by the initial expansion of such channels is minimal. Trend data on the changes in programme types since the early 1970s indeed suggest less than dramatic change: there is less sport on the terrestrial channels, but more feature films and drama series, a slight decline in children's and religious programming, and a change (especially on ITV) of what factual programming actually represents. For ITV the decline of the documentary has been countered by the rise of other factual programming like daytime magazine shows. Perhaps the most significant changes – and these too are not yet entrenched – are on Channel 4 which has, as we have already seen, recently produced an increasing amount of entertainment programming at the expense of news, documentaries, current affairs and religion.[53] Whether it is able to adhere to its well-defined remit is an open question. Across all terrestrial channels it is possible to perceive a change that aesthetically there has been a shift towards 'style over content': experimentation for the sake of it, an over-emphasis on graphics and, overall, shorter internal segments of programmes, perhaps produced in the belief that the average viewer's attention span is a matter of seconds.

Satellite and Cable

In terms of the foreseeable future the available evidence *suggests* that national terrestrial channels will continue to be the dominant force in broadcasting. Consider the case of the USA where the three network channels take more than half of the viewing in cable homes despite sustained competition from over 40 such cable channels. In the long term, however, the precise shape of UK broadcasting will surely be determined by the cumulative impact of satellite and cable.

Supporters of the proliferation of satellite and cable channels argue that the four terrestrial channels are somewhat unfocused compared to the 'branded' channels of satellite-born competition. They predict a major shift to so-called 'narrowcasting': many channels transmitting specialized programmes to small but enthusiastic and committed audiences. Such a change would, of course, depend on viewer demand and the money to pay for such programming.[54] The long-term prospects for subscription TV cannot of course be accurately predicted neither can the availability of possible advertising budgets. Interestingly, it has been argued, on the basis of evidence from the UK, Germany, Sweden and France, that an increase in the number of available channels does not seem to lead to an appreciable increase in individuals' viewing time. It appears that the most likely determinant of more viewing is not additional choice at times when television is already available, 'but the provision of television at times when none was previously scheduled'. So once 24-hour programming is available on any channel, the potential for increased viewing time is severely limited.[55] There is also – given the European context – the vexed question of the different domestic regulations concerning advertising, in addition to which some advertising will simply not travel. One estimate is that cultural differences across Europe will result in 80 per cent of advertising being aimed at local markets – for example, a UK, French or Spanish market.[56]

One more issue concerning advertising is quite pertinent: advertisers have shown themselves reluctant to be associated with 'undesirable' programming, even if such programmes deliver substantial audiences. This should not, however, be a problem for the majority of new channels. As Collins has remarked, satellite television may well deliver to UK audiences 'access to more erotic television' than it has previously been accustomed to, but it is very unlikely to provide such material as *Driller Killer* or *Deep Throat*. The staple diet of mainstream satellite television will remain the recycling of existing programmes and movies from the UK and USA. Collins' views as to the future of satellite television highlight the importance of public-broadcasting television remaining intact, properly funded and aware of its values:

> The key to the future of satellite television is the terrestrial television regime. If the present UK terrestrial services are maintained (still more so if expanded), satellite television, a higher-cost, lower-funded medium with difficulties of establishing a place in the market, is unlikely to make a serious impact on UK viewing.[57]

From its humble beginnings in the 1940s USA cable television is now dominated by corporations and an extensive pattern of cross-ownership has emerged, with multiple-system operators coming from a variety of industries.[58] Similarly, in the UK major US corporations, like NYNEX, are heavily involved in building the cable future. A major incentive for such companies to invest in the UK is the regulatory divide between cable and telecommunications in the USA; unlike the UK it is predicted that, despite current regulatory restrictions, cable TV and voice telephony will ultimately be integrated.[59]

Stuart Hood rightly points out that cable 'in itself' is neither better nor worse than any other technology, rather what matters is how such a technology is used, and for what ends.[60] Commercially and politically-minded utopians have talked of 'cabling the nation' and of such ominous scenarios as 'the wired society'. Currently, UK cable is being bought by subscribers for access to BSkyB packages and, importantly, telephony. *Alternative* uses for cable, however, could include local television services which might result in a 'multiplicity of voices'. Supporters of such local – as distinct from regional – programming believe there is a misconception as to what such a service represents. To many viewers, they argue, the mere mention of cable television suggests 'pornography, openly biased campaigning programmes by wacky or extremist groups, on-the-street strippers, and performing dogs, cats and goldfish'.[61] The local television services *they*, on the other hand, wish to see developed may be low on production values and with less than state-of-the-art sophistication, but high on relevance. In particular they point to the future potential of local interactive services with, for example, the opportunities given to citizens of responding to, say, a local politician's plans and decisions. It is an open question as to the viability of such channels, unless the programming is extremely short in duration and the studios manned by volunteers. However, given the multiplicity of religions, ethnic and cultural minorities in the UK together with the inability of terrestrial television to satisfy such communities' needs, perhaps a window is available there for such local television channels.

In the long-term it seems likely that both cable and satellite channels will need to offer more programmes for 'family audiences' in order to increase their overall viewing share. Niche broadcasting for specialist audiences may not be enough. The degree to which they will be able to satisfy this 'crisis of content'[62] will depend upon innumerable factors, not least the behaviour of the various regulatory bodies involved with their activities and the terrestrial companies in competition with them.

The question that occupies a number of industry forecasters is whether cable and satellite will, eventually, settle into some kind of profitable co-existence. Currently both services have certain advantages over each other. Sky TV's advantages include: proprietary equipment – once viewers have bought the dedicated decoder they are effectively locked-in to receiving Sky TV;[63] wide ownership of programming material; universal access (following the purchase of a dish); and a possible alliance with British Telecom. Cable's prime advantage over satellite services is the ability to provide cheap telephony which will, in turn, attract potential audiences of a higher social class perhaps more suited to an advertiser's needs.

Table 9.2 Cable and satellite services in the UK, 1993–2000

	1993	1994	1996	1998	2000
Average number of TV homes	22.2m	22.5m	23.1m	23.6m	24.2m
Average penetration of satellite into TV homes	11.6%	16%	18%	19%	22%
Average penetration of cable into TV homes	3%	4%	8%	15%	23%

Source: Adapted from Stewart and Laird (1994), p. 36.

Forecasts of the future deal with what has become known as 'anchorless data', none the less it has not prevented such speculative thinking taking place. Of course forecasters hope that simply by the act of forecasting they may bring a future scenario to life. One such forecast is that by the year 2000 cable services will catch up with satellite services, driven especially by telephony and integrated TV-based services.

'Television Without Frontiers'

'The audio visual future of Europe is not written in the stars', opined the European Institute for the Media in 1988.[64] What *is* certain, the Institute argued, was that the regulatory systems of the past were at an end, though it did not actively support systematic deregulation, as it believed that the free market could not guarantee real diversification of programming. The most important European initiative in broadcasting policy – the establishment of a single market in television – followed the EC's Green Paper, *Television Without Frontiers*.[65] Despite this initiative it is clear that the interests and beliefs of various EU member-states are radically different, for example, while the UK supports the integration of markets and an absence of intervention, France has taken the opposite view. The result at present is a 'policy' which, Richard Collins remarks, is referred to as one of 'unity in diversity'. Such euphemistic and somewhat ironic words describe the 'incompatible goals of establishing a single-Community broadcasting and audio-visual market and (not necessarily the same thing) a single-European culture and identity and, on the other hand, fostering cultural pluralism and protecting established broadcasting and audio-visual markets and institutions now organized at national and subnational levels'.[66]

The European television map is currently dotted with different regulatory systems which thus form a barrier to the development of large cross-media proprietors but which, ironically, act in favour of non-European groups not subject to European restrictions. The predominant themes of EU and national regulatory policy are towards the safeguarding of competition *and* the promotion of European programming. But as we have seen this is itself in dispute. There appears to be little demand for pan-European programming: MTV is offered on four satellites and reaches as far as Turkey and the Lebanon, but statistics suggest that only 2 per cent of total reported viewing is on pan-European stations.[67] And as we have seen the viewing that takes place is predominantly of national domestic channels.

It is surely the case that this new (and growing) era of broadcasting demands a new structure of regulation. Some commentators believe that such future regulatory bodies should ensure that quotas are met, but not be in a position to regulate what people actually watch: 'the aim should be that in the multi-channel environment there are a variety of channels between them providing a true variety of essentially British television'.[68] If the market is unable to meet such demands it would be the role of the BBC to satisfy such requirements. Other commentators, however, believe that such a *laissez-faire* approach would inevitably lead to a 'consumer sovereignty' of choosing the least-demanding programming and, therefore, to a decline in public-service broadcasting.

Neither is it easy to imagine how the rules of media and cross-media ownership are to be *either* restricted or liberalized. Presently News International, for example, can be said to control to some extent Sky TV and the encryption-system bar, which would allow anyone to challenge Sky, plus it exercises considerable influence over the national press whose advertising sells BSkyB packages. But would restriction of cross-media ownership limit the opportunities for international expansion of other British media players?[69] In fact contained in the 1995 Broadcasting Bill there are a number of proposals concerning alterations in media-ownership rules. The two-licence limit for ITV companies is to be abolished, replaced with a new ceiling of 15 per cent of television audience permitted; there is to be greater cross-ownership between newspaper groups, TV companies and radio, but with no retreat on the new rule preventing press groups with more than 20 per cent of the market from controlling ITV franchises; TV companies will be allowed to buy newspapers, up to a level of 20 per cent of UK circulation – whereas newspaper groups can control up to 15 per cent of TV audiences.

Tunstall and Palmer in their speculative analysis of the future of UK broadcasting argue that when deregulation in other fields has occurred it has been actually followed by re-regulation, and they believe the same process will occur in broadcasting – *regularization*. Corrective rather than prescriptive, regularization would be 'regulation with a lighter touch'.[70]

The multiplicity of channels does not at all guarantee a genuine diversity of programmes. The expansion of satellite and cable channels does not result in the growth of original programming, but rather an increase in the recycling and distribution of existing material. Thus, it could well be argued that the resultant 'choice' is somewhat mythical, merely a variation on a theme, rather than a different concerto, as Pam Mills succinctly argues.[71] There is, however, a need to be cautious on this issue. For, as she suggests, viewers do not necessarily think along the same lines as broadcasters.

For broadcasters, choice seems to imply high quality programmes of different genres shown at the same time. But for viewers, two channels showing similar programmes they might want to watch offer more effective choice than four channels showing programmes they do not want to watch. Moreover, most viewers have little interest in the overall situation or in the long term view.[72]

Mills suggests that research has indicated that in countries with well-established multi-channel television systems, as in the USA, the Netherlands, Denmark or Germany, viewers tend to watch only a half or a third of the total number of channels available to them. Substantively, something of the order of seven out of twenty. It is, therefore, apparent that any possible 'appetite for variety' does not necessarily increase in proportion to the available number of channels. None the less she believes it to be inevitable that the future will herald a multiplicity of channels and although not all viewers will partake of them many viewers will none the less value such freedom of choice, and perhaps consider the programming to be of sufficient quality to their needs; that terrestrial budgets will suffer as satellite and cable channels develop; and that the effect of 'pre-emptive scheduling' against satellite programming will be to reduce the quality and choice available to all viewers.

In other words, the terrestrial broadcasters will inadvertently deliver subscribers into the arms of such cable and satellite channels and ultimately, viewers will suffer the consequences.[73]

Postscript

'Don't ask what does people harm. Ask what does them good.'[1]

Broadcasting must not . . . patronise or underestimate the possibilities of its audiences, no matter how many disappointments it has on the way. Broadcasters should stand up for the common man's right to be respected, to recognise the highest when he sees it, and so to deserve being offered nothing but the best in all kinds of programme, to be capable of more than the superficial. The real patronage is to level down. Since the popular press has dived for the deepest ditch where lie the lowest common denominators, there is all the more reason for the freer network to aim higher.

Richard Hoggart (1995), *The Way We Live Now*

Richard Hoggart's welcome diatribe against the currency of contemporary television talk continues with his assertion that 'no programme is ever justified by the answer: "but they enjoyed it". So does a cat playing with a dying sparrow.'[2] In other words, he draws attention to the crucial pedagogic and moral role of television, and in so doing he expresses his distaste for the 'giving the punters what they want' philosophy. And quite right too – a minority of mainstream viewers would, after all, welcome all sorts of pornographic and violent material on their domestic sets. Witness, for example, the high sales of explicit sex-guide videos, hard-core porn and such items as the recently compiled video of *executions*.

In a deregulated and market-driven UK broadcasting culture the consumer – the viewer – is philosophically seen as *sovereign*. In theory such consumers would choose what they wished to watch from the multitude of channels on offer, and if the broadcaster does not meet their wants and needs they will consequently tune out. This is the apogee of consumer choice, a behaviour much valued across the Atlantic and, indeed, since the early 1980s, in the UK too.

Some viewers, however, may well be amply satisfied by the duopolistic system of public broadcasting that has been in place since the mid-1950s, but others may rarely watch mainstream programming and spend their hours tuned to channels they have personally subscribed to. The shape of things to come cannot, of course, be known in advance. No one can predict the cumulative effect of current changes on the public-broadcasting system of the future, neither can one predict whether the BBC licence fee will survive or, indeed, what the size and shape of advertising budgets will be. Nor can anyone accurately predict the 'quality' or otherwise of channels and individual programmes.

The language in which the future of television is discussed has all but been hijacked by economically-minded politicians. It is the lexicon not only of capitalism but more particularly of an affluent, competitive and consumer-driven society. In his seminal book, *The Affluent Society*, first published in 1958, John Kenneth Galbraith described such societies as ones in which a state of widespread and unprecedented abundance had resulted in economic resources being used in the somewhat wasteful gratification of trivial wants – artificially stimulated by advertising and through the provision of excessive credit – rather than in the necessary satisfaction of fundamental needs.[3] Central to the stimulation of such wants is television in the guise both of its advertising and also the overall values of materialism and consumerism that it so ably represents. The energy and time expended by the consumer for the procurement of goods and services inevitably displaces other activities and indeed alternative sensibilities. In the wise words of the psychoanalyst Erich Fromm we thus become creatures who must *have*, rather than *be*.[4] While we can shop 'till we drop, we know less about our inner experiences and thoughts, or our individuality and subjectivity. In such a consumer culture we are defined by what we consume. Indeed, advertisers earnestly search for television programmes which will deliver such *consumers*: ABC2s, 25–44-year-olds, or the very young are accordingly defined as simply an economic unit and in terms of their potential spending power. It may, therefore, come as no surprise then that in the near future many viewers might *want* to consume more channels and, perhaps, indeed feel that they *need* them.

The cultural air we breathe, however, is too important for our health and well-being to allow it to be polluted by free-market values. In a sense it is already polluted: and as Marina Warner has perceptively remarked there are plenty of *Jurassic Park* dinosaur lunch boxes at school but not many books in the library. She also laments the fact that children appear to have 'forgotten how to play',[5] though they can use CD-ROMs, manipulate computer games at high speed, understand the aesthetics of television and identify with a myriad screen characters. Such children inhabit a culture that encourages a *narrowing* of their experience. The growth of multiple television-set households means that, increasingly, people view with others of a similar age: adults view with adults, teenagers with teenagers and children with children. Or of course they view alone.[6]

To reverse the arguments of the 'consumer sovereigntists' and suggest that people should not be given what they *want* but what they *need*, unfortunately, sounds like paternalism.[7] But where do we draw the line? If enough viewers claim they wish to see live transmissions from countries which carry out executions, or want to see detailed voyeuristic interviews with rapists and child molesters do we actually give them what they want?

Neil Postman observes that this trend has even affected religious broadcasting, as in the case of the USA where, he adds, the unwritten law of television preaching is that the viewer has to be given 'something it wants'. As Postman remarks, this is an unusual religious credo: 'there is no great religious leader – from the Buddha to Moses to Jesus to Mohammed to Luther – who offered people what they want. Only what they need'.[8]

It is important not to concede to consumer sovereigntists because of other reasons: what is 'discursively equated with "what the audience wants" through ratings discourse is nothing more than an indication of what actual audiences have come to accept in the various, everyday situations in which they watch television'. As Ien Ang puts it, such ratings discourse tells us nothing of the mixed and indeed contradictory interminglings of 'pleasures and *frustrations*' that viewers feel.[9] Viewers come to accept what is actually already on offer, and are not necessarily in a position to know what possible alternative programming might well be available. In a future public-broadcasting system with potentially limited resources such alternative risk-laden programming is, of course, even more likely to be conspicuous by its absence. So-called mass-appeal programming will form the core of the television diet.

Fear over the possible development of mass culture is not a new phenomenon. Brantlinger identifies a number of critics who, in their quite different ways, believed that 'mass culture' was in fact opposite to 'the true way to live':

> Marx, Engels, and the Frankfurt Institute theorists on the left; existentialists from Kierkegaard and Nietzsche to Gabriel Marcel, Karl Jaspers, and Albert Camus; Freud, Jung, and the psychoanalysts; the 'cyclical historians'; and Baudelaire, Flaubert, Matthew Arnold, T.S. Eliot, José Ortega y Gasset, down to Marshall McLuhan, Christopher Lasch, Richard Sennett, and Daniel Bell among cultural critics and theorists.[10]

After years of a focus on what does audiences *harm*, on concentrating on the negative aspects of television – violence, bad language and exploitative sex – perhaps we should ask questions as to what might do audiences good. This is of course the terrain on which British critics like Matthew Arnold, F.R. Leavis and Richard Hoggart so determinedly walked. They all believed that mass culture was invariably hideous because it was produced for commercial ends alone. They, so they claimed, instead believed in a higher and more desirable culture. Leavis himself argued that the task of saving the masses from low culture was no easy matter – 'individuals cannot just be naturally educated *into* their own culture, they must be also educated *against* it'. Richard Hoggart's seminal *The Uses of Literacy* described the brutal and saccharine fantasies of popular culture, and its phoney and trivial language. Hoggart, writing predominantly of the pre-television age, describes libraries full of 'worthless fiction or of that kind of non-fiction which is really only a sort of fiction with the added pleasure of a "true-life story"' (modern docu-dramas?), and trenchantly argues that there is no virtue in the habit of reading for itself if it becomes merely an addiction separated from 'the reality of life' (heavy television viewing in the 1990s?).[11]

Of course one does not have to be a postmodernist to object to the opposition of high culture and popular (low) culture, especially as when presented by Arnold and Leavis. In their terms much of film, television and contemporary music would be trashed and deposited into the pit of popular, low culture: *NYPD Blue, Inspector Morse, Brookside, Groundhog Day, EastEnders, The Sweeney, When Harry Met Sally*, the music from Motown, Madonna, Bruce Springsteen and Bob Dylan would all be relegated to the dustbin of history. The list is endless. None the less such critics do have a point unless, like the postmodernist, all culture is considered equal. But television *is* different. It is so pervasive, so embedded in contemporary life and is such an important social force: it distracts, takes up time, may encourage mimicry and allows life to be lived vicariously. In an age when consumerism and technology have replaced religion as the organizing principles of daily life, television has a central role in contributing to our identities and behaviour.[12]

In his retrospective review of Hoggart's *The Uses of Literacy* Fred Inglis perceptively notes that while disapproving of the tabloid press, the girlie magazines and the sex-and-violence novels of the time, Hoggart also emphasized the strongly resistant energies of 'ordinary people in the face of the debilitating effects of mass media', and insisted that much material in the 'dismal culture' he criticized *was* of the kind that Leavis would have approved. Inglis concludes that Hoggart's book, first published in 1957, is still relevant today: 'He shows how to value and discriminate amongst the torrent of stories coming from the mass media . . . It shows us what, for our self-respect and our intelligent life in the future, we should want for ourselves'.[13]

Perhaps the era after 2000 will indeed be one in which viewers rationally choose freely from a multitude of channels, tuning to programmes which enhance their intelligence, sociability and ability to contribute to the cultural environment in which they and their children live. Or perhaps the post-2000 era will witness further privatization with children locked into rooms resplendent with multi-media paraphernalia; fragmented television audiences; a corresponding decline in a shared culture; a deregulated system resulting in the widespread access to porn of various types; a surfeit of information leading to chronic information anxiety and an inability to distinguish the interesting from the trivial; and lower budgets, varied quality and with all programmes barely watched with anything resembling attentiveness. But these are alternatives about which viewers and citizens can choose. Public dialogue is essential, urgently required and absolutely necessary.

Writing specifically in regard to video nasties Rosalind Miles laments that it will forever be a 'blight upon what we call twentieth-century civilisation and a reproach to us all, that in an era when technology offered unprecedented chances of opening magic casements on perilous seas and faery lands forlorn, all we could come up with was *Driller Killer* and *Huns Fucking Nuns*'.[14]

Notes

Introduction

1 Hoggart (1995), p. 133.
2 Barwise and Ehrenberg (1990), p. 175.
3 Ettema and Whitney (1994a), pp. 9–10. The authors go so far as to assert that: 'In technologically advanced societies, measurement technologies are an essential part of the apparatus for the social construction of reality' (p. 11).
4 See Gunter and Svennevig (1988), p. 2.
5 The results of a smaller sample of viewers from 'ethnic minorities' is reported in the author's *Not a Pretty Picture* (1996).
6 See Collins (1990), p.29.

Chapter 1   Audiences

1 Silverstone (1993), p. 575 and p. 594.
2 Barwise and Ehrenberg (1990), p. 20.
3 Source, BARB/Continental Research, *Marketing Week*, 1 July 1994.
4 Source, *The Guardian*, 4 February 1995. The audience in 100 countries for The Three Tenors Concert was 1.3 billion, while the average 1993 attendance at a live modern theatre production was 381. (*Variety* 8-14, 1994, *The Independent*, 27 October 1994.)
5 Seymour-Ure (1991), p. 1.
6 Kingsley and Tibballs (1990), p. 5 and p. 10.
7 Diaries of Coronation Day (1953) Mass-Observation Unit.
8 Kingsley and Tibballs (1990), p. 5 and p. 10.
9 Royal Wedding Diaries, 29 July, 1981, Mass-Observation Unit, University of Sussex.
10 Galbraith (1992).
11 McEwan (1988), p. 8.
12 Aukstakalnis and Blatner (1992), pp. 206–7.
13 Barwise and Ehrenberg (1990), p. 12 This source is invaluable to this section.
14 Barwise and Ehrenberg (1990), p. 12.
15 Ibid., p. 13.
16 Ibid., p. 5 and p. 8.
17 Ibid., p. 6.
18 Eckstein (1994), p. 39.

19 Ang (1994), p. 368.
20 Lull (1988b). See the work of Collett (1986).
21 Lindlof, Schatzer and Wilkinson (1988), pp. 177–8.
22 Barwise and Ehrenberg (1990), p. 123.
23 Quoted in Ang (1994), p. 371. See Morley (1986).
24 Cubitt (1985). Quoted in Morley (1988), p. 28.
25 Morley (1994), p. 475.
26 Lull (1988b), p. 253, reports that in China there is not the extensive pattern of male dominance in family television viewing reported by Morley, while evidence from India indicates that while men may have more *formal* say than women in programme selection, women may exercise greater *actual* influence. Lull also comments on Rogge and Jensen's (1988) research into one-parent families where such families may refer to the actions of television characters 'in order to symbolically play out the role of the missing parent, thereby extending the family itself' (1986, p. 246).
27 Taylor and Mullan (1986), p. 49.
28 Newcomb and Hirsch (1994), p. 511.
29 See Hall (1980). Also Bobo (1994), p. 304.
30 Condit (1994), p. 428. See especially the work of Fiske (1987).
31 Fiske (1987), p. 308.
32 Cf. Collins (1990), p. 20. See also McGuigan (1994), p. 548.
33 Schudson (1994), p. 492.
34 Schiller (1989), p. 149.
35 Livingstone (1991), p. 303.
36 Condit (1994), p. 445.

Chapter 2 Technology

1 Taylor and Mullan (1986), p. 205.
2 Barwise and Ehrenberg (1990), pp. 6–7.
3 Smith (1994), p. 7.
4 Kingsley and Tibballs (1990), p. 4.
5 O'Sullivan (1991), p. 164. `
6 Ibid., p. 164.
7 Ibid., p. 176.
8 All the entries are dated April 1949, Mass-Observation Unit, University of Sussex.
9 Kagan World Media (1994), p. 181.
10 Ibid., p. 181.
11 An estimate from Kagan World Media anticipates that British television advertising will double between 1993 and 2003, from £1,915m. to £4,063m. Satellite channels are forecast to take 1.69 per cent of TV advertising by 2003 (1994, p. 183).
12 Hughes (1990), pp. 165–6.
13 Ibid., p. 166.
14 IBA (1984), p. 2.
15 Barwise and Ehrenberg (1990), p. 78.
16 Barwise and Ehrenberg (1990), pp . 78–9.
17 Gray (1992), pp. 215–16.
18 Rogge and Jensen (1988), p. 95.
19 Lindlof, et al (1988), p. 180 and p. 183.
20 Lewis (1990), p. 58.
21 Ibid., p. 57.
22 Gray (1992), p. 236.
23 Walker and Bellamy Jr. (1993), p. 4.
24 Benjamin (1993), p. 17.

25   Ibid., p. 21.
26   Klopfenstein (1993), pp. 35–6.
27   Benjamin (1993), p. 22.
28   Barwise and Ehrenberg (1990) claim that teletext penetration had reached 15 per cent of UK homes, while the ITC 1994 survey reported a figure of 55 per cent penetration amongst its sample. Such numerical conundrums appear to be an inevitable aspect of media analysis.
29   Uses of Teletext:

	1990 %	1991 %	1992 %	1993 %	1994 %
Unweighted Base (viewers with teletext)	525	527	616	774	871
Weighted Base	405	401	460	494	552
Use teletext:					
Most days/everyday	47	41	49	44	42
Occasionally/hardly ever	39	40	37	39	41
Never/I don't know	15	18	13	17	17
Unweighted Base:					
(teletext service used most often)	436	433	538	640	734
Weighted Base:	346	327	399	411	460
Use Ceefax on BBC1/BBC2 most often	34	29	30	36	35
Use Teletext on ITV/CH 4 most often	33	34	37	49	47
Other cable/satellite teletext service	–	1	2	1	2
Use all equally	26	16	14	15	14
It depends	–	18	15	11	10
Don't know	6	4	2	1	1

30   Kyle (1992).
31   Stewart and Laird (1994), p. 1 and p. 7.
32   Ibid., p. 5.
33   Phelps (1995), p. 1.
34   Ibid., p. 9.
35   Number of satellite dishes in the UK, 1989–93:

	'000 dishes
Jan. 1989	30
Oct. 1989	350
Jan. 1990	497
Oct. 1990	1,017
Jan. 1991	1,278
Oct. 1991	1,906
Jan. 1992	2,130
Oct. 1992	2,607
Jan. 1993	2,596

Source: Continental Research (BARB/Taylor Nelson AGB, 1994)

36   Stewart and Laird (1994), pp. 15–16: 'In cable television, Belgium has the highest penetration rate in Europe with 97 per cent. Ownership of the network is a fragmented mix of private and public and mixed enterprises, although many are run under contract by Electrabel, the state electricity company. The Netherlands similarly has an extremely

high penetration rate of 90 per cent. The municipalities originally operated the networks but they have increasingly subcontracted operations to the private sector and utility companies.

'The only other country with a significant base of cable households is Germany and the high penetration there is a result of an extensive cabling plan carried out by the Deutsche Bundespost Telekom.'

37   Hilsman (1989), p. 17.
38   Phelps (1995), p. 4.
39   Stewart and Laird (1994), p. 23.
40   ITC, 27 January 1995, p. 1. ('ITC Publishes Latest Cable Telephone Figures'.)
41   The Broadcasting Act 1990 contains no requirements that the holder of a local delivery franchise should provide any kind of local service. Under the Cable and Broadcasting Act 1984, under which all cable franchises were granted between 1984 and 1990, there also was no requirement that those operating a franchise must provide a local service. However, in deciding whether and to whom to award a franchise, the Cable Authority was required to take into account the proposals for services contained in the applications submitted to it, and empowered to insert conditions in the licence referring to such services. Section 7 of the 1984 Act required the Cable Authority to take into account in deciding whether or to whom to grant a franchise all matters appearing to them to be relevant. Without prejudicing the generality of this requirement, the Section went on to specify that the Authority should take into account the extent to which each applicant proposed to do certain specified things. These included proposals to include a range and diversity of programmes; to include programmes of an educational nature, programmes calculated to appeal specially to the taste and outlook of persons living in the area and programmes in which such persons were given an opportunity to participate; to include programmes provided by local voluntary associations and to assist such organizations in the preparation and production of programmes; and to provide, or secure the provision of, related services. 'Related services' included interactive, telephone and data services. (ITC mimeo, *Local Television on Cable*, 1985, pp. 1–2.)
42   Phelps (1995), p. 5.
43   Wilson (1995) cites the examples of Nickelodeon which has challenged The Children's Channel effectively as the main channel targeted at the younger age group, and UK Living which, he asserts, has shown willingness to tackle 'difficult topics', and to occasionally be 'controversial'. He concludes that 'new channels which do not have something distinctive and unique to say about their offering in their marketing may have difficulty achieving a meaningful penetration'.
44   Stewart and Laird (1994), p. 30.
45   Ibid., p. 29.

Chapter 3   Programmes

1   Enright (1990), p. 46.
2   Schickel (1985).
3   Inglis (1990), p. 166.
4   Postman (1987), p. 125.
5   Inglis (1990), pp. 39–40.
6   Braudy (1986).
7   Boorstin (1961).
8   Lasch (1978), p. 21.
9   Quoted by Barrett (1972), p. 3.
10   Inglis (1990), p. 90.
11   Adam Sweeting, *The Guardian*, 9 February 1995, p. 8.
12   Eckstein (1994), p. 31.

13 Barwise and Ehrenberg (1990), pp. 25–6.

14 Morley (1988), p. 40.

15 Lull (1988b), p. 249.

16 IBA (1974a), p. 3.

17 Kingsley and Tibballs (1990), p. 144.

18 Hood (1989), p. 25.

19 Enright (1990), p. 85.

20 Kingsley and Tibballs (1990), p. 147.

21 Williams (1990: orig., 1975), pp. 75–6.

22 Sharkey (1995), p. 27.

23 Williams (1990), p.72.

24 Taylor and Mullan (1986), p. 166.

25 Stephenson and Phelps (1989: 205, 131) add that some film studios concentrate on material that is unsuited to broadcast television. 'In terms of commercial movies this means stories aimed at adolescents (the main cinema-going audience and age-group that has always been poorly served by television and those deemed too "adult" for the small screen). The result is the inclusion in films of material that would have been unacceptable in the past'. They also point out that some projects are 'in most respects, feature films but whose sheer length makes TV transmission the most suitable form of presentation . . . [for example] . . . Claude Lanzmann's nine and half hour *Shoah*'. But, they add, television is 'too competitive and rating-conscious to allow such luxuries except as rarities. To keep its huge audience the TV image must be constantly on the move, fearful always of boredom and channel-hopping. Its rhythm is naturally restless, its attention-span too often limited to the short period before the next advertising break.'

26 Schulze (1994), p. 173.

27 Whannel (1992), p. 106.

28 Taylor and Mullan (1986), p. 51.

29 Whannel (1992), p.107.

30 Whannel (1992), p. 181. This section relies heavily on Whannel (1990) and Whannel (1992).

31 Quoted in Whannel (1992), p. 181. See Black (1972).

32 Whannel (1990), p. 106.

33 Taylor and Mullan (1986), p. 106.

34 Clarke (1992), p. 237.

35 Ibid., p. 250.

36 See Wober and Gunter's (1990: p. ii) research on attitudes towards *Crimestoppers*. Some respondents claimed that the programme did not make them more fearful, although they conceded that violent reconstructions ought to be labelled beforehand. A minority of respondents claimed that they *were* made more fearful by the programme. At the same time a similar proportion of viewers claimed they were reassured by *Crimestoppers* that the police solve many crimes.

37 Taylor and Mullan (1986), p. 56. In their research the authors were only told of two programmes that viewers found unequivocally too fearful to watch – *Threads* and *The Day After* – both concerned with the consequences of nuclear war.

38 The attraction of national news programmes to both genders is discussed in chapter 5.

39 Seymour-Ure (1991), p. 119.

40 Enright (1990), p. 20.

41 Barrios (1988), p. 55. Barrios notes that telenovelas are watched by all audiences, independent of social class, educational level, age or sex.

42 Taylor and Mullan (1986), p. 133. See also Horton and Wohl (1956) on '*parasocial interaction*'.

43 Potter (1982), p. 124. See also Weber (1993), pp. 113–60.

44 Enright (1990), p. 26.

45   Kingsley (1988), p. 335. See also Simpson (1993), Enright (1990), p. 31, and Wober (1992).
46   Glaessner (1990), p. 121.
47   Geraghty (1992), p. 148.
48   Comstock (1991), p. 64.
49   Hodgson (1995). See also Lasch (1978), pp. 106–7. Lasch quotes one surfer: 'Television is destroying our sport. The TV producers are turning a sport and an art form into a circus'.
50   Whannel (1992), p. 202. Each sport has a quite different televisual history, as Comstock (1991, p. 76) points out in the case of boxing in the USA. 'In the 1950s, it was a popular and established part of the Wednesday and Friday evening schedules, with occasional Friday championship bouts. The exposure diminished grass-roots interest in boxing; local arenas were emptied, and fan interest dwindled. The televised bouts, except for those championships, lost appeal because of mismatches and the dubious credentials of opponents. By 1960, boxing was gone from television. Then, in the 1970s, the extravaganzas of Muhammad Ali on closed-circuit TV demonstrated that there was an audience for boxing. In the 1980s, it returned to broadcast and especially cable television.'
51   Whannel (1990), pp. 113–14.
52   Whannel (1992), p. 199.
53   Novak (1976), quoted in Lasch (1978), p. 122. See also Williams (1990), p. 67, and Barnett (1990), pp. 202–6.
54   Williams (1990), p. 59.
55   Ibid., p. 60.
56   Brooks (1995), p. 10.
57   Enright (1990), p. 42.
58   CSO (1994), p. 145.
59   Gunter and Viney (1994), p. 73. They report that for some religious groups, notably Christians, Hindus and Black Pentecostals, religious programmes were frequently seen as uplifting. Some Hindu respondents often regarded such programmes as 'exciting'.
60   Svennevig et al. (1988), pp. 57–8.
61   European Institute For The Media (1988), p. 112.
62   Bunting (1995), p. 29.

Chapter 4   'Quality Television'

1   Williams (1990), p. 95.
2   Morley (1994), p. 481.
3   Taylor and Mullan (1986), p. 169. See also Morley (1994), p. 493.
4   The following section relies heavily on Eckstein (1994), pp. 39–50.
5   See Eckstein (1994), p.49. The figures are for 1994, but clearly suggest a trend.
6   Paterson (1990), pp. 31–2.
7   Ibid., p. 36. Paterson points out that one of the most successful campaigns was that for *EastEnders* in 1985. It featured 59 completely separate trailers before the serial went on air – each only shown once.
8   Ibid., p. 38.
9   Ibid., p. 40.
10   Barwise and Ehrenberg (1990), p. 19.
11   McGuigan (1994), p. 554.
12   Brunsdon (1990), p. 89.
13   *Cutting Edge*, 23 January, 1995: 'Growing Apart'.
14   Brunsdon (1990), p. 77.
15   Broadcasting Research Unit (1989), pp. 10–11.
16   Ibid., p. 16.

17 Warnock (1990), pp. 10–11, and p. 14. See also the Broadcasting Research Unit (1989), p. 1: 'Quality programming does not pre-judge audiences by presumed height of brow. It assumes rather that we can all at some time and in some ways find our imaginations touched. So it seems constantly to renew, not to repeat formulae; it explores, takes risks, pushes the boat out, extends the frontiers, takes itself and us by surprise as to what is possible in good television.'

18 Warnock (1990), p. 15.

19 Brunsdon (1990), p. 77.

20 HMSO (Cmnd 517), 1988.

21 Brunsdon (1990), p. 73.

22 Brunsdon also includes *'entertainment and leisure codes'*, but adds that such codes are more difficult to conceptualize. Much of the discussion on quality television relies heavily on Brunsdon's article.

23 Brunsdon (1990), p. 86. Brunsdon notes that *Boys from the Blackstuff* (BBC, 1982) achieved the quickest repeat in television history.

24 Ibid., p. 88 and p. 89.

25 IBA (1974a), p. 13. See also IBA (1984a).

26 Thorburn (1994), p. 546.

27 The figures are inevitably prone to fluctuation. In 1993 repeat transmissions made up 26 per cent of BBC1's schedule and almost 40 per cent of BBC2's. Channel 4's has risen to almost 35 per cent in the same year. For ITV the figure is approximately the same as that for Channel 4, although the precise numbers are difficult to obtain. See Eckstein (1994) and Kagan World Media (1994).

28 Inglis (1990), p. 117.

29 Williams (1994), pp. 141–2.

30 Ibid., p. 152.

31 See Eckstein (1994), p. 19.

32 See Warnock (1990), pp. 18–19.

33 Schudson (1994), p. 492. Also note Judith Williamson's comments on what she terms 'postmodern populism':

One of the big tenets of 'post-modernism' is subjectivity. People are 'allowed' to be subjective 'again', to enjoy, to say what they feel. But the new yuppie-left pop culture craze is peculiarly phoney and non-subjective, for while it centres on other people's subjectivity (all those TV watchers who love *The Price is Right* or *Dynasty*) it allows the apparently left-wing practitioners of it to conceal theirs. How about a radical left critique of *The Price is Right*? With all our education, have we nothing more to say than 'people like it'? (quoted in McGuigan, 1994, p. 553)

Chapter 5   News

1 Gall (1994), p. 15.

2 Postman (1987), p. 8.

3 Inglis (1990), p. 149.

4 Taylor and Mullan (1986), p. 154.

5 Barnett (1989a), p. 49.

6 Svennevig and Wober (1988).

7 Barnett (1991), p. 72

8 Barwise and Ehrenberg (1990), p. 130.

9   Ignatieff (1985), p. 57. See also Philo and Lamb (1987, p. 29): 'The Western Media did not have a very deep interest in the issue of famine or a sustained commitment to explaining its causes. Once the disaster had reached catastrophic proportions in Ethiopia, the BBC took the story and finally treated it as a major story . . . '. Individual reporters *were* interested. But, they added, 'If we take interest in the Western media to mean the commitment of major resources by major organisations, then this simply did not happen until the tragedy had already struck.'

10 Ignatieff (1985), p. 73. Ignatieff adds: 'There is no reason to suppose that the new media lack the same capacity of representation (as Goya's *Horror of War* and Picasso's *Guernica*) to make them real and to force the eye to see and the heart to recognise what it has seen.' It is possible that Ignatieff is mistaken in believing such a *comparison* is possible. See also Lasch (1985), p. 141.

11 Ignatieff (1985), p. 72.

12 Ibid., p. 74.

13 Morrison (1992), pp. 93–4.

14 Traynor (1995), p. 27. Traynor points out that in Croatia too, tight control of the media remains central to the longevity of President Franjo Tudjman's regime.

15 Ibid., p. 27.

16 Lasch (1978), p. 76.

17 See Schudson (1991), p. 143 and p. 145. See also Herman and Chomsky (1988).

18 Collins (1990), p. 235.

19 See Hood (1989), p. 128 and Lichtenberg (1991), p. 225.

20 Eldridge (1993), p. 156.

21 Collins (1990), p. 246.

22 Alasdair Milne, interviewed for the *London Evening Standard* (12 May 1982), quoted in Eldridge (1993), p. 157.

23 Ibid., p. 158. Eldridge adds that in some respects the very mark of its (the BBC's) professionalism is that it has access to such sources.

24 Collins (1990), p. 251.

25 Quoted in Hood (1989), pp. 127–8.

26 Toffler and Toffler (1995), p. 27.

27 Grace Aaron (of Peace Action, USA) quoted in Toffler and Toffler (1995), p. 27.

28 Quoted in Schudson (1991), p. 142.

29 Hood (1989), p. 9.

30 Or see *The Independent*, *The Times* or *The Daily Telegraph*. The 1 December 1994 issue of *The Sun*, in contrast, featured 9 human interest stories, 9 domestic political items, 2 foreign news stories, 12 crime items, 7 on entertainment and 10 on TV, in addition to the usual TV listings, a National Lottery special, a motoring page, sports pages, and the obligatory half-nude woman photograph. The Achille Lauro sinking featured midway in the publication.

31 See *Jane's Weekly*, issue for December 1994.

32 Sorlin (1994), p. 145.

33 Seymour-Ure (1991), p. 141.

34 Ibid., p. 126.

35 Young (1988), p. 209.

36 Ignatieff(1985), p. 76.

37 Ibid., p. 70.

38 Ibid., p. 70.

39 Inglis (1990), p. 85.

40 Ibid., p. 89. See also Kumar (1975).

41 See, for example, Turow (1991), p. 173. Also Amidon (1995), p. 11.

42 Postman (1987), p. 112.

43 Ibid., p. 105.

44   Ibid., p. 109

45   Schlesinger (1988).

46   Goodwin (1990), p. 54. See Williams (1990), p. 48. Williams argues, that 'when we add the general facts of visualisation to the altered selections and priorities of the broadcast bulletins, we have to see a qualitative difference, and almost certainly a qualitative gain, in television as compared with printed news'. He adds that print none the less retains its 'incomparable advantages as a way of collecting, recalling and checking information'.

47   Hoggart (1982), p. 154.

48   See Eldridge (1993), and Goodwin (1990), p. 54. See also Lichtenberg (1991), pp. 226–8.

49   Gurevitch (1991), p. 190.

50   Philo (1990), pp. 198–9.

51   See *Jane's Intelligence Review*, Volume 7(2), February 1995, pp. 50–7 for a discussion on Chechnia and, on Bhopal see, for example, 'Greenpeace Submission To The Fourth Session of The London Tribunal On Industrial Hazards and Human Rights on the Occasion of the Tenth Anniversary of the Bhopal Tragedy', by Kenny Bruno (November 1994, Greenpeace International: Amsterdam).

52   Morley (1994), p. 494. Morley adds that such a preference for local news connects directly to 'their other expressed interest – in programmes like *Police Five*, or programmes warning of domestic dangers'. See also Morley (1988), p. 45.

53   See Comstock (1991), p. 81.

54   Williams (1990 orig. 1975), p. 46.

55   Postman (1987), p. 113.

56   Schudson (1991), p. 152, paraphrasing R. D. Laing.

57   Barnett (1989a), p. 55.

58   Ibid., p.55.

59   Schudson (1991), p. 156.

Chapter 6   Television, Politics and Impartiality

1   Barwise and Ehrenberg (1990), p. 147.

2   Postman (1987), p. 7.

3   Rees (1992), p. 171. See also Schickel (1985).

4   Postman (1987), p. 4.

5   Philo (1993), p. 417.

6   Young (1988), p. 211.

7   Sennett (1977), p. 283. He adds: 'impulses to withdraw from public life began long before the advent of these machines; they are not infernal devices, according to the usual scenario of technology as monster; they are tools invented by men to fulfil human needs. The needs which the electronic media are fulfilling are those cultural impulses that formed over the whole of the last century and a half to withdraw from social inter-action in order to know and feel more as a person. These machines are part of the arsenal of combat between social interaction and personal experience.'

8   Ibid., p. 285.

9   Lasch (1978), p. 78.

10   Rees (1992), p. 175.

11   Seymour-Ure (1991), p. 161. I rely heavily on his detailed account of political broad-casting.

12   Ibid., p. 167.

13   Ibid., p. 169.

14   Ibid., p. 171.

15   Ibid., p. 172. Seymour-Ure comments that the satire programmes built up anger which, occasionally, would lead to outbursts: 'Most famous was Harold Wilson's explosion over the BBC documentary *Yesterday's Men* (1971). This had been intended as an innocent enquiry into the feelings and doings of ministers unexpectedly thrown out of office by the electorate. Wilson thought it tendentious, malicious, biased and quite contrary to the virtues of "balance". This very vulnerability, however, illustrates the underlying strength of the broadcasters by the mid-1960s: they might lose battles, but the TV medium was now too entrenched to lose the war.'

16   Lasch (1978), p. 75.

17   Ibid., p. 74.

18   Gurevitch (1991), pp. 186–7.

19   Ibid., p. 187.

20   A *Washington Post* columnist, quoted in Gurevitch (1990), p. 187.

21   Ibid., p. 188.

22   Postman (1987), p. 16 and p. 81.

23   Ibid., pp. 92–3.

24   Ibid., pp. 94–5.

25   Hood (1989), p. 3. See also Collins (1990), p. 257.

26   The Broadcasting Act (1990), Section 6(1) (b) and (c).

27   Barnett (1990a), p. 65.

28   Seymour-Ure (1991), p. 206.

29   Tunstall (1983), p. 238.

30   Seymour-Ure (1991), p. 206.

31   Ibid., p. 206. He itemizes a number of policies: 'the structure and organization of whole industries (film, TV) or of particular parts (Channel 4); finance (no VAT on newspapers); content (official secrets and contempt laws); and audiences (compulsory TV licence fees)'.

32   Ibid., p. 207.

33   Ibid., p. 214.

34   Ibid., p. 124.

35   IBA (1974a), p. 7, and IBA (1984a), p. 10.

36   Barnett (1990a), p. 640.

37   Ibid., p. 650.

Chapter 7   Offensive Television

1   Tynan (1988), p. 236.

2   Quoted in Tynan, p. 236.

3   Warnock (1990), p. 9.

4   Cosgrove (1995), p. 16.

5   Hood (1989), p. 8.

6   Under the current legislation Section 6(1) (a) of the Broadcasting Act 1990 requires that the ITC does all it can to secure that every licensed service includes nothing in its programmes which offends against good taste or decency or is likely to encourage or incite to crime or lead to disorder or be offensive to public feeling. A pretty tall order.

7   IBA (1974a), p. 8.

8   Groups of children discussing television with the author (five groups of eight children in each, recruited from schools).

9   Allan and Burridge (1991), p. 234.

10   Arango (1989), p. 193.

11   Ibid., p. 3.

12   Millwood-Hargrave (1991b).

13   Ibid., p. 21.

14   Redmond (1991), p. 45.
15   Curteis (1991), p. 49.
16   Brophy and Partridge (1931), p. 16.
17   Jackson (1991), pp. 61–2.
18   Ibid., p. 53.
19   Morris (1991), p. 81.
20   Ibid., p. 84.
21   Terrestrial output (between 6 p.m. and midnight) was monitored during the two weeks between 16 April and 29 April 1994, and Sky Movies and The Movie Channel for the same time period between 7 May and 20 May 1994. (*Violence on Independent Television*, A Summary Report of an ITC Monitoring Exercise, Annex A to ITC Paper 135 (94), pp. 5–26.) The same exercise had previously been carried out in 1993.
22   Plater (1992), p. 79.
23   Paul Johnson, 'Just why is TV so obsessed with sex?', *Daily Mail*, 18 January 1995, p. 10.
24   Millwood-Hargrave (1992), p. 71. See also Barwise and Ehrenberg (1990), p. 143 and Taylor and Mullan (1986), p. 38.
25   Haste (1992), p. 92.
26   See Morrison (1992), pp. 87–91.
27   Steinem (1980), p. 38.
28   Ibid., p. 37.
29   Bart and Jozsa (1980), p. 217.
30   Plater (1992), p. 80.
31   Ibid., p. 80.
32   Ibid., p. 78.
33   See Hurard (1992), p.106.
34   Moore Jr. (1972), pp. 68–9.
35   *BBC Programme Complaints Bulletin*, February–September 1994, BBC (The Board of Governors), December 1994.
36   Ibid., p. 7.
37   Ibid., p. 7.
38   Ibid., p. 8.
39   Ibid., p. 37.
40   Ibid., p. 13.
41   ITC (1995b), p. 10.
42   Armstrong (1995), p. 17.
43   Ibid., p. 17.

Chapter 8   Children, Regulation and the 'Effects' of Television

1   See Williams (1990 p. 69), where he describes commercial television as 'a sequence in which the advertisements are integral rather than as a programme interrupted by advertisements'.
2   Seymour-Ure (1991), p. 121.
3   Enright (1990), p. 48. He adds that some 'genius conceived the idea of calling a brand of soap powder "Biological", even (as I recall) "biological (pat. pend.)", though I don't see how you patent the word: we are all of us biological. Before long all soap powders became "biological", and copy-writers had to come up with a "New Biological" label, something more efficient, as it were more biological, than "ordinary Biological powders".'
4   Kingsley and Tibballs (1990, orig. 1989), p. 40.
5   Barwise and Ehrenberg (1990), p. 173.
6   Quoted in Comstock (1991), pp. 142–3.
7   Goethals (1981), p. 136 and Barnouw (1978), pp. 82–3.

8   Slinger (1993), p. 202.
9   Communication with Abbott Mead Vickers BBDO Ltd., February 1995.
10   This section relies heavily on Phelps (1995a).
11   Ibid., p. 9.
12   Ibid., p. 11.
13   Ibid., p. 13.
14   Ibid., p. 13.
15   Phelps (1995b), p. 11.
16   See Packard (1960, orig. 1957). The term 'embedded persuasions' is taken from Murdock (1992), p. 205.
17   Murdock (1992) p. 206.
18   The Pilkington Committee on Broadcasting (1962), p. 81. Quoted in Murdock (1992), p. 213.
19   Seymour-Ure (1991), p. 122.
20   ITC (1994b), p. 5. Principles 7 and 3 of the Code.
21   Murdock (1992), p. 223.
22   Ibid., p. 224.
23   Ibid., p. 225.
24   Ibid., p. 227.
25   Quoted in Murdock (1992), p. 228.
26   The phrase used by Michael Grade, and quoted in Brown (1989), p. 4.
27   The programme Code also applies to the contents of acquired material, including films, as well as to the production of programmes. British Board of Film Classification (BBFC) certifications of the versions of films or programmes proposed for transmission may be used as a guide to scheduling where they exist. Stricter rules apply to video classification than cinema classification since the former includes a test of suitability for viewing in the home. An even stricter classification applies to material intended for transmission on a subscription television service.
28   IBA (1984a), p. 19.
29   IBA (1974a), p. 12.
30   See Holman and Braithwaite (1982).
31   Gunter and Svennevig (1987), p. 32.
32   All extracts are from interviews carried out by the author.
33   *Los Angeles Times*, 27 February 1995.
34   Tucker (1994), p. 19.
35   Warner (1994), pp. 45–6.
36   Ariès (1962). See also Pollock (1983) who disagrees with the Ariès thesis, and believes there was indeed a 'childhood' in the sixteenth century.
37   Kline (1993), p. 13.
38   *Earth Island Journal*, quoted in *The Guardian*, 4 March 1995, p. 8. The precise figure is 30.6 billion hours.
39   Dawn Airey quoted in *Television Today*, 9 December 1993, p. 205, and *Sunday Telegraph*, 5 December 1993, p. 14.
40   Information from Bandai UK Limited, distributors of *Power Rangers* toys.
41   See Wober (1990), p. 1.
42   See Driscoll (1994); 68 per cent of all advertisements aimed at children appear between October and the end of December.
43   Kline (1993), p. 167.
44   Ibid., p. 314.
45   Ibid., p. 317.
46   Ibid., p. 327. See also Sutton-Smith (1986), p. 190.
47   Kline (1993), p. 330.
48   Holt (1967), p. 239.
49   Kline (1993), p. 336 and p. 350.

50 See for example Lasch (1978), p. 128.
51 Inglis (1990), p. 9.
52 Ibid., pp. 10–11.
53 Quoted in Cruz (1992), p. 177. See also Enright (1990, p. 228), who comments, 'can it be that now, with television and its passion for chat shows and off-the-cuff pontificating, we are returning to orality, to the illiterate society foreshadowed by Melvyn Bragg? Is the race heading for its second childhood?'
54 Enright (1990), p. 16. The view expressed is one made by Melvyn Bragg in debate with Michael Holroyd.
55 PASCS Survey (1994); ALBSU, (1995) reported in *The Guardian*, 7 February, 1995; CSO (1995) *Social Trends 25*, pp. 52–3.
56 Coopers and Lybrand (1994), p. 7.
57 Mintel (1995), p. 80.
58 Katz (1990), p. 50. Quoted in Provenzo, Jr. (1991), p. x.
59 Provenzo, Jr. (1991), p. 97.
60 Reported in *The Times* (20 December 1995) – the work of Colwell and Sigger.
61 CSO – Central Statistics Office (1994), table 3.35, p. 55.
62 Heppell (1994), p. 2.
63 Warner (1994), pp. 23–4.
64 Referred to in Provenzo, Jr. (1991), p. 121.
65 See Wagg (1992), p. 174. See also Davies (1989), pp. 204–5, and Barwise and Ehrenberg (1990), p. 145.
66 Postman (1987), p. 147.
67 Macdonald (1994), p. 27.
68 CSO (1994a), p. 53.
69 See Gunter and Svennevig (1987), p. 49. See also the Annual Report of The Broadcasting Standards Council. A related issue is the concern of the Advertising Standards Authority over companies targeting teenagers with slimming products, and the subsequent number who diet unnecessarily.
70 Wagg (1992), p. 163.
71 Ibid., p. 167.
72 Ibid., p. 169. Such programmes are perfectly matched with younger-teenage age groups: 'teenage culture is a contradictory mixture of the authentic and the manufactured: it is an area of self-expression for the young and a lush grazing pasture for the commercial providers' (Hall and Whannel, 1994, p. 71).
73 Buckingham (1995), p. 83.
74 Wood (1993), p. 194.
75 Ibid., p. 91.
76 Young (1993/4), p. 9.
77 Barwise and Ehrenberg (1990), p. 139.
78 Hoggart (1971), p. 225.
79 Newson (1994).
80 Bazalgette and Buckingham (1995a), p. 2.
81 Ibid., pp. 5–6. The specific conclusion is drawn from a document presented to the Broadcasting Group, House of Lords, by A. Sims and P. Gray (1993), 'The media, violence and vulnerable viewers.'
82 Miles (1994), p. 175 and p. 185.
83 Gauntlett (1995).
84 Barwise and Ehrenberg (1990), p. 140.
85 Gauntlett (1995), p. 32 and p. 33.
86 Radio 4's *Violence Files*.
87 Gauntlett (1995), p. 40 and p. 41.
88 Ibid., p. 67.

89   Ibid., p. 71.
90   Interviewed in *Time Out*, 1–8 February 1995, p. 20.
91   Tracey (1984), p. 3.
92   Home Office statistics, reported as table 9.3, in CSO (1995), p. 154.
93   Source OECD, reported as table 4.25, in CSO (1995), p.76. See also the Rowntree Foundation Survey, 1995. Inglis (1990), p. 146, points out that 'the mass media fill up unoccupied space and time . . . They therefore exert their strongest direct influence on the lonely, the ill, the elderly, the very young, the workless, the bored, the itinerant'.
94   Warner (1994), p. 47.
95   French (1992), p. 167.
96   Tracey, (1984), p. 3.
97   Enright (1990), p. 37.

Chapter 9   Television's Uncertain Future

1   Cumings (1992), p. 25.
2   Source, The Henley Centre, reproduced as table 13.2, in CSO (1995), p. 216.
3   Dunkley (1985), p. 128.
4   Seymour-Ure (1991), p. 250.
5   Arthur (1993), p. 60.
6   Lasch (1978), p. 181.
7   Quoted in Puner (1978), p. 270.
8   Halbwachs (1980), pp. 89–90. Quoted in Young (1988), p. 115.
9   Young and Schuller (1991), p. 165.
10   BFI (1995).
11   Cumberbatch and Negrine (1992), p. 136 and p. 138.
12   See Rogge and Jensen (1988), p. 103.
13   Ibid. p. 122.
14   Midwinter (1991), p. 19.
15   Davis and Davis (1985), quoted in Midwinter (1991), p. 1.
16   Midwinter (1991), p. 28.
17   Liz Forgan, quoted in Midwinter (1991), p. 4.
18   Naomi Sargant, quoted in Midwinter (1991), p. 1.
19   Laslett (1989), p. 4.
20   Kreitzman (1994), p. 19. See also Silman and Poustie (1994).
21   Lannon (1994), p. 34.
22   Latest available figures.
23   Central Statistics Office (CSO) (1994), 'Overseas transactions of the film and television industry 1993', 5 October 1994, CSO (94) 210, London.
24   Quoted in Masters (1994), p. 22.
25   Hoggart (1978), p. 2.
26   Quoted in Hoggart (1978), p. 2.
27   Yadava and Reddi (1988), p.130.
28   Behl (1988), p. 153.
29   Lull and Se-Wen Sun (1988), p. 231.
30   Ruthven (1995), p. 6.
31   Ahmed, in Schlesinger (1993), p. 34.
32   Williams (1990), p. 132.
33   See Morley (1992), p. 74.
34   Phelps (1995), p. 14. There are also problems in acquiring programmes from British companies because of the policies concerning residual payments.
35   Collins (1994b), p. 388.
36   Ibid., p. 388.

37 For an extensive discussion of the complex issues involved see Strinati (1992) and Collins (1990), pp. 151–65.
38 See also David Hume's *Treatise on Human Nature*. See also Schiller (1989), p. 6, and Berger (1988), p. 28.
39 Hüber (1994), p. 15.
40 Quoted in *The Observer*, 30 September 1951, p. 8.
41 Donnelly (1986), p. 182.
42 Strinati (1994), p. 429. See also Strinati and Wagg (1992a).
43 See Fiske (1991), p. 58.
44 Strinati (1994), p. 429.
45 Seymour-Ure (1994), p. 65.
46 Inglis (1990), p. 123.
47 Seymour-Ure (1991), p. 107.
48 Inglis (1990), p. 131.
49 Rowland Jr. and Tracey (1990), p. 110.
50 25 January 1995.
51 Stewart and Laird (1994), p. 19.
52 Blumler (1991), p. 208.
53 Eckstein (1994), pp. 18–23.
54 See Collins (1992), p. 121 and Barwise and Ehrenberg (1990), pp.154–5.
55 Barnett (1989), pp. 40–1.
56 Hood and O'Leary (1990), p. 226.
57 Collins (1990), p. 88.
58 Hilsman (1989), p. 24.
59 See Tunstall (1992), p. 252, and Stewart and Laird (1994), p. 10.
60 Hood (1989), p. 116.
61 Wilson (1994), p. 56.
62 See Hüber (1994), p. 56, and the WOAC Communications Company (1994), p. 103.
63 Stewart and Laird (1994), pp. 25–7. They add that there are 'moves afoot in the EC towards regulating decoder supply whereby all decoders have the facility to accept a number of different broadcasters' cards, thus preserving the viewer's ability to choose between satellite services . . . '
64 The European Institute for the Media (1988), p. 11.
65 Commission of the European Communities (1984).
66 Collins (1994a), p. 99. See also Collins (1990), pp .46–7.
67 Stewart and Laird (1994), p. 20. See also Collins (1995), p. 9.
68 Dyke (1994), pp. 39–40.
69 Ibid., pp. 40–1. See also Sorlin (1994), p. 150, who comments that media is 'singular in as much as, unlike other industries, its primary aim is not making money. The owner-ship as well as the production of any medium brings fame . . . [But] those who own it and use it to strengthen their social domination are less concerned with money than with reputation; they are keen to separate possession from management and some-times to face heavy losses'.
70 Tunstall and Palmer (1991), p. 44.
71 Mills (1994), p. 140. See also Murdock (1992a), p. 36.
72 Mills (1994), p.144.
73 Ibid., p. 147.

Postscript

1 Enright (1990), p. 71. The phrase is from the dedication of Pamela Hansford Johnson's (1967) *On Iniquity*, and spoken by her daughter.
2 Hoggart (1995), pp. 153–4.

3   See Galbraith (1958).

4   Fromm (1978). Also see Weisskopf (1965).

5   Warner (1994), p. 47.

6   Comstock (1991), p. 139.

7   See Warnock (1990), p. 23.

8   Postman (1987), p. 123.

9   Ang (1994), p. 382.

10   Brantlinger (1983), p. 42. See for example the comments of Inglis (1990), p. 38 on the Frankfurt School: 'they saw cultural production as an industry like any other in most respects, whose function was to sedate the masses and keep them quiet so that the real beneficiaries of capitalism, the male bourgeoisie, could go on drawing the profits and kidding themselves that they were the civilized ones'. This view is but a modern version of the classic conspiracy theory of giving the people 'bread and circuses' to keep them preoccupied and amused with trivia, first described by Juvenal. See also Seldes (1950).

11   See Hoggart (1990, orig. 1957), p. 332. See also Inglis (1990), pp. 35–6.

12   For an illuminating account of the relationship between modern technology and personal identity see Barrett (1972), pp. 20–8.

13   Inglis (1990), pp. 36–7.

14   Miles (1994), p. 173.

Bibliography

AGB (1994) *The AGB Television Yearbook 1994*, London: AGB.

AGB (1995) *The AGB Television Yearbook 1995*, London: AGB.

Allan, Keith and Burridge, Kate (1991) *Euphemism and Dysphemism*, New York: Oxford University Press.

Allen, Edward (1989) *Straight Through the Night*, New York: Soho Press.

Allen, Woody (1983) *Four Films of Woody Allen*, London: Faber and Faber.

Ang, Ien (1991) *Desperately Seeking the Audience*, London: Routledge.

Ang, Ien (1994) 'Understanding television audiencehood', pp. 367–86, in Newcomb, Horace (ed.) (1994).

Amidon, Stephen (1995) 'Don't write off the story', *The Sunday Times*, 29 January, pp. 11–12.

Arango, Ariel (1989) *Dirty Words: Psychoanalytic Insights*, Northvale, New Jersey: Jason Aronson.

Arendt, Hannah (1975) 'Home to Roost: A Bicentennial Address', *New York Review*, 26 June, p. 3.

Ariès, Philippe (1962) *Centuries of Childhood*, Harmondsworth: Penguin.

Armstrong, Karen (1995) 'No room for catholic views?', *The Sunday Times*, 5 February, p. 17.

Arthur, Chris (ed.) (1993) *Religion and the Media*, Cardiff: University of Wales Press.

Aukstakalnis, Steve and Blatner, David (1992) *Silicon Mirage*, Berkeley: Peachpit Press.

Barnett, Steven (1989a) 'European broadcasting in the 1990s: Europudding or Eurocaviare?', *ADMAP*, pp. 40–1.

Barnett, Steven (1989b) 'Broadcast news', *British Journalism Review*, vol. 1(1), Autumn, pp. 49–56.

Barnett, Steven (1990a) *Games and Sets*, London: BFI.

Barnett, Steven (1990b) 'TV: The political bias?' *British Journalism Review*, vol. 1(3), Spring, pp. 63–7.

Barnett, Steven (1991) 'An average war for television', *British Journalism Review*, vol. 2(3), Spring, pp. 71–3.

Barnouw, Eric (1978) *The Sponsor, Notes on a Modern Potentate*, New York: Oxford University Press.

Barrett, William (1972, orig. 1958) *Irrational Man*, London: Heinemann Educational Books.

Barrios, Leoncio (1988) 'Television, telenovelas, and family life in Venezuela', pp. 49–79, in Lull, James (ed.) (1988).

Bart, Pauline B. and Jozsa, Margaret (1980) 'Dirty books, dirty films, and dirty data', pp. 204–17, in Lederer, Laura (ed.) (1980).

Barthes, Roland (1957) *Mythologies*, London: Paladin.

Barwise, Patrick and Ehrenberg, Andrew (1990, orig. 1988) *Television and its Audience*, London: Sage.

Bazalgette, Cary and Buckingham, David (eds) (1995a) *In Front of the Children*, London: BFI.

Bazalgette, Cary and Buckingham, David (1995b) 'Introduction: the invisible audience', pp.1–14, in Bazalgette and Buckingham (eds) (1995).

BBC (1974) *BBC Handbook*, London: BBC.

BBC (1984) *Annual Report*, London: BBC.

BBC (1994a) *Annual Report and Accounts*, London: BBC.

BBC (1994b) *Programme Complaints Bulletin*, December 1994, London: BBC.

Behl, Neena (1988) 'Equalizing Status: television and tradition in an Indian village', pp. 136–57, in Lull, James (ed.) (1988).

Benjamin, Louise (1993) 'At the touch of a button: a brief history of remote control technology', pp. 22–39, in Walker and Bellamy Jr. (eds) 1993

Bennett, Tony (1994) 'Popular culture and "the turn to Gramsci"', pp. 222–9, in Storey, John (ed.) (1994).

Berger, John (1988) 'For Raymond Williams – from "who governs" to "how to survive"', *New Statesman*, 11 March, p. 28.

BFI (British Film Institute) (1995) *Television and the Household*, London: BFI.

Black, Peter (1972) *The Mirror in the Corner*, London: Hutchinson.

Blumler, Jay G. (1991) 'The new television marketplace: imperatives, implications, issues', pp. 194-215, in Curran and Gurevitch (eds) (1991).

Bobo, Jacqueline (1994) '*The Color Purple*: Black women as cultural readers', pp. 302–10, in Storey, John (ed.) (1994).

Bolter, David (1984) *Turing's Man*, Chapel Hill: The University of North California Press.

Boorstin, Daniel (1961) *The Image*, London: Weidenfeld and Nicholson.

Brandt, George W. (ed.) (1993a) *British Television Drama in the 1990s*, Cambridge: Cambridge University Press.

Brandt, George W. (1993b) 'Introduction', pp. 1–18, in Brandt, George W. (ed.) (1993).

Brantlinger, Patrick (1983) *Bread and Circuses*, Ithaca: Cornell University Press.

Braudy, Leo (1986) *The Frenzy of Renown*, New York: Oxford University Press.

Broadcasting Research Unit, The (1989) *Quality in Television*, London: John Libbey.

Brooks, Richard (1995) 'Blood in a throwaway cup', *The Guardian*, 31 January, p. 10.

Brophy, John and Partridge, Eric (1931) *Songs and Slang of the British Soldier: 1914–1918*, London: Routledge and Kegan Paul.

Brown, Maggie (1989) 'Advertisers "set to exert greater influence on TV"', *The Independent*, 29 August, p. 4.

Brunsdon, Charlotte (1990) 'Problems with quality', *Screen*, vol. 31(1), Spring, pp. 67–90.

Buckingham, David (ed.) (1993) *Reading Audiences*, Manchester: Manchester University Press.

Buckingham, David (1995) 'Television and the definition of childhood', pp. 79–96, in Mayall, Berry (ed.) (1995) *Children's Childhoods*, London: Falmer Press.

Bunting, Madeline (1995) 'TV channels with God on their side', *The Guardian*, 18 November, p. 29.

CCIS (1989) *Democracy and Broadcasting Pluralism*, London Centre For Communication and Information Studies, PCL.

Central Statistics Office (CSO) (1994) *Social Trends 24*, London: HMSO.

Central Statistics Office (CSO) (1994a) *Social Focus on Children*, London: HMSO.

Central Statistics Office (CSO) (1995) *Social Trends 25*, London: HMSO.

Clarke, Alan (1992) '"You're nicked!": Television police series and the fictional representation of law and order', pp. 232-53, in Strinati and Wagg (eds) (1992).

Collett, Peter (1986) *Watching the TV Audience*, paper presented to the International Television Studies Conference, London.

Collins, Richard (1990) *Television: Policy and Culture*, London: Unwin Hyman.

Collins, Richard (1992) *Satellite Broadcasting in Western Europe*, London: John Libbey.

Collins, Richard (1994a) 'Unity in diversity? The European single market in broadcasting and the audiovisual, 1982–92', *Journal of Common Market Studies*, vol. 32(1), pp. 89–102.

Collins, Richard (1994b) 'Trading in culture: the role of language', *Canadian Journal of Communication*, vol. 19, pp. 377–99.

Collins, Richard (1995) 'Convergence between telecommunications and television. Technological change, regulatory lag and the case of satellite television in the European Community'. Paper presented at *Le symposium international sur la convergence des techniques de communication*, University of Quebec, Montreal, 29–30 September, 1994.

Commission of the European Communities (1984) 'Television without frontiers'. Green Paper on the Establishment of the Common Market for Broadcasting especially by satellite and cable. COM (84) 300 final (Luxembourg: OOPEC).

Comstock, George (1991) *Television in America*, Newbury Park, Calif.: Sage.

Condit, Celeste Michelle (1994) 'The rhetorical limits of polysemy', pp. 426–47, in Newcomb, Horace (ed.) (1994).

Coopers and Lybrand (1994) 'Video and computer games', *Media Climate Briefing*, Issue 44, Autumn, pp. 7–8.

Corner, John (ed.) (1991) *Popular Television in Britain*, London: BFI.

Correct Public Affairs Ltd (1994) *21st Century Media Conference*, Transcript of Proceedings, Queen Elizabeth II Conference Centre, 13 July, London.

Cosgrove, Stuart (1995) '4-letter words', *The Guardian*, 13 January, pp. 16–17.

Cruz, Juan (1992) 'Octavio Paz', *Leonardo*, pp. 176–7.

CSO *see* Central Statistics Office.

Cubitt, Sean (1984) 'Top of the Pops: The politics of the living room' pp. 46–8 in Masterman, Len (ed.) (1984).

Cumberbatch, Guy and Negrine, Ralph (1992) *Images of Disability*, London: Routledge.

Cumings, Bruce (1992) *War and Television*, London: Verso.

Curran, James and Gurevitch, Michael (eds) (1991) *Mass Media and Society*, London: Edward Arnold.

Curran, James (1991) 'Mass media and democracy: A reappraisal', pp. 82–117, in Curran and Gurevitch (eds) (1991).

Curteis, Ian (1991) 'A television dramatist's view', pp. 53–6, in Millwood-Hargrave, Andrea (ed.) (1991).

Davie, C.E. et al. (1984) *The Young Child at Home*, New York: NFER-Nelson.

Davies, Máire Messenger (1989) *Television is Good for Your Kids*, London: Hilary Shipman.

Davis, R.H. and Davis, J.A. (1985) *Television's Image of the Elderly*, Lexington, Mass.: Lexington Books.

Delclós, Tomás (1992) 'The screen comes of age', *Leonardo*, pp. 186–8.

Donnelly, William J. (1986) *The Confetti Generation*, New York: Henry Holt.

Driscoll, Margarette (1994) 'Crazy toys, crazy children, crazy parents', *The Sunday Times*, 18 December.

Dunkley, Christopher (1985) *Television Today and Tomorrow*, Harmondsworth: Penguin.

Dyke, Greg (1994) 'Ownership and control', pp. 38–41, in Correct Public Affairs Ltd. (1994).

Eckstein, Jeremy (1994) *Cultural Trends 1994: 21*, London: Policy Studies Institute.

Edwards, Richard C., Reich, Michael and Weisskopf, Thomas E. (eds) (1972) *The Capitalist System*, New Jersey: Prentice Hall.

Eldridge, John (1993) 'Ill news comes often on the back of worse', pp. 147–61, in Arthur, Chris (ed.) (1993).

Enright, D.J. (1990) *Fields of Vision: Literature, Language, and Television*, Oxford: Oxford University Press.

Ettema, James S. and Whitney, D. Charles (eds) (1994a) *Audiencemaking: How the Media Create the Audience*, London: Sage.

Ettema, James S. and Whitney, D. Charles (1994b) 'The money arrow: an introduction to audiencemaking', pp. 1-18, in Ettema and Whitney (eds) (1994).

Euromedia Research Group (1992) *The Media in Western Europe*, London: Sage.

European Institute for the Media (1988) *Europe 2000: What Kind of Television?*, European Institute for the Media, Manchester.

Fiddick, Peter (1994) 'Early day motion', *Ariel*, 31 August, p. 7.

Fiske, John (1987) *Television Culture*, Methuen: London.

Fiske, John (1991) 'Postmodernism and television', pp. 55–67, in Curran and Gurevitch (eds) (1991).

Fore, William (1993) 'The religious relevance of television', pp. 55–67, in Arthur, Chris (ed.) (1993).

French, Marilyn (1992) *The War Against Women*, London: Hamish Hamilton.

Fromm, Erich (1978) *To Have or To Be?*, London: Jonathan Cape.

Galbraith, John Kenneth (1958) *The Affluent Society*, Harmondsworth: Penguin.

Galbraith, John Kenneth (1992) *The Culture of Contentment*, London: Sinclair-Stevenson.

Gall, Sandy (1994) 'Refugee situation worsens in continuing Afghan stalemate', *Jane's Defence Weekly*, vol. 22(22), 3 December, p. 15.

Gauntlett, David (1995) *Moving Experiences: Understanding Television's Influences and Effects*, London: John Liberty.

Geraghty, Christine (1992) 'British soaps in the 1980s', pp.133–49, in Strinati and Wagg (eds) (1992).

Geraghty, Christine (1994) 'Soap opera and utopia', pp. 317–25, in Storey, John (ed.) (1994).

Gitlin, Todd (1983) *Inside Prime Time*, New York: Pantheon.

Glaesnner, Verina (1990) 'Gendered fictions', pp. 115–27, in Goodwin and Whannel (eds) (1990).

Goethals, Gregor (1981) *The T.V. Ritual*, Boston: Beacon Press:

Goodwin, Andrew (1990) 'TV news: striking the right balance?', pp. 42–59, in Goodwin and Whannel (eds) (1990).

Goodwin, Andrew and Whannel, Garry (eds) (1990) *Understanding Television*, London: Routledge.

Gray, Ann (1992) *Video Playtime*, London: Routledge/Comedia.

Gunter, Barrie and Svennevig, Michael (1987) *Behind and in Front of the Screen*, London: John Libbey.

Gunter, Barrie and Svennevig, Michael (1988) *Attitudes to Broadcasting Over the Years*, London: John Libbey.

Gunter, Barrie and Viney, Rachel (1994) *Seeing is Believing: Religion and Television in the 1990s*, London: John Libbey.

Gurevitch, Michael (1991) 'The globalization of electronic journalism', pp. 178–93, in Curran and Gurevitch (eds) (1991).

Halbwachs, Maurice (1980) *The Collective Memory*, New York: Harper and Row.

Hall, Stuart (1980) 'Encoding/decoding', pp. 128–38, in Hall et al. (eds) (1980).

Hall, Stuart et al (eds) (1980) *Culture, Media, Language*, London: Hutchinson.

Hall, Stuart and Whannel, Paddy (1994) 'The Young Audience', pp. 69-75, in Storey, John (ed.) (1994).

Haste, Cate (1992) 'Sexual standards', pp. 92–6, in Millwood-Hargrave (ed.) (1992).

Heppell, Stephen (1994) 'Children's technological capabilities not recognised' (according to new research), press release.

Herbert, Hugh (1995) 'The fly that lies on the wall', *The Guardian*, 20 January.

Herman, Edward S. and Chomsky, Noam (1988) *Manufacturing Consent*, New York: Pantheon.

Hilsman, Hoyt R. (1989) *The New Electronic Media*, Boston: Focal Press.

Hodge, Bob and Tripp, David (1988) *Children and Television*, New York: Polity Press.

Hodgson, Guy (1995) 'TV's power behind the screens', *Independent*, 21 December, p. 22.

Hoggart, Richard (1971) *Speaking to Each Other*, London: Chatto and Windus.

Hoggart, Richard (1978) *The Mass Media: A New Colonialism?* The Eighth STC Communication Lecture, Standard Telephone and Cables Ltd, London.

Hoggart, Richard (1982) 'Closing observations', pp. 150–60, in Hoggart, Richard and Morgan, Janet (eds) (1982).

Hoggart, Richard (1990, orig. 1957) *The Uses of Literacy*, Harmondsworth: Penguin.

Hoggart, Richard (1995) *The Way We Live Now*, London: Chatto and Windus.

Hoggart, Richard and Morgan, Janet (eds) (1982) *The Future of Broadcasting*, London: Macmillan.

Holman, J. and Braithwaite, V. (1982) 'Parental lifestyles and children's television viewing', *Australian Journal of Psychology*, vol. 34. pp. 375–82.

Holt, John (1967) *How Children Fail*, Harmondsworth: Penguin.

Hood, Stuart (1982) *The Ghost Behind the Screen*, Ninth Annual Convocation Lecture, The New University of Ulster, 27 May.

Hood, Stuart (1989, orig. 1980) *On Television*, London: Pluto Press.

Hood, Stuart and O'Leary, Garret (1990) *Questions of Broadcasting*, London: Methuen.

Horton, Donald and Wohl, Richard (1956) 'Mass communication and para-social interaction', *Psychiatry*, vol. 19, pp. 215–29

Hüber, Roland (1994) 'Superhighway or superhype?', *The Journal of the Royal Television Society*, November/December, pp. 12–16.

Hughes, Patrick (1990) 'Today's television, tomorrow's world', pp. 165–85, in Goodwin and Whannel (eds) (1990).

Hurard, François (1992) 'Sex on French television', pp. 97–106, in Millwood-Hargrave (ed.) (1992).

IBA(Independent Broadcasting Authority) (1974a) *Annual Report* London: IBA.

IBA (1974b) *Attitude to Television: A Survey of Public Opinion*, London: IBA.

IBA (1984a) *Annual Report*, London: IBA.

IBA (1984b) *Attitudes to Broadcasting*, London: IBA.

Ignatieff, Michael (1985) 'Is nothing sacred? The ethics of television', pp. 57–78, *Daedalus*, Fall.

Inglis, Fred (1990) *Media Theory*, Oxford: Basil Blackwell.

ITC (1994a) *Annual Report*, London: ITC.

ITC (1994b) *The ITC Code of Programme Sponsorship*, London: ITC.

ITC (1994c) *Terrestrial Channel's Recapture Viewers in Cable Homes*, December 16, London: ITC.

ITC (1994d) *Violence on Independent Television*, a summary report of an ITC monitoring exercise, Annex A to ITC Paper 135(94), pp. 5–25.

ITC (1995a) *ITC Publishes Latest Cable Television Figures*, 27 January, London: ITC.

ITC (1995b) *Programme Complaints and Interventions Report*, 18 January, London: ITC.

Jackson, Paul (1991) 'Language in Comedy', pp. 58–64, in Millwood-Hargrave, Andrea (ed.) (1991).

Johnston, Wendy M. and Davey, Graham C.L. (1995) *The Psychological Impact of Negative TV News Bulletins: The Catastrophising of Personal Worries*, mimeo.

Kagan World Media (1994) *Kagan's European Television Country Profiles*, London: Kegan World Media.

Katz, Donald (1990) 'The new generation gap', *Esquire*, February, p. 50.

Kingsley, Hilary (1988) *Soap Box*, London: Macmillan.

Kingsley, Hilary and Tibballs, Geoff (1990, orig. 1989) *Box of Delights*, London: Macmillan.

Kline, Stephen (1993) *Out of the Garden*, London: Verso.

Klopfenstein, Bruce C. (1993) 'From gadget to necessity: the diffusion of remote control technology', pp. 22–39, in Walker and Bellamy, Jr. (eds) (1993).

Kreitzman, Leon (1994) 'Quantifying the "third age"', *Admap*, July/August, pp. 19–24.

Kumar, Krishnan (1975) 'Holding the middle ground', *Sociology*, (9), pp. 67–88.

Kyle, J. (1992) *Switched On: Deaf People's Views on Television Subtitling*, London: BBC/ITC.

Lannon, Judie (1994) 'How they're different', *Admap*, July/August, pp. 30–6.

Lasch, Christopher (1978) *The Culture of Narcissism*, New York: W.W. Norton.

Lasch, Christopher (1985, orig. 1984) *The Minimal Self*, London: Picador.

Laslett, Peter (1989) *A Fresh Map of Life*, London: Weidenfeld and Nicolson.

Lederer, Laura (ed.) (1980) *Take Back The Night*, New York: WWM Morrow.

Lewis, Justin (1990) *Art, Culture, and Enterprise*, London: Routledge/Comedia.

Lichtenberg, Judith (1991) 'In defense of objectivity', pp. 216–31, in Curran and Gurevitch (eds) (1991).

Lindlof, Thomas R., Shatzer, Milton J. and Wilkinson, Daniel (1988) 'Accommodation of video and television in the American family', pp. 158–92, in Lull, James (ed.) (1988a).

Livingstone, Sonia (1991) 'Audience reception: the role of the viewer in retelling romantic drama', pp. 285–307, in Curran and Gurevitch (eds) (1991).

Lull, James (ed.) (1988a) *World Families Watch Television*, Newbury Park, Calif.: Sage.

Lull, James (1988b) 'The family and television in world cultures', pp. 9–21, in Lull, James (ed.) (1988a).

Lull, James (1988c) 'Constructing rituals of extension through family television viewing', pp. 237–60, in Lull, James (ed.) (1988a).

Lull, James and Sun, Se-Wen (1988) 'Agent of modernization: television and urban Chinese families', pp. 193–236, in Lull, James (ed.) (1988a).

Macdonald, Deidre (1994) *Times Educational Supplement*, 6 May (section 2), p. 27.

McEwan, Ian (1988) *The Child in Time*, London: Picador.

McGuigan, Jim (1994) 'Trajectories of cultural populism', pp. 547–59, in Storey, John (ed.) (1994).

McLaughlin, Carmel (1994) *What Do Customers and Potential Customers Think About Cable?*, CTA Marketing Conference, 17 February, 1994.

Masterman, Len (ed.) (1984) *Television Mythologies*, London: Comedia.

Masters, Nick (1994) 'A star too far', *Spectrum*, Autumn, p. 22.

Mayall, Berry (ed.) (1995) *Children's Childhoods*, London: Falmer Press.

Medved, Michael (1993) *Hollywood Versus America*, Zondervan: HarperCollins.

Midwinter, Eric (1991) *Out of Focus: Old Age, the Press and Broadcasting*, London: Centre for Policy on Ageing.

Miles, Rosalind (1994) *The Children We Deserve*, London: HarperCollins.

Miller, Nod and Allen, Rod (eds) (1994) *Broadcasting Enters the Marketplace*, London: John Libbey.

Miller, Nod, Norris, Cresta and Hughes, Janice (eds) (1990) *Broadcasting Standards*, Manchester: Manchester Monographs.

Mills, Pam (1994) 'More channels equal happier viewers?', pp. 140–8, in Miller and Allen (eds) (1994).

Millwood-Hargrave, Andrea (ed.) (1991a) *A Matter of Manners?*, London: BSC.

Millwood-Hargrave, Andrea (1991b) *Taste and Decency in Broadcasting*, London: BSC, Annual Report.

Millwood-Hargrave, Andrea (1991c) 'A matter of manners?', pp. 7–44, in Millwood-Hargrave, Andrea (ed.) (1991a).

Millwood-Hargrave, Andrea (1992) *Sex and Sexuality in Broadcasting*, BSC Annual Report, London: John Libbey.

Minois, George (1989) *A History of Old Age: from Antiquity to the Renaissance*, Oxford: Basil Blackwell.

Mintel (1995) *British Lifestyles 1995*, London: Mintel International Group Limited.

Moore, G. E. (1903) *Principia Ethica*. Cambridge: Cambridge University Press.

Moore Jr., Barrington (1972) *Reflections on the Causes of Human Misery*, London: Allen Lane.

Morley, David (1986) *Family Television: Cultural Power and Domestic Leisure*, London: Comedia.

Morley, David (1988) 'Domestic Relations: the framework of family viewing in Great Britain', pp. 22–48, in Lull, James (ed.) (1988).

Morley, David (1992a) 'Electronic communities and domestic rituals', pp. 65–83, in Slovmand and Schrøder (eds) (1992).

Morley, David (1992b) *Television Audiences and Cultural Studies*, London: Routledge and Kegan Paul.

Morley, David (1994) 'Television and gender', pp. 474–97, in Newcomb, Horace (ed.) (1994).

Morris, Colin (1991) 'Blasphemy', pp. 80–4, in Millwood-Hargrave, Andrea (ed.) (1991a).

Morrison, David (1992a) 'Homosexuals and television', pp. 87–91, in Millwood-Hargrave (ed.) (1992).

Morrison, David E. (1992b) *Television and the Gulf War*, London: John Libbey.

Mulholland, Clare (1991) 'Codename quality', *Spectrum*, Spring, pp. 4–5.

Mullan, Bob (1996) *Not A Pretty Picture*, Aldershot: Avebury.

Murdock, Graham (1992a) 'Embedded persuasions: the fall and rise of integrated advertising', pp. 202–31, in Strinati and Wagg (eds) (1992).

Murdock, Graham (1992b) 'Citizens, consumers and public culture', pp. 17–41, in Slovmand and Schrøder (eds) (1992).

Newcomb, H. (ed.) (1982/1994) *Television: The Critical View*, New York: Oxford University Press.

Newcomb, Horace and Hirsch, Paul M. (1994) 'Television as a cultural form', pp. 503–15, in Newcomb, Horace (ed.) (1994).

Newson, Elizabeth (1994) *Video Violence and the Protection of Children*, mimeo.

Novak, Michael (1976) *The Joy of Sports*, New York: Basic Books.

O'Sullivan, Tim (1991) 'Television memories and cultures of viewing 1950–65', pp. 159–181, in Corner, John (ed.) (1991).

Outhwaite, William et al. (eds) (1996) *The Blackwell Dictionary of Twentieth-Century Social Thought*, Oxford: Basil Blackwell.

Packard, Vance (1960: orig. 1957) *The Hidden Persuaders*, Harmondsworth: Penguin.

Paterson, Richard (1990) 'A suitable schedule for the family', pp. 30–41, in Goodwin and Whannel (eds) (1990).

Petrie, Duncan and Willis, Janet (eds) (1995) *Television and the Household*, London: BFI.

Phelps, Guy (1995a) *VCC Presentation on Cable and Presentation*, mimeo (ITC).

Phelps, Guy (1995b) 'Sex on the box', *Spectrum*, Summer, pp. 10–11.

Philo, Greg (1990) *Seeing and Believing*, London: Routledge.

Philo, Greg (1993) 'Political advertising, popular belief and the 1992 British general election', *Media, Culture and Society*, vol. 15, pp. 407–18.

Philo, Greg and Lamb, Robert (1987) *Television and the Ethiopian Famine*, London: UNESCO.

Plater, Alan (1992) 'Sex, television drama and the writer', pp. 77–81, in Millwood-Hargrave (ed.) (1992).

Pollock, Linda A. (1983) *Forgotten Children: Parent–Child Relations from 1500–1900*, Cambridge: Cambridge University Press.

Postman, Neil (1982) *The Disappearance of Childhood*, New York: Dell Publishing.

Postman, Neil (1987, orig. 1985) *Amusing Ourselves To Death*, London: Methuen.

Potter, Dennis (1982) 'Soap time: thoughts on a commodity art form', in Newcombe, H. (ed.) (1982).

Provenzo, Jr., Eugene F. (1991) *Video Kids: Making Sense of Nintendo*, Cambridge, Mass.: Harvard University Press.

Puner, Morton (1978, orig. 1974) *To The Good Long Life*, London: Macmillan.

Randall, Elaine (1995) 'Switching on at 60-plus', pp. 49–64, in Petrie and Willis (eds) (1995).

Rees, Laurence (1992) *Selling Politics*, London: BBC Books.

Redmond, Phil (1991) 'Class, decency and hypocrisy', pp. 45–52, in Millwood-Hargrave, Andrea (ed.) (1991).

Rogge, Jan-Uwe and Jensen, Klaus (1988) 'Everyday life and television in West Germany: an empathic–interpretive perspective on the family as a system', pp. 80–115, in Lull, James (ed.) (1988).

Rowland, Jr., Willard D. and Tracey, Michael (1990) 'Worldwide challenges to public service broadcasting' *Journal of Communication*, Spring, vol. 40(2), pp. 8–28.

Ruthven, Malise (1995) 'The west's secret weapon against Islam', *The Sunday Times*, 1 January.

Schickel, Richard (1985) *Common Fame: the Culture of Celebrity*, London: Pavilion/Michael Joseph.

Schiller, Herbert I. (1989) *Culture Inc.*, New York: Oxford University Press.

Schleifer, S.A. (1993) 'An Islamic perspective on the news', pp. 163–75, in Arthur, Chris (ed.) (1993).

Schlesinger, Philip (1988 rev. edn) *Putting 'Reality' Together*, London: Sage.

Schlesinger, Philip (1993) 'Islam, postmodernity and the media: an interview with Akbar S. Ahmed', *Culture and Society*, vol. 15, pp. 29–42.

Schudson, Michael (1991) 'The sociology of new production revisited', pp. 141–59, in Curran and Gurevitch (eds) (1991).

Schudson, Michael (1994) 'The new validation of popular culture: sense and sentimentality in academia', pp. 486–94, in Storey, John (ed.) (1994).

Schulze, Laurie (1994) 'The made-for-TV movie: industrial practice, cultural form, popular reception', pp. 155–75, in Newcomb, Horace (ed.) (1994).

Seldes, Gilbert (1950) *The Great Audience*, Westport, Conn.: Greenwood.

Sennett, Richard (1977) *The Fall of Public Man*, Cambridge: Cambridge University Press.

Seymour-Ure, Colin (1991) *The British Press and Broadcasting Since 1945*, Oxford: Basil Blackwell.

Sharkey, Alix (1995) 'The doctor prescribes death', *The Independent*, 1 February, p. 21.

Shils, Edward and Young, Michael (1953) 'The meaning of the Coronation', *Sociological Review*, December, pp. 63–81.

Silman, Richard and Poustie, Richard (1994) 'What they eat, buy, read and watch', *Admap*, July/August, pp. 25–8.

Silverstone, Roger (1993) 'Television, ontological security and the transitional object', *Media, Culture and Society*, vol. 15, pp. 573–98.

Simpson, Neil (1993) 'Popular religion on TV', pp. 101–13, in Arthur, Chris (ed.) (1993).

Singer, Jerome L. (1973) *The Child's World of Make-Believe*, New York: Academic Press.

Slinger, Peg (1993) 'Television commercials: mirror and symbols of societal values', pp. 199–207, in Arthur, Chris (ed.) (1993).

Slovmand, Michael and Schrøder, Kim Christian (eds) (1992) *Media Cultures*, London: Routledge.

Smith, Joan (1994) 'Tuned in, clued up and switched off', *The Guardian*, 10 December, p. 7.

Sorlin, Pierre (1994) *Mass Media*, London: Routledge.

Steinem, Gloria (1980) 'Erotica and pornography: a clear and present difference', pp. 35–9, in Lederer, Laura (ed.) (1980).

Stephenson, Ralph and Phelps, Guy (1989, orig. 1965) *The Cinema As Art*, Harmondsworth: Penguin.

Stewart, Cathy and Laird, Julian (1994) *The European Media Industry*, London: Financial Times.

Storey, John (ed.) (1994) *Cultural Theory and Popular Culture*, London: Harvester Wheatsheaf.

Strinati, Dominic (1992) 'The taste of America: Americanization and popular culture in Britain', pp. 46–81, in Strinati and Wagg (eds) (1992a).

Strinati, Dominic (1994) 'Postmodernism and popular culture', pp. 428–38, in Storey, John (ed.) (1994).

Strinati, Dominic and Wagg, Stephen (eds) (1992a) *Come On Down?*, London: Routledge.

Strinati, Dominic and Wagg, Stephen (1992b) 'Introduction', pp. 1–8, in Strinati and Wagg (eds) (1992a).

Sutton-Smith, Brian (1986) *Toys as Culture*, New York: Gardner Press.

Svennevig, Michael, Haldane, Ian, Siers, Sharon and Gunter, Barrie (1988) *Godwatching: Viewers, Religion and Television*, London: John Libbey.

Svennevig, Michael and Wober, J.M. (1988) *The Chernobyl Disaster*, London: IBA Research Paper.

Taylor, Laurie and Mullan, Bob (1986) *Uninvited Guests*, London: Chatto and Windus.

Thorburn, David (1994) 'Television melodrama,' pp. 537–50, in Newcomb H. (ed.) (1994).

Toffler, Alvin and Toffler, Heidi (1995) 'Where were the peace broadcasts?', *The Guardian*, 28 January, p. 27.

Tracey, Michael (1984) 'Television affects everything we do, everything we think', *Listener*, 19 January, pp. 2–3

Traynor Ian (1995) 'A question of who calls the shots', *The Guardian*, 28 January, p. 27.

Tucker, Nicholas (1994) 'Man child', *The Guardian*, 28 December.

Tunstall, Jeremy (1983) *The Media in Britain*, London: Constable.

Tunstall, Jeremy (ed.) (1992) 'The United Kingdom', pp. 238–55, in The Euromedia Research Group (1992).

Tunstall, Jeremy and Palmer, Michael (1991) *Media Moguls*, London: Routledge.

Turow, Joseph (1991) 'A mass communication perspective on entertainment industries', pp. 160–77, in Curran and Gurevitch (eds) (1991).

Tynan, Kathleen (1988) *The Life of Kenneth Tynan*, London: Methuen.

Wagg, Stephen (1992) '"One I made earlier": media, popular culture and the politics of childhood', pp. 150–78, in Strinati and Wagg (eds) (1992a).

Walker, James R. and Bellamy, Jr., Robert V. (eds) (1993) *The Remote Control in the New Age of Television*, Westport, Conn.: Praeger.

Walker, James R. and Bellamy, Jr, Robert V. (1993) 'The remote control device: an overlooked technology', pp. 3–14, in Walker and Bellamy, Jr (eds) (1993).

Warner, Marina (1994) *Managing Monsters*, London: Vintage.

Warnock, Mary (1990) 'Quality and Standards in Broadcasting', pp. 5–26, in Miller et al. (eds) (1990).

Weber, Derek (1993) 'Everybody needs good neighbours: soap opera as community of meaning', pp. 113–23, in Arthur, Chris (ed.) (1993).

Webster, James G. and Phalen, Patricia F. (1994) 'Victim, consumer, or commodity? Audience models in communication policy', in Ettema and Whitney (eds) (1994).

Weisskopf, Walter (1965) 'Economic Growth Versus Existential Balance', *Ethics*, LXXV(2), January.

Whannel, Garry (1990) 'Winner takes all: competition', pp. 103–14, in Goodwin and Whannel (eds) (1990).

Whannel, Garry (1992a) *Fields in Vision*, London: Routledge.

Whannel, Garry (1992b) 'The price is right but the moments are sticky: television quiz and game shows, and popular culture', pp. 179–210, in Strinati and Wagg (eds) (1992).

Wildman, S. and Siwek, S. C. (1988) *The International Trade in Films and Television Programmes*, Cambridge, Mass.: Ballinger.

Williams, Betsy (1994) '"North to the Future": *Northern Exposure* and Quality Television', pp. 141–54, in Newcomb, Horace (ed.) (1994).

Williams, Raymond (1950) *Reading and Criticism*, London: Muller.

Williams, Raymond (1990, orig. 1975) *Television: Technology and Cultural Form*, London: Routledge.

Wilson, Roger (1994) *Local Television*, Shropshire: Dragonflair.

Wilson, Roger (1995) 'Understanding the Cable Audience', *Inside Cable*, February, pp. 8–9.

WOAC Communications Company, The (1994) *The Cable TV and Telecom Yearbook 1994*, London: WOAC.

Wober, J.M. (1990) *Advertising Toys at Christmas Time*, London: IBA Research Paper.

Wober, J.M. (1992) *Neighbours at Home and Away*, ITC Research Reference Paper.

Wober, J.M. and Gunter, B. (1990) *Crime Reconstruction Programmes*, London: IBA Research Paper.

Wood, Julian (1993) 'Repeatable Pleasures: notes on young people's use of video', pp. 184–201, in Buckingham (ed.) (1993).

Yadava, J.S. and Reddi, Usha V. (1988) 'In the midst of diversity: television in urban Indian homes', pp. 116–35, in Lull, James (ed.) (1988).

Young, Michael (1988) *The Metronomic Society*, London: Thames and Hudson.

Young, Michael and Schuller Tom (1991) *Life After Work*, London: HarperCollins.

Young, Toby (1993/4) 'Beavis and Butt-Head, ha ha ha', *The Modern Review*, p. 9.

Index